AF324891

BOOKSALE

WORLD WAR II

On September 1, 1939, the tanks of Nazi Germany rolled into Poland, and Europe was plunged into war. Behind this event lay two tragic decades of shattered hopes for peace; ahead lay six years of savage global conflict. Never before had a war been fought on so grand a scale over so great an area. This is the story of the grim chain of events that led to the rise of Nazi Germany, fascist Italy and Imperial Japan, of the vital turning points that led to the final Allied triumph and of the leaders of both sides in whose hands lay the lives of millions and the fate of nations.

WARSAW COMMUNITY PUBLIC LIBRARY
WARSAW, INDIANA

WORLD WAR II

by Thomas Weyr

Maps

BOOKSALE

Julian Messner
New York

940.54
W549w

Published simultaneously in the United States and Canada by
Julian Messner, a division of Simon & Schuster, Inc.,
1 West 39 Street, New York, N.Y. 10018. All rights reserved.

Copyright, ©, 1969 by Thomas Weyr

*For Teddie and Garret
in memory of what they were spared*

Printed in the United States of America

SBN-671-32177-3 Cloth Trade
671-32178-1 MCE

Library of Congress Catalog Card No. 74-79702

part I

EUROPE

WESTERN FRONT
Boundaries and names are those
of Sept. 1939.
0   miles   200   400
Arrows indicate direction of major Allied
offensive campaigns.
Axis Powers
Area controlled by Axis
Powers in July, 1942.
NORWAY
SWEDE
Oslo
Stockholm
SHETLAND
IS.
North
Sea
DENMARK
Copenhagen
Baltic S.
GREAT
BRITAIN
IRELAND
Hull
Coventry
The
Hague
Berlin
London
NETH.
ATLANTIC
Dunkirk
Cologne
Cherbourg
BELGIUM
GERMANY
Bastogne
St.
Caen
Remagen
Lo.
Falaise
LUX.
OCEAN
Paris
Prague
Munich
FRANCE
Vienna
SWITZ.
AUSTRIA
HUNG.
Lyon
Milan
Bologna
YUGOSLAVI
PORTUGAL
Gulf of
Genoa
Adriatic
SPAIN
Marseilles
ITALY
Madrid
Rome
Sea
Monte
CORSICA
Anzio
Cassino
BALEARIC IS.
(Fr.)
Naples
Foggia
Salerno
Taranto
GIBRALTAR
SARDINIA
(Br.)
MEDITERRANEAN
Tyrrhenian Sea
SPANISH
MOROCCO
Bizerte
Casablanca
Oran
Messina
SICILY
Tunis
MOROCCO
TUNISIA
MALTA
(Fr.)
ALGERIA
Casserine
(France)
Pass
Tripoli
from Egypt
Map by William Jaber

Chapter

The first of September, 1939, dawned clear and bright and hot across the flat Polish fields. It was a day much like the others that had preceded it in August, when the sun had baked the earth into a firm, hard crust and kept the level of rivers low. In the fullness of summer, autumn still seemed far away.

As light paled the early sky that morning, it suddenly picked out the shadow of planes streaking east: hundreds and thousands of them. And on the ground, across the horizon, an armada of snout-faced tanks rolled as swiftly and easily as if they were driving down a concrete highway. Conditions could not have been more perfect for armored operations or for the sudden bolt of death flung from the sky as Adolf Hitler's German Third Reich struck at neighboring Poland—without warning and without provocation.

Purposefully, the three thousand Nazi planes fanned across the tragic nation squeezed between the German mammoth to the west and the Russian giant in the east. Bombers swooped low over Polish airfields to carpet them with high explosives. Fighters dipped their wings and screamed across the tarmacs at treetop level to machine-gun anyone or anything still moving. On the ground three German army groups crunched into the country along a 1200-mile front. The thunder of bombs and guns deafened the countryside. The fires of war were lit and would not burn out for nearly six years.

Yet for all the abrupt surprise of the German attack, the war had not come unexpectedly. There were many who thought it had been under way for years—without force in Central Europe, where Hitler had not needed it, and with force in Africa and Spain. And few doubted that the war had been in the making for much longer, ever since the end of World War I. Most of the causes of the second great conflict of our century had their roots in the Versailles Treaty that settled the first one.

It was a document written by vengeful and frightened victors. Britain and France had almost lost the 1914-1918 war and in the end won it only because the United States joined the allied cause. President Woodrow Wilson had helped speed the German surrender by offering an idealistic peace, embodied in his famous fourteen points, that would assure justice and fair treatment for all. But London and Paris would not allow what they considered wishful dreams to clutter up the peace treaty. Both nations had lost millions of dead and much of the treasure that made them rich and powerful. Now they wanted their money back and iron-clad guarantees that the Germans would not again invade France and drag England into war. Wilson's idealism cracked and broke against the self-centered determination of his allies. The League of Nations, which the President hoped would keep the peace, did not even win support in his own country and started its brief life foredoomed.

Thus the harsh peace terms the victors forced on the Germans crippled from birth the Weimar Republic that followed the Kaiser's empire. In the immediate postwar years, hunger, disease, revolution, unemployment and stagnation were found from one end of Germany to the other. In the early 1920s maddening inflation tore through the country. The price of bread doubled in an hour. The savings of a lifetime vanished in an afternoon. A bitter and desperate mood beset the German people. They had so often been near victory. The Kaiser's troops had knocked Russia out of the war and twice come close to bringing France to her knees. Even with American in the war, the Germans had almost captured Paris in their great April offensive of 1918. Many simply could not believe that the Empire had been defeated, and blamed treachery and treason.

Germany quickly turned into a dark and brooding land with a populace willing to listen to any myth that put the blame elsewhere. And myth-makers there were aplenty in those years. It is Germany's —and the world's—tragedy that the bleakest of them would ride the wave of discontent to absolute power over this skilled, energetic and resourceful people, and then use that power to plunge mankind into horrible slaughter. Adolf Hitler was destined to enter history as one of the most villainous men who ever lived—a mass murderer whose evil deeds were so immense that only a computer could measure them, and whose legacy was a string of death factories across Europe.

Adolf Hitler was born in Braunau, Austria, a town near the German border, on April 20, 1889. As a young man he moved to Vienna. Fired with artistic ambition, he hoped to become a great painter. But he couldn't even pass the entrance exam into the Vienna Academy of Fine Arts, and for five years he lived in abject poverty, drifting through Viennese flophouses and earning a little money selling the picture postcards he painted. These were important years for Hitler, years that formed his personality and his prejudices. He hated the languid city on the Danube that would not let him make his way, and he hated all the diverse people who lived in it: Poles, Czechs, Serbs, Hungarians, Croats, Slovenes and Jews. Only the Germans were pure and great and creative. And so in 1913 Hitler moved to Munich, ostensibly to breathe the purer German air and avoid Vienna's "racial stench." More prosaically, there is good evidence that he moved simply to avoid the Austrian draft.

But when war broke out in 1914, the young Austrian volunteered for the German army. (He was not to become a German citizen until shortly before assuming power as Chancellor eighteen years later.) He was a good soldier, twice wounded and twice decorated with the Iron Cross. When the war ended, Adolf Hitler was a PFC—a man as bitter, as frustrated and as desperate as millions of other Germans.

Back in Munich, he quickly found work as a political informer for the army and for other right-wing groups. One day he was sent to attend a beerhall meeting of a new organization called the German Workers Party. Hitler expected a Socialist group, and found instead men who thought like himself. They hated the Jews, blamed sinister agents for Germany's defeat and hoped for national rebirth. Hitler had already decided on politics as his future career, and now he saw his chance. He moved in on the Workers Party with speed and skill. A spellbinding orator, he quickly drew large crowds and sizable contributions of money. The Party moved to a bigger beer hall. Hitler hired a secretary and bought a typewriter on the installment plan. Other disgruntled misfits joined him. Among the most important was Ernst Roehm, a former army officer who organized goon squads of ex-soldiers. The storm troopers, or brown shirts (SA), protected Hitler's meetings and broke up those of his enemies. Now Hitler gave his own flavor to the Party's name. He called it the National Socialist German Workers Party (German initials: NSDAP).

Over the next few years the NSDAP prospered, and by 1923 it was a force in the local politics of Bavaria, the south German state of which Munich is the capital. It was a good year for agitators. Inflation struck like a whirlwind, boosting the value of the dollar from 7000 marks in January to more than a million in August and close to a billion in November. The French occupied the Ruhr. Local rebellions exploded across the face of Germany like firecrackers. Only the army kept the central government in Berlin from collapsing.

As Hitler watched the growing chaos, he felt sure he could pull off a coup in Bavaria and, if he moved fast enough, seize power in the Reich. Fortified by the support of General von Ludendorff, one of the great German heroes of the war, Hitler acted on the night of November 8, 1923. At quarter to nine a flying wedge of storm troopers burst into the Buergerbraeukeller, where the leaders of the Bavarian government were addressing a crowd of three thousand. Brandishing a revolver, Hitler herded the speakers off the platform and tried to force them at gunpoint to join him in forming a new Bavarian government. At first they refused, but gave in when Hitler produced Ludendorff as an ally. Then Hitler blundered: he left the beer hall. As soon as he was gone, the Bavarian leaders appealed to the army for help. The next morning Munich was full of troops.

Nevertheless, Ludendorff persuaded Hitler to march into the center of town and try and take over the city. Police and soldiers met the marchers in a downtown square. Shots rang out. Hitler dropped to the ground and, as the fusilade worsened, was among the first to flee. Only Ludendorff marched, stiff and erect, through the police lines as bullets whizzed round his head. Not a single Nazi followed him.

Hitler was sentenced to five years' imprisonment for his beer hall putsch, a light sentence for open and violent rebellion. And in fact he only spent nine months in Landsberg prison, just enough time to write his book, *Mein Kampf*, while living in a comfortable prison room with a view of the river below. Prison authorities were among his sympathizers.

The book was a remarkably accurate blueprint of how Hitler would seize power in Germany and make war beyond its borders. Domestically, he planned to "purify" the German race and make of it a nation of blue-eyed, blond supermen. This meant eradicating the Jews and other "inferior" racial stock. Abroad, he planned to settle the score with France "once and for all" and then turn his attention to Russia. Out of that nation's vast land masses, he was sure, the Germans could carve the *Lebensraum* (living space) they needed to grow and prosper. He was not much interested in return of Germany's pre-war colonies in Africa—a disinterest that ultimately helped him lose the war—and was convinced that expansion in that direction had been a mistake and that Germany should return to the path charted by the Teutonic knights 600 years before, when they first fell upon Russian lands.

Mein Kampf was a dull, long and badly written book. Few people bothered to read it, and those who did thought it a joke—to their own and the world's sorrow.

Hitler left jail towards the end of 1924 to find a vastly changed Germany. Inflation was over. Billions in American loans were pouring into the country. Factories were rebuilt. Prosperity began to spread. For a few short years it seemed there was hope for the Weimar Republic and its democratic future. In a climate of growing political stability, the prospects of rabblerousers and street-corner orators dwindled. Hitler was forced to bide his time. In 1928 the NSDAP won 810,000 votes and a dozen seats in the Reichstag, the German parliament. It seemed as much as the Nazis would ever get.

But Hitler's fortune changed in an unexpected place and manner. The 1929 stock exchange crash in New York tumbled money markets around the world. Millions lost their jobs. Depression stalked the Western world. Germany was among the hardest hit, with six million unemployed. Young people looked bitterly to a future without hope. The misery and chaos of the postwar years returned and with it the old, sharp resentment against the Versailles Treaty.

The Nazis were quick to exploit this discontent and the political instability it brought. New elections were called for the fall of 1930. Hitler and his henchmen, most notably the fat and flashy former air ace Hermann Goering and the propaganda genius Joseph Goebbels, mounted a fast and tightly knit political campaign, perhaps the first of the modern kind. They promised bread and jobs, played heavily on anti-Semitic prejudice, and denounced the Versailles Treaty. Their platform won them six and a half million votes and 107 seats in the 600-odd seat parliament. As the nation's second strongest party, the Nazis had the political base to mount their drive to the top. It took them 28 months of worsening political chaos to do it.

By 1931 Hitler was considered for the chancellorship. But aged President Hindenburg disliked the crude Nazi and refused to offer it to him. Amid rising political turmoil new elections were called in the summer of 1932. This time the NSDAP emerged as the strongest party, with 230 seats, but was still short of a majority in a parliament where a dozen parties were represented.

Chaos now ruled German streets. Brawling was common, political murder almost routine, the degree of lawlessness frightening. The government had passed into the hands of extreme nationalists and right-wingers who ruled by presidential decree. A few months later the electorate was again asked to decide, and in the November, 1932, elections the NSDAP lost 34 seats but remained the largest party. For the next 57 days General Kurt von Schleicher served as chancellor. Then he too fell, and at last Hindenburg turned to Hitler. On a gray, overcast winter day, Monday, January 30, 1933, the hack painter from Braunau left the presidential palace with the chancellor's decree in his hands. German democracy was dead.

For the next two months the Nazis consolidated their hold on power. Hitler called for new elections, confident that now he would win them overwhelmingly. Goebbels manufactured an imminent communist uprising, and to make the danger more real, Goering decided to burn down the Reichstag building. He even found a demented Dutch communist, Marinus van der Lubbe, who had boasted in a bar that he would set parliament on fire. Goering's agents encouraged van der Lubbe, and on February 27 he walked into the Reichstag building. Storm troopers had already soaked it with gasoline and had even set a few fires. Van der Lubbe started some of his own and watched the flames lick the ceiling. Goering had him arrested on the spot. The next day the Nazis trumpeted news of bloody insurrection and coming civil war. Thousands of Communists, Socialists and other non-Nazis were arrested on the spot. Street violence mounted. Storm troopers broke into homes at midnight to make arrests, and the Nazi propagandists told lurid tales of imminent Bolshevik revolt. In the week before the March 5 elections no other voice but that of the Nazis was heard in Germany.

Incredibly, the NSDAP did not win a majority. The elections, though rigged, were not controlled, and the Nazis ended up with only 44 percent of the vote and 288 seats. But Hitler had had enough of this democratic nonsense. He barred 81 Communist deputies from taking their seats, "detained" a dozen Socialists and had the majority he needed for an "enabling act" that gave a legal facade to his dictatorship. The 84 Socialists still in the Reichstag voted "nay." It was their final gesture of defiance.

Even before these last elections, Hitler bent his mind to making Germany ready for war. He met in February with the nation's leading industrialists and promised to start rearming in earnest, not furtively the way the Weimar Republic had done. The steel and coal barons were delighted and eager to pour money into the Nazi coffers. Hitler raised three million marks in one night alone.

Purposefully, the wheels of German industry began to turn towards the production of guns, tanks and planes. Still, Hitler dared not rattle his sabers too openly—yet. The allies remained much stronger than Germany militarily and could have crushed his weak forces in a day if he provoked them into action. Moreover, the brutal tactics he had used to club his way into power revolted and sickened the whole world. Anti-German feelings ran high. Hitler would first have to soothe them. On May 17, 1933, he did just that in a speech denouncing war as "madness" and pledging a "hands off" policy on foreign territory. It worked. The West believed him, and Hitler saw the pattern for the yo-yo foreign policy he would follow for the next six years—alternating threats and professions of peace.

That fall Hitler shifted tactics. On October 14 he quit the League of Nations and walked out of disarmament talks. At the same time, he told his generals to fight should the allies attack Germany. It was the first of many bold and fearfully dangerous risks Hitler took with the icy coolness of a riverboat gambler. For the allies now had the tailor-made opportunity to topple his regime if they wanted to. It was only the first of many such opportunities, but the weak and unsure Western governments failed to take advantage of a single one.

When they finally and reluctantly stood up to the German bully, he had grown stronger than they.

Next, Hitler showed the carrot. He signed a non-aggression treaty with Poland. Again the gullible West swallowed the Nazi version of what in our day has become known as "peaceful coexistence." The treaty took some of the sting from Germany's withdrawal from the League.

By the spring of 1934, Hitler could look back on solid achievement. He had made Germany once again a power to be reckoned with abroad, and he had solidified the Nazi hold on government. He had started a drive to rid Germany of Jews that included construction of the first concentration camps. And he had begun to rearm in earnest.

Hitler then met a challenge from within his own ranks. Ernst Roehm and his SA storm troopers were unhappy. They had hoped for a true national rebirth that would drive out the old military-industrial complex of Junker generals and Ruhr steel bosses which had dominated Germany for so long. Instead, they saw Hitler deal with both of them: big business and the military would back Hitler as Hindenburg's successor if he curbed the SA. A showdown between Hitler and Roehm neared.

But the Fuehrer, as he now called himself, never let it reach a climax. Early in the morning of June 30, 1934, he found Roehm in a small Bavarian hotel, dumped him into a car and drove him through columns of hostile brown shirts to a Munich jail. Ironically, it was the same jail cell Hitler and Roehm had shared after the 1923 putsch. The Fuehrer left Roehm a pistol in his cell. When the SA leader refused to kill himself, two blackshirts (the Fuehrer's personal storm troopers—the dreaded SS, which Heinrich Himmler had built up as a counterweight to the SA) walked in and emptied their revolvers into Roehm's shirtless torso. Hitler then moved to settle every personal score built up in his 15-year struggle to power. In the next 24 hours, which are recorded in history as the Night of the Long Knives, Hitler had nearly 7000 people murdered. Firing squads worked overtime. The pattern of brutality and murder would hold all through his reign.

The brown shirt threat broken, Hitler again turned to foreign affairs. Three weeks after Roehm's murder, he organized a putsch against the government of neighboring Austria, his homeland. It was the first Nazi intervention in a foreign country, and chances for success looked favorable. The Nazis had built a strong underground party in Austria, and only four months earlier the country had had a bitter civil war between Socialists and Catholics. The Catholics had won, but the conflict had left a legacy of hatred and distrust.

The Nazis murdered Chancellor Engelbert Dollfuss and occupied the seat of government. The Austrian army, however, remained loyal to the Catholic regime and forced the insurgents to surrender. Moreover, German plans to intervene were foiled when Italian dictator Benito Mussolini pointedly moved three divisions to the Brenner Pass to back up Italian guarantees of Austrian independence.

Undaunted, Hitler changed tactics. He poured money and agents into Austria to undermine the government. It would take four years, but finally Austria fell right into his lap.

Meanwhile, Germany continued to rearm at breakneck speed. Hitler's generals quickly realized the importance of fast movement on the ground and control of the skies. Accordingly, German war production focused on planes and tanks. In order to challenge Britain on the seas, Hitler also began to build a large navy, including the world's biggest battleship. All these activities were in brazen violation of the Versailles Treaty, but neither Britain nor France nor the League of Nations was inclined to call the German dictator's wrath upon themselves. The Western countries were haunted by memories of war and had become deeply pacifist, convinced that if they only wished hard enough for peace it would come of itself. They neglected their defenses and failed to keep up with modern technological and strategic advances.

In those despairing years of the mid-thirties, only one voice in the Western world was raised against the dictators—first against Hitler, later against Mussolini. It belonged to a moon-faced, pudgy Englishman near sixty who had held most jobs in British government save that of Prime Minister, and who was believed well over the political hill: Winston Leonard Spencer Churchill.

Again and again Churchill would rise in the House of Commons to warn against the danger of German aggression, to plead with successive British governments to stop Hitler before it was too late, to rebuild British defenses and do it with modern technology. His words were in vain. In 1934 Churchill said flatly that Hitler would soon have an air force to match Britain's and in a few years one twice its size. Nonsense, the government replied, and remained complacent even when, in early 1935, it was forced to admit that Churchill had been right. By achieving air parity, Germany had taken a giant stride towards return as a world military power.

In 1935 German political strength, too, grew significantly. Hitler gained a powerful friend when Italy attacked primitive Ethiopia in Africa, thus alienating Britain and France, her World War I allies, and the League of Nations. The stage was set for formation of a Rome-Berlin axis.

Benito Mussolini had seized power in Italy in 1922 and imposed a dictatorial, fascist regime on the country. His rule was as authoritarian as Hitler's, but his methods not as harsh and his government not as efficient. In fact, after a dozen years of power, Italian fascism had begun to look shopworn. Mussolini needed a diversion to take his people's minds off domestic problems. Dictators have always found war a good way to do this, and they rarely have far to look for a cause. Il Duce found his in Africa when Italian soldiers stationed in Eritrea and Somaliland fought border clashes with Ethiopian tribesmen. Italian demands on Ethiopia for reparations quickly escalated, and in October, 1935, Mussolini's troops marched out of the two Italian colonies to seek booty and conquest across the border in Ethiopia.

The League was revolted at this display of naked aggression and quickly adopted economic sanctions against Italy. But the sanctions did not include oil, and such non-League members as the United States and Japan ignored them altogether. The Italian war machine was not impaired. In May, 1936, Italian troops entered Addis Ababa, the capital. Emperor Haile Selassie, the legendary Lion of Judah, fled, and King Victor Emmanuel III of Italy was proclaimed Emperor of Ethiopia. The League had watched a member state die without taking any military action to keep it alive.

A short time later Haile Selassie stood on the rostrum of the League's palace in Geneva to tell the assembled nations that "international morality" was at stake in the death of his country. It was not. The democracies had already surrendered it. To Hitler and Mussolini, who had also quit the League, the international body's "do-nothing" attitude was revealing. Both dictators were now convinced they could defy the League with impunity, and both did.

Hitler gambled on League inaction even before the African war was over. On March 7, 1936, German soldiers goose-stepped into the demilitarized Rhineland, between the Rhine and the French border, in yet another violation of the Versailles Treaty. France appeared paralyzed. Instead of sending soldiers to stop the German advance, the French high command moved another 13 divisions into the Maginot Line, a wall of forts, bunkers and heavy guns built in the 1920s along the Franco-German frontier. And there the troops sat and watched. Yet the German generals were so frightened at even this mouselike response to aggression that they pleaded with Hitler to withdraw his three battalions. They knew that the German Wehrmacht was as yet no match for a French Army that in 1936 numbered a hundred divisions.

Hitler refused to yield and was proved right. The French and British wrung their hands—and said hopefully that this latest example of German treaty-breaking might be the new beginning of peaceful reconstruction in Europe. After all, had not Herr Hitler said so in several of his recent speeches? Once again they were grabbing like drowning men for the withered carrot the Fuehrer held out to them.

Dutifully, Winston Churchill pointed out that annexation of the Rhineland had put German troops along the Belgian and Luxembourg frontier and in a position to outflank the Maginot Line (which stopped at the Luxembourg border) by thrusting through the Low Countries. Moreover, Hitler could now build a wall of his own within shouting distance of the French fortifications. Again nobody listened, and of course the Germans did exactly what Churchill predicted. They called their wall the Siegfried Line. Once completed, it would provide Germany with a shield against attack from the west and leave Hitler free to go about his business of conquest in Central Europe without worrying about French intervention.

With the Rhineland again in German hands and the war in Ethiopia ended, the conflict shifted to Spain, where civil war had broken out in July, 1936. Francisco Franco, a general with a fascist political outlook similar to that of Hitler and Mussolini, rallied the Spanish army and the Falange Party against the weak Republican government in Madrid. Hitler and Mussolini promptly supported him, hoping not only to win a new ally but also to test their war machine under combat conditions and on neutral soil. Axis help to the Spanish insurgents was swift and massive. Hitler first sent thirty transport planes to Spanish Morocco, where Franco had started the rebellion, so he could ferry his troops to the mainland. Then Mussolini sent thousands of Italian troops to fight alongside the Falange— 100,000 men before the war was out. Hitler sent only 12,000 troops, but he provided Franco with the use of an air force, the Kondor Legion. The Republicans got a little help from Russia and some moral support from public opinion in Britain and France. But the Western governments sat on the fence and in the end refused to sell arms to the Republicans or let weapons for them pass through their territory. That settled the Loyalist fate, though they fought on bitterly until the spring of 1939.

For Hitler, Spain was the testing ground of his Luftwaffe. Here his fliers could develop dive-bombing techniques, perfect fighter operations and practice battle formation flying. It was war in a test tube. The most blatant and most cynical of these battle "demonstrations" came on April 27, 1937, when the Kondor Legion's planes attacked the sleepy little market town of Guernica in northern Spain. It was a Monday afternoon. The town was jammed with farmers who had put their chickens, eggs and salad greens on sale in the main square. At 4:30 P.M. church bells stormed a warning: enemy air strike. Within minutes five Heinkel 111 fighter bombers were overhead. They dropped their bombs, then swooped low to machine-gun houses and streets. Then the dive bombers, the Stukas, roared across town, a new wave every twenty minutes, and dropped their bombs. More than 1,600 persons died in little more than three hours; 900 were left wounded. The center of town was a heap of gutted rubble. The purpose of the exercise: a clinical experiment to test the efficacy of mass bombing on town-sized targets.

Again the West professed shock and outrage. Pablo Picasso painted a flaming mural depicting Guernica's destruction. But no one bothered to turn words into action, to help the Republicans stop Franco and the dictators.

Politically Spain provided Hitler with a screen. The world watched the Civil War and paid scant attention to what the Nazis did, including Hitler's conclusion of an anti-Russian pact with Japan which laid the groundwork for the later Berlin-Rome-Tokyo axis and the Nazi undermining of Austrian independence. Admittedly Spain was a convenient screen. The French government continued incapable of making the hard decisions needed to rebuild French defenses. In Britain an avowed appeaser, Neville Chamberlain, had taken office as Prime Minister in the spring of 1937. Chamberlain was convinced Germany had been handed a raw deal at Versailles, and he was equally sure that Hitler would stop stirring trouble if the wrongs done Germany were set right. So for the next two years the British leaned over backwards to give the Fuehrer anything he asked for, just as long as he promised to keep the peace.

The next thing Hitler wanted was Austria. Already in November, 1937, Mussolini inclined to the view that things should "take their course" in that country. Thus Chancellor Kurt von Schuschnigg could no longer count on Il Duce's support, which had saved him three years before. Early in 1938 Nazi agitation in Austria rose to a deafening crescendo, as did police efforts to suppress it—and Hitler's threats to support the Austrian Nazis.

In mid-February, Hitler summoned Schuschnigg to his Berchtesgaden retreat in the Bavarian Alps. For a whole day he tongue-lashed the civilized, 41-year-old Austrian unmercifully. Schuschnigg offered concessions. Hitler wasn't interested. He wanted to frighten his guest. At one point Hitler ordered Schuschnigg out of the room while he called loudly for General Keitel, his army commander. The Austrian was sure that invasion—and his own arrest—were imminent. Finally, Hitler let him go, with a list of demands that spelled the end of an independent Austria—among other things, legalization of the Nazi Party, three cabinet posts for Nazi ministers and amnesty for all jailed Nazis.

In the weeks that followed, the fabric of Austrian government disintegrated. Street demonstrations increased. Nazi activities grew more brazen. Open sympathy for Hitler's cause grew in the police force and in the army. The Germans began to shuttle troops along the Austrian border. France and Britain continued to wring their hands, but did nothing. With each passing day Schuschnigg's position grew more desperate and more isolated. Finally he had a brainstorm. He would call for a plebiscite on Austrian independence.

It was a master stroke. The Germans were stunned. Hitler fumed. He knew Schuschnigg would win easily. For all their thunder and smoke the Nazis remained a minority, and Hitler could not afford such a loss of prestige. The Germans swiftly readied an invasion force to prevent the plebiscite with guns if need be. On the morning of March 11, the day before Austria was to vote on its future, the Germans closed the border. At ten o'clock local Nazis relayed Hitler's demands that the plebiscite be canceled. Four hours later Schuschnigg capitulated, convinced that the police would not obey him and that order could not be maintained. By then, however, Hitler had upped the ante. That night Arthur Seyss-Inquart, the Austrian Nazi leader, replaced Schuschnigg as Chancellor. The next morning, March 12, German tanks lumbered across the Austrian border. At noon Hitler himself followed them into the land of his birth, where he was given a hero's reception. The main square of Linz was crowded with people when he arrived, and the cheering did not stop.

But Hitler got no further than Linz that night and had to delay his triumphant entry into Vienna until March 14. The reason for the delay is curious and instructive: half the German tanks and trucks in the invasion force broke down on the highway to Vienna. As his generals had warned, the Wehrmacht still wasn't ready for war. Had Mussolini or the West intervened then, the Nazi march of conquest could have been stopped, as it could have been so often in the past.

But a cabinet crisis paralyzed the French government in Paris, and in London Chamberlain sent a polite and diplomatic note of protest. The Germans rejected the note and bluntly told the British that Austria was none of their business.

German and local Nazis quickly wrought vengeance on their political and racial enemies in Austria. Jews were hunted down like animals. Thousands of them were jammed into concentration camps, as were thousands of Catholics and Socialists. Austrian storm troopers soon proved more vicious than their German brothers.

Heady with his Austrian triumph, Hitler determined on the quick conquest of his next target, Czechoslovakia. Britain had refused to guarantee Czech independence. Édouard Daladier and his foreign minister, Georges Bonnet, had just formed an appeasement government in France. Thus neither London nor Paris was likely to make much trouble for him. Moreover, Hitler had a ready-made political issue in the grievances of the 3,000,000-strong German minority in Czechoslovakia. Accordingly, orders went out to the Wehrmacht to plan for an attack. Again Hitler's generals demurred. The Czechs had an army of 35 divisions, as large as their own, and manned fortifications as strong as the Maginot Line. But the Fuehrer insisted —and stumbled.

The allies got wind of his plans, and Paris, London and Moscow expressed solidarity with Prague. The Czechs ordered partial mobilization. Alarmed, Hitler pulled back and assured the Czechs that no attack was planned, that he only wanted to improve the lot of the Germans there. For once his timing had been off. He now set himself a deadline of October 1, 1938, for a military solution of the "Czech problem." It was a deadline he met.

British firmness in May had only been an act of bravado. Chamberlain remained desperate to keep the peace, at just about anybody's expense. In July he resumed pressure on Prague to make concessions. The crisis came in September. On the 7th the *London Times,* in a government-inspired editorial, suggested that the Czechs cede the Sudetenland, the German-speaking area, to the Reich and thus make Czechoslovakia a more homogenous state. What the editorial failed to mention was the fact that such a move would slice away the mountain fortress the Czechs had built and leave the "homogenous" country defenseless. On the 12th, Hitler delivered a harangue that stopped just short of a declaration of war. The Sudetenlaenders promptly revolted, and it took Czech authorities two days of bloody fighting to put down the uprising.

Thoroughly alarmed by events, Chamberlain now cabled Hitler to ask him for a face-to-face meeting. His wish was granted, and on September 15, 1938, Chamberlain, umbrella securely furled and homburg plastered neatly on his thin forehead, arrived in Berchtesgaden. After tea the British Prime Minister had little difficulty in agreeing that Germany should get the Sudetenland—naturally on the basis of self-determination. The loss of Czech defensive installations would not matter, since Hitler had promised that this would be his last territorial demand in Europe.

A week later Chamberlain was back in Germany. The Czech government had resigned in face of British and French pressure to accept Hitler's terms and had agreed to surrender the Sudetenland. The British Prime Minister had even sweetened the package for Hitler. The German-speaking areas would join the Reich without a plebiscite; a three-power commission would determine the future of "mixed" areas. But, as he had done in Austria six months earlier, Hitler upped the stakes. Now he wanted unconditional cession of the Sudetenland, with Czech evacuation completed by September 28 at 2 P.M.

For the next six days the world watched tensely. The Czechs rejected the German demands and mobilized their army. Hitler remained intransigent. France mobilized. Reluctantly Chamberlain concluded that he had better prepare even Britain for war. London evacuated its schoolchildren and began digging trenches. With Hitler's deadline 24 hours away, orders went out to mobilize the British fleet. But through it all Chamberlain clung to the idea of appeasing Hitler, undaunted by the Fuehrer's refusal to heed British pleas. Finally, on the evening of September 27, Chamberlain tried one more time. Would Hitler agree to a four-power meeting of Germany, Italy, Britain and France to iron out details of the Sudetenland's surrender? At noon on the 28th, just two hours to war, Hitler acquiesced. He suggested Munich as the site and the next day, September 29, as the time.

Secretly, the Fuehrer was relieved. There wasn't much popular support for war just then. His generals were adamantly against it. Some even plotted to oust him, shelving their plans only when the Munich conference was arranged. For they, like Hitler, were convinced they could win hands down at any bargaining session with the democracies. And indeed the Germans did.

The talks began at noon on the 29th and lasted for 14 hours. The result? An agreement to evacuate the Sudetenland in five stages, beginning October 1 and ending ten days later. The final Czech frontiers were to be settled by an international commission. After the document was signed it was shown to the Czech representative, who had waited outside, barred from the conference room itself.

Before flying back to London, Chamberlain met Hitler privately and got him to sign a declaration proclaiming the importance of good German-English relations and pledging that the two would never go to war against each other. Back home Chamberlain told a grateful nation that the Munich agreement would ensure "peace in our time." Of course it did not, and "Chamberlain's umbrella" and "Munich" have entered the dictionary of history as definitions of spineless appeasement.

With Czechoslovakia reduced to the status of a defenseless rump state ripe for German occupation at Hitler's pleasure, the Nazi leader again turned to domestic matters, specifically a speed-up in war production and the rigorous persecution of the Jews. A pretext for brutally cracking down on German Jewry came about a month after Munich. On November 7 a young Jewish refugee gunned down a German diplomat on a Paris street. Two days later Goebbels and Goering decreed "spontaneous" anti-Semitic demonstrations across Germany. The pogrom of November 9, known as the *Krystallnacht,* resulted, by Nazi count, in the murder of 36 Jews. Another 36 were badly wounded. Storm troopers arrested 20,000 and set 119 synagogues, 815 shops and 171 homes on fire. Nazi estimates were low, however. Repair of broken glass—the slaughter was called "crystal night"—alone ran into millions. But Goering found a way to pay for the losses: he fined German Jews a billion marks for crimes against the Reich. New anti-Jewish regulations were issued which in effect stripped Jews of their last civil and legal rights.

On the *Krystallnacht* the Nazis turned a bitter corner: extermination of the Jews became official government policy carried out by government officials. Until that night German authorities had merely done nothing to protect Jews from the brown shirts' beating and plunder; now they themselves swung the whip.

Six months after Munich, Hitler judged the time ripe to finish off the Czechs. On March 15, 1939, the Wehrmacht goose-stepped across the ancient cobblestones of Prague. Again Chamberlain wrung his hands, but this time the British people didn't wring theirs with him. Public opinion hardened and swung strongly against appeasement. Chamberlain, a politician dependent on public support and keenly aware of the sudden change, swung with it. On March 31 he rose in the House of Commons to give Hitler's obvious next victim —Poland—the kind of guarantees he had refused Czechoslovakia. Britain as well as France was now solemnly committed to fight should Hitler attack Poland.

But Hitler paid little attention. Had not France refused to live up to equally solemn commitments to help the Czechs? Purposefully the Fuehrer began his sniping campaign against Poland. There was, for example, the free city of Danzig on the Baltic, a German town, nominally independent but obviously under Polish control. Would the Poles give it back? And would the Poles please allow him to build a four-lane highway and a rail line across the Polish corridor to the sea that separated East and West Prussia? For months these and similar demands rained down on Warsaw.

Thoroughly alarmed, the Poles began strengthening their Western alliances. It wasn't all that easy, for Poland had played along with Hitler for several years. The Poles had signed a nonaggression treaty with Germany and had helped themselves to a slice of dismembered Czechoslovakia. Talks and discussions with the West were held often in the next few months, but no concrete plans emerged to coordinate defenses should Hitler strike Poland. Nor did the Poles and the West pay any heed to the giant on Poland's eastern borders —Russia.

Ever since Communism had taken power there in 1917, the Soviet Union had been suspect in the West, and only rarely did Paris or London consent to talk international politics with Moscow. Thus Chamberlain and Daladier could not bring themselves to bring Russian dictator Josef Stalin into the Czech crisis, although throughout the '30s the Soviets had pleaded over and over for a system of collective security against Nazism. Stalin did not take the slap of Munich lightly.

In the spring of 1939 he began to shift Soviet foreign policy away from offers of cooperation with the West. He fired Maxim Litvinov, his pro-Western foreign minister, and replaced him with hammer-hard V. M. Molotov. On May 20, 1939, Molotov proposed improving relations between Russia and the Reich. Hitler, who had already interpreted the shift in personalities as a shift in policy, was willing to listen.

For the next few months Germany and a suddenly alarmed West began serious talks with the Russians. But although both sides were confirmed anti-Communists, Hitler hysterically so, it was London and Paris who could not leave their shell of prejudice, and the Fuehrer who could shuck it as easily as an overcoat. After all, the Nazi leader had never been burdened with principles.

His pragmatic approach paid off in August, when Molotov and German Foreign Minister von Ribbentrop negotiated the Nazi-Soviet Pact. Germany and Russia agreed on Soviet intervention in a war against Poland and on Poland's partition—down to drawing the demarcation lines between their zones on a map. In addition, Germany promised to deliver machinery to Russia in return for strategic raw materials the Reich would not get if Britain joined the war and imposed a naval blockade. The agreement was signed on August 23, 1939. Hitler no longer cared if war could, or indeed should, be avoided. The remaining week of peace was devoted to frantic and futile exercises in allied diplomacy. Hitler was bent on attacking Poland. If the allies reneged on their commitments, so much the better. But if they went to war, Germany was ready.

Chapter

☆ 2 ☆

The Nazi-Soviet pact sent shock waves through the allied world. Within hours of its publication Britain had mobilized the first reserves, requisitioned ships, canceled military leaves and readied anti-aircraft defenses. The most hidebound appeasers now realized that war was imminent—even Neville Chamberlain. And to make that point as strongly as he could, he fired off a letter to Hitler with this blunt warning: Britain would stand by her commitment to Poland. "No greater mistake could be made" than believing she would not.

Hitler was unimpressed and sent back an equally tough answer. Britain's guarantees would only encourage Polish terrorism against Germans living in Poland. Germany could not tolerate such atrocities. If Britain went to war "Germany . . . will be found prepared and determined." And the Fuehrer moved quickly to show his determination. On August 25 he issued orders that the Wehrmacht roll against Poland at 4:30 the next morning.

Yet only three hours after that command went out, Hitler canceled plans for the attack. That very afternoon Britain had signed a formal assistance treaty with Poland, and Mussolini had made unmistakably clear that all Germany could expect from Italy in case of war was benevolent neutrality, not open intervention. The double blow had shaken the Fuehrer's "iron determination" enough for him to decide on postponement. But he remained convinced that the extra few days of peace could be used for talking Britain out of her pledge to help Poland.

And so the wheels of diplomacy spun furiously. A flurry of notes was exchanged. The British ambassador met constantly with Hitler and his top aides. The Germans offered to keep talking to the Poles. The British urged Warsaw to reciprocate. The Poles said they would. Germany rained down offers of peace and cooperation—including a guarantee of the safety of the British Empire itself. But the Poles had heard guarantees before. On August 30 they ordered partial mobilization. The next day Hitler made up his mind to attack.

Shortly after noon on August 31, the Fuehrer once again studied his first directive on the conduct of the war. "Since . . . all political possibilities of peaceful settlement have been exhausted," it began, "I have decided on a solution by force. . . . The date of attack— September 1, 1939." Then Hitler picked up a red pencil and wrote "Time of attack—4:45 A.M." And promptly at H-hour the Germans unleashed the furies of war.

But the habits of appeasement died hard. The first British ultimatum was not issued until 9:30 on the evening of September 1, hours after the attack had begun. Hitler ignored it. The next afternoon Chamberlain made a temporizing speech in the House of Commons, only to find the House in no mood to temporize. Suspicious of another Munich, the members of his cabinet cornered Chamberlain at dinner that night—Saturday, September 2. Britain had to act now to keep her pledge, they told him. If France would not coordinate her policy with Britain's, she would have to follow the British lead. Reluctantly, Chamberlain agreed.

Accordingly, at nine o'clock Sunday morning, September 3, the British ambassador delivered a second ultimatum to the German Foreign Office: If the Germans didn't start withdrawing from Poland by 11 A.M., Britain and Germany would be at war. Glumly the top Nazis stared at the document. Hitler was furious. To the end he was convinced the British could be bluffed into staying out. "If we lose this war," Hermann Goering said, downcast, "may heaven be merciful to us." The clock ticked off two hours, and at eleven Germany and Britain were indeed at war. A few hours later an even more hesitant France followed suit.

For Poland, on whose behalf the reluctant allies had finally redeemed their word, the declarations came too late. Hitler's pounding had sent the Polish army reeling back on all fronts. Nothing short of a prompt and massive allied offensive in the west could now save that beleaguered land. And although the French army could have

WARSAW COMMUNITY PUBLIC LIBRARY
WARSAW, INDIANA

cakewalked into Germany then—Hitler had gambled again and left only a token force manning the Siegfried Line—allied statesmen were too exhausted by their own courage in going to war even to contemplate such a course of action.

And so the world watched Poland die while Hitler's generals unfolded their new practice of warfare: lightning war, or blitzkrieg.

The Germans had hewed rigidly to Hitler's timetable. Punctually at 4:45 A.M. the first Luftwaffe planes streaked across Poland and the German armies began a concerted attack along a great crescent, from the Masurian Lakes of East Prussia in the north to the Carpathian mountains in the south. Within 48 hours the Germans had wiped out the 700-plane Polish air force, most of it destroyed on the ground. The Stukas were now free to fly close support for tanks and infantry. A giant umbrella of several thousand planes protected the 1,500,000-man German attacking force.

The Germans had divided their troops into two army groups. Colonel General Fedor von Bock commanded Army Group North, composed of the Third Army under General von Kuechler in East Prussia and the Fourth under von Kluge in eastern Pomerania. Colonel General Karl Gerd von Rundstedt had three armies in his Army Group South: the Eighth under Blaskowitz in central Silesia, the Tenth under von Reichenau in Upper Silesia and the Fourteenth under General List, which manned a front running from Upper Silesia to western Slovakia.

Western Poland jutted like a huge salient into German-held territory and the Wehrmacht could attack it from three sides. The Nazi objective was clear: cut Poland in two. Accordingly, von Kluge first drove his tanks across the Polish corridor, which divided East Prussia from the rest of Germany. Once across it he linked up with Kuechler's Third Army. Now von Bock could wheel his forces south and east. He sent one column crashing towards Warsaw, and an armored force under General Heinz Guderian towards Brest-Litovsk, a hundred miles east of the capital. The first arm of what would be a double pincer was to meet the Tenth Army tanks, storming up from the south. Guderian would link up with the Fourteenth Army's tank corps, under General Kleist, driving east from the Carpathians. Once the pincers closed, the bulk of Poland's forces would be trapped inside two pockets: one between Warsaw and the western front, the other between Brest-Litovsk and the capital.

In Rundstedt's sector the Eighth Army headed for the gap between the Polish Poznan and Lodz army groups and at the same time guarded the left flank of Reichenau's Tenth Army. Reichenau packed Rundstedt's big armored punch—seven mechanized divisions in all —and he sent his panzers barreling down the middle of the southern front. In four days he tore a fifty mile deep gash into Polish lines and pulverized the Lodz army group. Striking from Slovakia, the Fourteenth army headed for the river San.

The speed of Reichenau's tanks was dazzling. On September 6 he entered Cracow, Poland's second city. Three days later his armored patrols operated near the outskirts of Warsaw itself. Polish armies, already sensing the trap about to be sprung in the Warsaw area, marched about almost helplessly. Prospects for moving them back to the Vistula-Narew line, where they could make a more orderly stand, were dim indeed. Horses and vehicles kicked up so much dust that German spotter planes could no longer report on Polish troop movements, and the Polish commanders themselves often didn't know where to find their armies.

Yet the only effective Polish counterattack of the war was launched in the midst of this chaos. About September 8, Lieutenant General Kutrzeba saw a chance to strike back hard: the left flank of the German advance on Warsaw had suddenly become vulnerable. Reichenau's tanks and motorized infantry had outrun their support units; they were low on fuel and their mobility much reduced. Quickly Kutrzeba gathered elements of the Poznan and Pomorze armies (the latter decimated in the Corridor battles) and on the 9th attacked across the river Bzura with conspicuous success. He shattered one of Blaskovitz' Eighth Army divisions and sent several others reeling back for many miles. The Polish advance continued almost unchecked for the next two days as the Germans paid little attention to what they considered a diversionary maneuver. Not until September 11 did Rundstedt and his chief of staff, von Manstein, wake up to the danger. And then they decided on a bold gamble: to meet the Polish threat without abandoning their momentum towards Warsaw. They sent three of Reichenau's divisions racing back to the Bzura and threw in additional reserves from the west, but the bulk of the Tenth Army stayed on the road to Warsaw. It proved a sound gamble. The Germans forced Kutrzeba to regroup and then, when he tried to wheel east and drive towards Warsaw so he could help in the capital's defense, prevented his breakthrough even though the Poles mauled two German divisions badly. Soon the Poles were contained in the narrow Bzura pocket. On September 19, after German planes had dropped 358 tons of bombs on their positions, Kutrzeba's troops surrendered.

In the end the valiant Polish battle had only been able to slow the German advance on Warsaw a little. By the 13th the first pincers closed. On the 17th Guderian and Kleist's tanks met at Brest-Litovsk to close the second. Other German units had taken Lwow. The Polish army in the western half of the country had been smashed. Only isolated units were able to hold on to such fortresses as Modlin. In Warsaw itself resistance was so fierce that Hitler decided against a direct assault, relying instead on heavy bombardment. Largely because the whole population pitched in to fight the enemy the capital did not fall until September 30.

How had Hitler done it and done it so quickly? A Polish army of two million men had been destroyed as an effective fighting force by the second week of the invasion. It had been a good enough army by the old standards, and certainly a courageous one. But German blitzkrieg had set new standards where courage and determination counted for little—and the concepts and strategies of other wars for even less. The Poles had strung only thirty divisions along their whole immense frontier and had strung them too thinly. Strategic reserves able to bottle up a breakthrough quickly had not been called up in time; once the enemy had cracked a defensive position, there was nothing to stop him. But even if the Poles had completed mobilization they would not have been able to halt this German army. For blitzkrieg demanded an awesome concentration of firepower at one point, able to pulverize an opponent and leave his flanks dazed and disorganized. That the Germans had. Stukas softened up the defense with aerial pounding. Tanks shot Polish cavalry to bits. Self-propelled guns brought up heavy artillery much more quickly than the Poles had believed possible. Motorized infantry rode right behind the tanks to secure areas cleared by armor. This German army was the finest military machine yet devised, and it functioned with clock-work precision.

Perhaps nothing better symbolized the hopeless Polish cause than a battle fought early in the campaign in the Polish corridor. As German tanks swept eastward they ran into a counterattack by the Pomorska brigade of Polish cavalry. It was an incredible scene. Across the broad plain the Polish horsemen lowered their long lances. The pennants of red and white, Poland's colors, fluttered from the lance tips. Galloping hooves struck sparks from the stones as the Poles rode into the mechanical monsters, silent and unyielding against the sky. For a moment only the thunder of horses filled the air. Then came the dry chatter of machine guns and the bark of cannon. Minutes later the battlefield resembled the stockyards. The bloated carcasses of horses littered the area for days, and the stench of decay lingered even longer.

Perhaps the Poles might have re-formed their lines in the eastern half of their country, hoping for a miracle in the west, had not Stalin now made good on his promise to Hitler. On September 17, the day the second pincer closed, the Red Army crossed the Polish frontier. Stunned by this treachery and too weary from defeat in the west, the Poles could offer only scattered resistance. On the 18th the Soviets took Vilna and met the Germans at Brest-Litovsk. Except for the scattered fighting that would go on until the end of the month, the Polish campaign was over. It was up to the victors now to divide the spoils.

This they did promptly. On September 29 the agreement was ready. Germany annexed some 36,000 square miles of western Poland outright and left a triangular wedge of another 36,000 square miles (including such major Polish cities as Warsaw and Cracow) as a German-dominated "Government General" with the brutal and sadistic Hans Frank as Governor. Russia received the eastern half of Poland and, in exchange for a minor Polish province, inclusion of Lithuania in the Soviet sphere of influence.

This was a heavy price for Soviet intervention, but the Germans paid it for sound reasons. In 1914 the Kaiser had fought on two fronts, in the east and the west, and although he had defeated Russia he had lost the war. It was a mistake Hitler was determined to avoid. As he had written in *Mein Kampf*, the score with France would be settled first. Then Germany could turn on Russia. Meanwhile, her neutrality was worth the spoils.

As for Stalin, he had got what he wanted most: a buffer of land between Germany and the Soviet Union that ran from the Baltic to the Balkans. For German agreement to stay out of Lithuania gave him a free hand in the three Baltic states of Estonia, Latvia and Lithuania. Moscow promptly negotiated mutual defense treaties with all three which allowed establishment of Soviet military bases on Baltic territory. Thus the Soviets had fortified one of the classic western invasion routes into Russia. In the summer of 1940, when Hitler was busy in the west, the Russians formally annexed the three nations.

But one threat remained—a thrust against Leningrad, Russia's second city, across the Karelian Isthmus, which divides Lake Ladoga from the sea. The Finnish frontier was only 20 miles from Leningrad; should Finland ever fall into the Nazi orbit, an attack might well come from there. So in October the Soviets opened negotiations with the Finns aimed at winning concessions similar to those granted Moscow in the Baltic states. Specifically, the Russians wanted to set up a naval base at Hangoe, a port astride the entrance to the Gulf of Finland. Together with the Estonian base of Paldiski, this would give them control over the entry to the vital waterway. At the same time, they wanted the frontier pushed back about 20 miles in order to put Leningrad out of range of the guns mounted in the Mannerheim Line: the fortifications the Finns had built across the Isthmus. In exchange, the Russians offered Finland more than 2000 square miles of land along the northeastern Finnish-Soviet frontier. The Finns were willing to make concessions, but balked at giving Moscow the naval base. Negotiations broke down in mid-November. On November 28 the Russians claimed that Finnish soldiers had fired across the frontier (one of those convenient incidents aggressors seem to have no trouble in arranging), and on November 30 the Red Army struck against the Mannerheim Line and simultaneously attacked the 750-mile Soviet-Finnish border at five points.

It should have been no contest—on paper. The Red Army had a huge superiority in men and equipment: 45 divisions, 1500 tanks, 3000 planes, a fleet of trucks. The Finns could only field a force of 16 divisions—just a little more than 200,000 men—a hundred planes, a few outmoded guns of World War I vintage. To make matters worse, they suffered from a shortage of ammunition. Yet in the beginning at least the winter war turned into another replay of the David and Goliath legend.

The Mannerheim Line built across the Karelian Isthmus was a creaking copy of the Maginot defense system, with only 44 concrete bunkers. Further north, Soviet armor bogged down in the snow. Infantry columns trained to fight in open plains found themselves stymied by the deep Finnish forests. Nor did they know how to fight in the snow. Forced to slog through high drifts, the Russians were soon exhausted and unable to push on.

The Finns, on the other hand, were superbly fitted for winter warfare. Dressed in white cloaks that made them all but invisible in the snow, the defenders fell back from Russian attack and disappeared into the woods—only to glide out of them on skis and annihilate stalled Soviet divisions. Russian efforts to use ski troops of their own proved too little and too late.

As 1939 ended, the Russian losses were many times greater than in the Polish campaign. Public opinion in the West was shocked and outraged, pressure to help the Finns strong. London and Paris even prepared an expeditionary force.

Meanwhile, the Russians were determined to win the war, no matter what the cost. They had already been expelled from the League of Nations and now cared little for what others thought of them. Marshal Timoshenko, the new Soviet commander, began to devise more effective battle techniques. New armies were formed and fearsome concentrations of artillery placed in strategic places. On February 11 Russian guns began to pulverize the Mannerheim Line, dumping 300,000 shells on the Finnish defenders within 24 hours. Ten days later Timoshenko had pushed halfway across the Isthmus. Early in March the Russians had established a beachhead south of Viipuri, a major Gulf of Finland port, and on March 4 they had begun to shell the main highway from Viipuri to Helsinki.

Marshal Mannerheim, the Finnish commander, urged the Helsinki government to sue for peace. He saw little hope of continuing successful resistance without massive allied help. Since Sweden had turned down two British requests for sending troops across her territory, that would not be forthcoming. Moreover, Mannerheim thought the Finns could now do better at the conference table than on the battlefield. Certainly Russian losses had been heavy enough—up to 200,000 dead according to some estimates, massive destruction of military equipment and a very bruised prestige. Talks began in Stockholm, and on March 11 a peace treaty was concluded. Soviet terms were harsh: Lake Ladago, the Karelian Isthmus and Viipuri were ceded outright, and Russia got a 30-year lease on Hangoe. In all, the Finns gave up 16,000 square miles of territory. It was enough to complete Stalin's buffer.

The situation was much less dramatic in the west. When the war began, a hundred French divisions sat hunched in the concrete bunkers of the Maginot Line facing 43 German divisions entrenched in the Siegfried Line. Only once did the French sally forth. On September 7, 1939, several French columns crossed the German border in the Lauterbourg-Trier area without meeting any opposition. But the French generals quickly got cold feet and did not advance any further. When the German armies poured back into the Siegfried Line from Poland, the French pulled back.

And for the next seven months both sides sat still in their trenches, only occasionally sending out patrols during this period of the "phony war." Corporal T. W. Priday, the first British soldier to die, was not killed until December 9. Air action was minimal. In fact, both sides treated each other as if they were cartons of raw eggs, not soldiers.

The war at sea, however, was a different story. Fighting began the day war was declared, and the crucial battle of the Atlantic raged on until the end of the great conflict itself.

At about eight P.M. on September 3 the commander of the German submarine U-30 looked through his periscope and sighted the 13,000-ton British liner *Athenia,* then some 200 miles from the Hebrides Islands at the tip of Scotland. German torpedoes streaked silently through the water. Heavy explosions rocked the ship, and she sank quickly, with the loss of 112 lives, including 28 Americans. The incident embarrassed the Germans. Goebbels promptly cooked up a story that Winston Churchill, who had just joined the Chamberlain government and had taken over as First Lord of the Admiralty only three hours before the U-30's torpedoes struck, had ordered the

Athenia blown up in order to create anti-German feeling in the United States.

With Nazi submarines strung across the North Atlantic shipping lanes days before the war began, the U-30's attack was only the first of a series. Three more British ships were sunk in the next three days. And on September 18, the U-29 sank the aircraft carrier *HMS Courageous* in the Bristol Channel. The British Navy reacted quickly. It swept German surface ships from the oceans and reimposed its World War I blockade. Within three weeks the Royal Navy had bottled up two million tons of enemy shipping in German and neutral ports. Moreover, as Churchill told the House of Commons a month after war started, seven U-boats out of a total of 60 enemy submarines had been sunk.

It was not enough, however, to end the German naval threat. On October 14, a stunned Britain learned that a U-boat had sunk the battleship *Royal Oak*. Lieutenant Commander Heinz Prien, in command of U-47, had sneaked his ship right past the "impenetrable" defenses of Scapa Flow, the very headquarters of the British fleet in the Orkney Islands. Once inside, Prien glued his torpedo sight onto the gray hull of a battleship. "Must be the *Royal Oak*," he whispered to his executive officer. The first salvo of torpedoes failed to detonate. Icily calm, Prien ordered his tubes reloaded and fired a second time. Great columns of smoke and water shot into the sky. The 29,000-ton *Royal Oak* sank in a matter of minutes, with the loss of 786 men, including the admiral in command. Prien took the U-47 back out of Scapa Flow and won a knight's cross for his exploit.

Germany's surface fleet was not strong enough to challenge the Royal Navy on the high seas. But Hitler had built a number of powerful capital ships that he could send out to raid allied shipping lanes in the North and South Atlantic and even beyond. These included three 10,000-ton pocket battleships equipped with six 11-inch guns, the *Admiral Graf Spee, Admiral Scheer* and *Deutschland;* two 26,000-ton battle cruisers, the *Scharnhorst* and the *Gneisenau;* and the 10,000-ton, eight-inch gun cruisers *Hipper* and *Prinz Eugen.* Two 45,000-ton battleships with 15-inch guns, the *Bismarck* and the *Tirpitz,* were still being built when war broke out.

Two of the pocket battleships had sailed on raiding missions in late August—the *Deutschland* close to home in North Sea and the

North Atlantic, the *Graf Spee* into the South Atlantic. The *Deutschland* stayed out for two months playing hide and seek with the Royal Navy. She sank only two ships, but her furtive presence tied down large British squadrons out hunting for her. In mid-November she slunk home. A week later *Gneisenau* and *Scharnhorst* took to the high seas. On November 23 the *Scharnhorst* encountered the armed British merchant ship *Rawalpindi* off Iceland and quickly sunk her. The two German ships then turned tail and ran for home.

The saga of the *Admiral Graf Spee* in the South Atlantic was a much more daring one. Working in tandem with her supply ship, the *Altmark*, which brought fuel and food and took off prisoners, the *Graf Spee* terrorized shipping lanes between Africa and South America for two and a half months. In addition to sinking nine allied ships and taking hundreds of prisoners, the *Graf Spee* forced Churchill to put half his fleet out in pursuit. Nine hunting groups combed the oceans looking for the German raider. Their only clues were radio messages from ships that the *Graf Spee* had sunk or sighted. But when the raider sank the *Doric Star* off the Atlantic coast of Africa, a British commander 3000 miles away played a hunch. Commodore Harwood figured that the *Graf Spee* would head next for the teeming shipping lanes off South America. Accordingly he took three of his cruisers into the River Plate estuary, several hundred miles from the Uruguayan coast.

On the morning of December 13 a lookout saw a sudden belch of black smoke on the horizon. Harwood quickly sent the cruiser *Exeter* steaming to the left to investigate. Three minutes later, at 6:17, the *Graf Spee*'s big 11-inch guns opened up. A German lookout, perched on a higher mast, had seen the British ships first, and Captain Hans Langsdorff decided to attack. He had recognized the *Exeter* but mistakenly thought the two smaller cruisers were destroyers and that the British force protected a convoy. Minutes later Langsdorff realized his error and was faced with a split-second decision: turn back and pound the enemy with his big guns at long range or press the attack. He bore on. Shells plastered the *Exeter* and quickly knocked out a gun turret. The bridge ripped apart, the wheel lay smashed. But the *Exeter*'s cannon kept firing. A shell tore through the *Graf Spee*'s funnel. In the meantime Harwood had sailed *Ajax* and *Achilles* past the raider's bow. Langsdorff now faced attack from two sides and swung his big guns back and forth, thus slowing down his rate of fire. Twenty minutes after the battle began, the *Graf Spee* laid down smoke and wheeled northwest. Coming out of the screen, the Germans resumed bombarding the now stricken *Exeter*. Fires crackled across the British ship. Most of the superstructure was wrecked. The ship listed badly. Only a single turret was intact.

The battle now shifted to the two smaller cruisers. Gradually the British ships closed the range so they could bring their six-inch guns to bear. Shooting with great accuracy, they destroyed the *Graf Spee*'s seaplane and did some damage to the superstructure. But they took fearful punishment too. By 7:30 that morning the *Ajax* had only two guns left and both ships were running low on ammunition. Ten minutes later Harwood decided to disengage. He laid down smoke and turned from battle expecting the *Graf Spee* to pursue. But Langsdorff didn't. Instead he kept on a westerly course, rather than trying to break out into the Atlantic. The British stayed a respectful distance of 15 miles behind, just out of range of the *Graf Spee*'s guns. For the next 15 hours the ships sped towards the distant coast of Uruguay, only occasionally exchanging gunfire. Harwood hoped to resume the attack under cover of darkness with a torpedo strike. But before he could, the *Graf Spee* made it into Montevideo Harbor. International law gave Langsdorff only 72 hours to make repairs and get out of port. The German captain felt he needed more time—at least two weeks. The British kept up physical and propaganda pressure. *Ajax* and *Achilles* patrolled the Plate estuary. The cruiser *Cumberland* steamed up to support them. And the radio was full of British reports that a battleship and an aircraft carrier were not far distant (in fact, they were five days away). Amid the turmoil Langsdorff was left with three choices: internment of his crew, scuttling the *Graf Spee* or risking a fight.

Sunday, December 17, was his day of decision. A crowd of 300,000 Uruguayans jammed every available quay as the *Graf Spee* slid away from dockside and out towards the sea. Moments later a great explosion rocked the proud ship and, as the German sailors watched from lifeboats, it settled quietly into the Plate estuary. Two days later, in a Buenos Aires hotel room, Langsdorff wrapped the flag of the Imperial German Navy (not of Hitler's navy) around his body and put a bullet through his temple.

The battle of the River Plate is a milestone in naval history, for it closed a whole chapter of war at sea that had begun nearly 80 years before off the coast of the Carolinas when the Union ship *Monitor* had blasted the Confederate ironclad *Merrimac* to bits. The Battle of the River Plate was the last full-fledged engagement between armor-plated ships trading gunfire across open stretches of water. Henceforth the airplane would determine the fate of fighting ships and air-sea action would mold the shape of naval battles.

The scuttling of the *Graf Spee* had more immediate political impact as well. An enraged Hitler began to pay some attention to naval affairs and became interested in a project his admirals had long favored—a strike against Norway. German conquest of Norway's ports and thousand-mile coastline would bring the Nazis a bushel of strategic advantages. For one thing it would roll back the British blockade for many hundreds of miles. All that Britain had to do at present was close the Straits of Dover and the relatively narrow mouth of the North Sea. For another, German surface ships and U-boats would be able to strike directly at the vital convoy lanes across the North Atlantic.

Grand Admiral Raeder wanted Norway for his fleet, but he was worried the British might get there first. Rumors that the allies planned to send an expeditionary force to Finland across Norway and Sweden increased his concern. Then in mid-December Raeder met a man whose name has become a synonym for treason: Major Vidkun Quisling, a former Norwegian defense minister who now headed a Nazi-style party there. Quisling wanted help for a pro-German coup and he fed Raeder's suspicion of a British plot against Norway. The admiral took Quisling to see Hitler. The timing was good—the high point of the emotionally exhausting *Graf Spee* crisis, when Hitler's normally landlocked mind became more receptive to naval action. He promised Quisling support and ordered the German high command to study the chances for carrying out an invasion.

Then, on February 16, Hitler was galvanized into action by the fate of the *Altmark*, the *Graf Spee*'s supply ship. For two months after the River Plate battle, the *Altmark*, with 300 British prisoners aboard, had hidden out in the South Atlantic. Finally it made a successful dash through the British blockade and reached Norwegian waters. Churchill determined to rescue the prisoners. He ordered the destroyer *Cossack* to sail into the Norwegian fjord where the *Altmark* had anchored. Once alongside the German ship, the British ship put a boarding party on it and quickly subdued resistance by the *Altmark* crew. Shouting "The navy's here," British sailors searched the vessel and found the prisoners locked in storerooms and even in an oil drum. Norway protested this breach of her neutrality. But for Churchill it was just confirmation that he should take some action in the north, preferably mining the approaches to Narvik harbor.

In Berlin, Hitler was finally convinced that the British meant business. He appointed General Nicholas von Falkenhorst as commander of the Norway operation and told him to work out a plan of attack. Armed with a Baedeker guide of the country, Falkenhorst, who had never been to Norway, set to work. Hitler liked the result and committed five divisions to the attack. On March 1 he decided to enlarge the operation to include Denmark. Initial plans called for a fast sea strike against the five major Norwegian ports—from Oslo on the Baltic to Narvik, more than a thousand miles away on the Arctic coast. Denmark would be invaded overland and by sea. Most of the German fleet was committed to the action.

In London, meanwhile, the British government also pondered the future of Norway. With the Finnish armistice signed on March 11, the allies had to abandon plans to send a force across Norway and Sweden to help Finland. (The force had actually been readied and some of the men placed aboard ship.) Now Churchill won his point about mining the approaches to Narvik harbor. This would effectively block shipment of iron ore from Sweden through Narvik down the Norwegian coast to German ports. At the same time, the British readied an assault force to land in Norway in case the Germans retaliated with an invasion. Thus, throughout March, both sides prepared for action in the high north, but as usual at this stage of the war the Germans did it better and more thoroughly.

On April 2, Hitler gave final orders for the attack. The landings would take place on April 9. About the same time, the British had selected a date to mine Narvik: April 8. Preparations on both sides now reached fever pitch. At two A.M. on April 3 the first German merchant ship loaded with supplies for the Narvik expedition nosed out of Hamburg harbor. Shortly after midnight on the 7th the cruiser *Hipper* and 14 destroyers, two-thirds of the German destroyer force, were at sea taking 3,700 soldiers up to Narvik and Trondheim. By the 8th, task forces destined for Oslo, Bergen and Kristiansand had also left port. The British moved into action on April 5, when 12 destroyers, protected by the battle cruiser *Renown*, set out for the mining operation.

Off Trondheim on the morning of the 8th, the Germans divided their task force. *Hipper* and four destroyers headed for Trondheim, the rest of the flotilla up towards Narvik. That night the *Hipper* force reached Trondheim, and early on the morning of the 9th the German commander ran his ships past coastal guns and took the town. A lucky shell had knocked out cable lines so that the Norwegian defenders could not use searchlights in predawn darkness.

The German destroyers had as easy a time of it at Narvik, quickly shooting two old ironclads out of the water and landing General Dietl's 2000 Alpine troops, who occupied the town in short order. But the supply ships sent out a week earlier had not arrived, and the Germans were soon short of equipment and fuel, shortages that would hurt badly later on.

Norwegian opposition was stiffer in the south. But despite heavy shore fire at Bergen and Kristiansand, which badly damaged a number of German ships, both towns fell in a matter of hours. Airborne troops took the important seaplane base at Stavanger without a fight.

In Oslo the German attack almost failed. The ships made it safely past the entrance of the 50-mile long Oslo fjord, but did not get by the 19th-century Oscarberg fort 20 miles below the capital. The fort's big 11-inch guns plastered the German fleet with shells, and a flock of torpedoes raced through the water. The cruiser *Bluecher* caught fire, exploded and sank. The pocket battleship *Luetzow* (the renamed *Deutschland*) and several other ships were badly damaged. German troops had to disembark well below the fort and fight their way into Oslo the next day.

Meanwhile, the German minister had awakened the Norwegian government and presented an ultimatum: the Germans were coming to protect Norway from Britain. Resistance, he said, would be useless. The Norwegians rejected the ultimatum and quickly got king, government and the nation's gold reserves to Hamar, 70 miles away. Bad weather helped their flight. The Germans had planned an air assault to coincide with the seaborne invasion, but it was not until 9 A.M. that a few transport planes managed to land at Oslo airport and the troops on them overcome local resistance. At noon two German companies marched into town behind an army band. There was no fighting.

As for Denmark, it took the Germans just five hours to force king and government to surrender. The operation began on the night of the 7th when Brigadier General Kurt Himer, charged with carrying out the "conquest," doffed his uniform for mufti and boarded the Berlin-Copenhagen express. On the 8th Himer inspected the Copenhagen harbor and selected a pier for his troopship, due the next morning. That night Himer told the German minister about the planned invasion, and at 4 A.M. the two Germans woke up the Danish foreign minister with another ultimatum. Before dawn the Nazi ship docked without incident. To the south a Germany infantry division crossed the Danish frontier. The Danish king and his cabinet met for several hours, trying to decide whether to fight or surrender. Himer hastened their decision: he picked up the phone and called Berlin for a show of Luftwaffe strength. At seven o'clock the king capitulated and ordered Danish troops to stop shooting. The Danes lost 13, and the German had 20 casualties.

By midday on the 9th the Germans had achieved all their initial objectives with almost ridiculous ease and right under the nose of the powerful British fleet. Troops poured into Oslo to prepare a drive across the country and into the north. German planes beat back an attempted attack by the British fleet in the Bergen area. Still, Hitler was not yet home free. His position in the north, especially around Narvik, was most precarious. The Norwegian government resolved to fight, especially after pro-German Quisling proclaimed himself Prime Minister in Oslo. And the Germans had to count on some kind of Allied intervention. But the Fuehrer's campaign was marked by luck and skill and that of the Allies by bungling and delay.

The British almost nailed the Germans at Narvik. A destroyer flotilla entered the fjords on the 10th and shot five enemy destroyers out of the war. The British lost two ships in an ensuing battle with the remaining five German vessels, but the rest escaped. Three days later the battleship *Warspite* sailed back into the Narvik fjord and sank every German ship in sight. Survivors scrambled ashore to swell the ranks of Dietl's men. The action cost the German navy half her destroyer strength.

The British did not follow up this naval victory with a prompt landing, as they could easily have done. Instead, on the 15th, they landed some troops at Harstad, on the Lofoten Islands off the coast. British army and navy commanders could not decide on a concerted attack, and the Allies did not mount a land drive against Narvik until a month later. Dietl, meanwhile, fought a tough and skillful campaign against Norwegian troops in a setting of ice and snow.

In the south, Falkenhorst briskly set to work mopping up areas south and east of Oslo. He completed that operation on April 12. The next day he sent half a dozen battlegroups knifing north and west towards Bergen and Trondheim. At the same time, German troops set out from Bergen to cross the difficult and mountainous terrain. The drive from Oslo made good progress. By April 18 the 196th mountain division was astride the two routes that led through the mountains to Trondheim. By the 21st the 196th was attacking stubbornly fighting Norwegian units in the Lillehammer and Amot Rena areas, 180 miles from Oslo. The Germans now headed for a direct confrontation with British troops, the first of the war.

After much debate the British had decided to land two brigades (and three French battalions) at two small Norwegian ports: Namsos, a railhead 80 miles north of Trondheim, and Andalsnes, a 100 miles to the south of it. Initial plans called for a pincer attack on Trondheim. But by the time the Andalsnes brigade had completed landing operations on the 19th, German pressure to the south had become so strong that the British troops were rushed to help defend Lillehammer, 140 miles away.

Undaunted, the commander of the Namsos force decided to attack Trondheim alone, and he began moving his men south through snow four feet deep. None of the soldiers had ever fought in such conditions before. Nevertheless, they got to within 30 miles of Trondheim before the Luftwaffe arrived to pound them unmercifully and to destroy Namsos' port facilities. Slowly the British and Norwegians fighting with them retreated. On April 27 the British decided to clear out of central Norway altogether and the Namsos brigade prepared for evacuation, which was completed on the night of May 2.

The Andalsnes brigade had not helped the Norwegian defenders of Lillehammer much. Two days after they had arrived at the front the Allies were forced to give up the town. From the 22nd to the 27th, British and Norwegians fought desperately and at times skillfully to protect the rail line to Trondheim. But the Germans ground on steadily, again and again outflanking Allied positions. On April 29 the Germans stood just south of Trondheim. On the 30th, with the British preparing to board ship at Andalsnes, columns of the 196th division linked up with forces coming down from Trondheim. The campaign in central Norway was over. On the 28th a British destroyer had taken King Haakon, his government and gold aboard and headed for the northern counties, where the struggle was to continue.

The battle in the north lasted another six weeks, but in the end became only a sideshow to the German blitzkrieg in the west. There was some irony to this, for on May 14 an Allied force from Harstad, now swollen to 25,000 men, made a landing north of Narvik. Two weeks later General Dietl's men were driven out of town. It proved a meaningless victory. The deteriorating situation in the west did not leave the Allies enough strength for such operations. Thus Narvik's capture proved only a tactical move to cover yet another retreat. By June 9 the last Allied soldier was out of Norway and General Dietl re-entered Narvik a hero. A few days earlier King Haakon and his government had fled once again, this time to England and five years of exile. Night fell on Norway as a vengeful Hitler moved to punish the Norwegians for daring to challenge his power. It was a challenge that would last through the war, for the Norwegians put up a vigorous underground struggle until the Nazi defeat, when the pro-German traitor Quisling was shot.

By any yardstick of the time, Norway had proved a brilliant German victory. The British had been humiliated at sea and on land. Their blockade rolled back hundreds of miles, just as the admirals predicted. New air and naval bases were made available for strikes against the convoy routes. And later in the war the mere presence in Norway of a battleship like the *Tirpitz* could threaten Arctic convoys sent to Russia. Most important, perhaps, the Nazi myth of invincibility had been strengthened and German stock rose among the neutrals, even in the United States.

In the long view, however, the Norwegian campaign was a different story. The German navy, which had planned and executed it, emerged a shattered force. Half her destroyers had been lost at Narvik alone. *Scharnhorst* and *Gneisenau* were so badly damaged in a final battle in June that they were laid up for the rest of 1940. Coastal batteries had damaged many of the attacking ships, and Allied submarines prowling the North Sea and the Skagerrak had sunk many more. When Hitler readied the invasion of England that summer, his effective fleet consisted of three cruisers and four detroyers. Moreover, the Norwegian bases lost much of their importance after the German conquest of France, which gave Hitler excellent Atlantic and Mediterranean ports. The final analysis of military historians, therefore, is that Germany paid more for Norway's conquest than the prize was worth.

And certainly it had one result that the Germans would regret for the rest of the war: defeat in Norway made Winston Churchill Prime Minister of England.

British public reaction to the disaster was loud and bitter. In the House of Commons the opposition Labor and Liberal parties demanded a debate on the conduct of the war. It opened on May 7 with members of Neville Chamberlain's own Conservative Party sharply critical of how the "man of Munich" handled the affairs of a nation at war. One of them dug back three centuries to Oliver Cromwell's call to another parliament: "Depart, I say, and let us have done with you. In the name of God, go." Harsh words, but they fitted the mood of the House. Chamberlain determined to form a national government of all parties, but he soon learned that no one wanted him to lead it. On May 10 Chamberlain called Churchill to 10 Downing Street, the home of Britain's Prime Ministers, and admitted defeat. At six o'clock that evening King George VI summoned the First Lord of the Admiralty to Buckingham Palace. As he walked through the palace gates to see his king, Hitler's armies had already splintered the western front. Holland stood in flames. Belgian neutrality was a shambles. The Nazis were about to show the world what blitzkrieg was really all about.

"His Majesty received me most graciously and bade me sit

down," Churchill wrote later. "He looked at me searchingly and quizzically for some moments, and then said: 'I suppose you don't know why I have sent for you?' Adopting his mood, I replied, 'Sir, I simply couldn't imagine why.' He laughed and said: 'I want to ask you to form a government.' I said I would certainly do so."

Three days later the new Prime Minister strode into the House of Commons to offer Britain nothing but "sweat, blood, toil and tears," and to give his countrymen a taste of that exhilarating oratory that would buoy them and the rest of the free world through the awful months and years that lay ahead.

Chapter

☆ 3 ☆

Back in the early 1900s Alfred Graf von Schlieffen, the chief of the German General Staff, thought up a bold and daring plan for the swift destruction of France: a great mass of German armies would sweep through Belgium and wheel down onto the French Channel ports before swinging west to attack Paris. The Kaiser used the plan in 1914 and in the first few weeks of fighting almost won the war with it. Twenty-five years later Hitler's generals still thought the plan a good one and set to work updating it to fit conditions of armored warfare.

The new version was a skillful variation on the old. It still called for an invasion of Belgium. But this time it would not be the major stroke, only a decoy to lure British and French armies out of their fortifications along the Belgian frontier and into a trap sprung by a massive thrust through the Ardennes. Flying wedges of German armor would hurtle through the dense forests of Luxembourg and southeastern Belgium, crack the French defense anchor at Sedan and then drive up behind the enemy to the coast. Allied troops who had rushed off to help Belgium would be trapped, and the Germans would be in a position to sweep across the rest of France and take the Maginot Line from behind.

Preparations for the attack were detailed and precise. Colonel General von Bock's army group B (30 divisions, two armies) would invade Holland and Belgium. In the center, Colonel General von Rundstedt's army group A (45 divisions gathered into three armies and an eight-division armored group) would punch through the Ardennes and then race down the Somme River to the sea. Finally, the 19 divisions in General Leeb's army group C would man the Siegfried Line and repulse any French attack from the Maginot Line. Hitler also kept 42 divisions in reserve for use later in the campaign and posted them right behind the Bock and Rundstedt sectors. Thus a total of 117 divisions were piled up along a front only 165 miles long. The resulting traffic jam reached many miles inland.

The Allies had about as many divisions as did the Germans. But they were scattered unevenly across the long front lines with little if any coordination among national commanders. Worst of all, Belgian and Dutch timidity had prevented formation of a common defense. When the code word "Danzig" was flashed to the German generals late on May 9, unleashing the predawn blitzkrieg explosion in the west, Allied resistance was scattered and generally ineffective. The Wehrmacht needed only five days to defeat Holland, 17 days for Belgium and six weeks for the conquest of France.

Goering masterminded the strike against Holland. His bombers were over Dutch airfields at four in the morning. Transport planes flew in close behind, and paratroopers dropped on key areas in western Holland hours before the Nazi ambassador got around to presenting the now-traditional ultimatum. The Germans quickly occupied three airfields around the Hague and secured them after a day's bitter fighting. An hour after German bombers had devastated the Waalhaven airbase across the Maas from Rotterdam, paratroopers captured it.

Even more spectacular was the German seizure of the bridges that spanned the islands of the Rhine estuary and led into Rotterdam. Fifty paratroopers landed in Feyenoord, across the Maas from the big port, and quickly made for the bridges. An hour later 12 old seaplanes with 150 men aboard landed in the water near the handful of attackers. Together this small force occupied and held the bridges against frantic Dutch attacks. Two more bridges further south were taken as easily.

That night the Germans were established inside "Fortress Holland," the inner defense perimeter anchored at Rotterdam, the Hague and Amsterdam, and they controlled the only overland route into it. The Dutch had surrounded their Fortress with a barrier of water: they had opened the dikes and flooded the lowlands around it.

While the air assault was in progress, General Kuechler's

Eighteenth Army struck across the Dutch frontier. A cavalry division rode into Holland north of the Rhine and occupied it in 48 hours. Kuechler's single armored division quickly smashed through the Grebbe line and reached the Rotterdam bridges on the morning of the 12th. Two days of fierce fighting followed. Then the Germans issued an ultimatum: surrender or face destruction from the air. The Dutch agreed to talk, but Goering didn't leave them enough time. He sent 100 bombers against the city and flattened it in a brutal terror raid. Thousands died and many more thousands were wounded. Nearly 80,000 were left homeless.

Holland surrendered the next morning. The Dutch army had suffered 100,000 casualties, a quarter of its strength. Queen Wilhelmina and her government fled to England. The Germans had scored another blitzkrieg victory. The dark night of Norway descended on the land of tulips and windmills.

But Holland was only a sideshow for the real German thrust through Belgium and Luxembourg to the sea. Once again the Luftwaffe showed the way, raining bombs on major Belgian cities and communications centers. Nearly a third of the 159-plane Belgian air force was destroyed on the ground before dawn on May 10. And the Germans cracked the first major Belgian defense along the Albert canal with an attack by troop-carrying gliders. Utterly silent, these "sailing" planes touched down near two key bridges and on the roof of a fort the Belgians thought impregnable. The Germans grabbed the bridges before they could be blown up and made short work of Fort Eben Emael.

Nine gliders landed on the fort's roof. The 85 men who climbed out in pitch darkness quickly stuffed explosives into gun turrets and observation posts. They used hand grenades to blow up ammunition elevators. Within a few hours the attackers held the upper floors of the fort. Incessant Stuka attacks kept the defenders from reaching the Germans on the roof. Paratroop reinforcements arrived later, and the 1200 Belgians, now trapped inside their own concrete prison, surrendered.

The Allies, meanwhile, had reacted to the German invasion just as the Nazi planners had predicted they would—by walking right into the trap. French and British armies joined Belgian soldiers in manning a line from Antwerp to Namour, where the major Allied stand in Belgium was planned. The strategy seemed to work for a while. After clearing most of northeastern Belgium, General Reichenau's Sixth Army failed to crack the Dyle River line and the Antwerp-Namour defenses held through May 15.

But Reichenau's attack was only a feint to screen the thrust through the Ardennes. Rundstedt's tanks rattled across the forests of Luxembourg and Belgium in 48 hours, disposing with ease of scattered French resistance. On May 12 the panzer generals reached the Meuse River from below Namour to Sedan. The next day General Erwin Rommel took his Seventh Armored Division across at Houx. Further south General Reinhardt forded the river at Montherme. And Guderian's tanks were stationed along the Meuse between Donchery and Sedan. Stukas blasted French defenses on the west bank of the river for three hours on the 13th. At seven that evening, the French quit Sedan without a fight, fearful that they were about to be outflanked. During the night Guderian bridged the Meuse, and by the morning of the 14th he had two divisions across it. All through that day the three German bridgeheads expanded rapidly. The Meuse defenses from Namour to Sedan lay shattered, and two French armies were all but destroyed. The German breakthrough grew wider by the hour. On the 15th, Reinhardt's tanks were 40 miles west of the Meuse, and the long guns of the panzers pointed menacingly towards the English Channel.

That same day French Premier Paul Reynaud called Churchill on the telephone and said in English: "We have been defeated, we are beaten." When Churchill flew to Paris the next day the news was worse. The Germans had opened a 50-mile-wide gap in the French lines. Their armor was racing for Arras and Amiens and from there could either wheel on Paris or head for the Channel. The Allies didn't know which course the enemy would take. Moreover, the French had no reserves to throw into the battle, but 42 divisions sat immobilized on the Maginot Line. It was typical of French thinking, mired in the tactics of World War I. Even in defeat they could not adjust to conditions of modern warfare.

Allied fortunes sagged everywhere. In Belgium, General Reichenau cracked the Dyle line, forcing the Allies to fall back to the River Escaunt. On the 17th the Sixth Army was in Brussels. In France relentless German tanks continued to build a corridor of armor to the sea that would split armies in Belgium from those in the rest of France. On the 18th, Guderian stood on the Somme at Peronne. Further north Rommel captured Cambrai. Both generals were now moving so fast that even the German High Command grew worried at the reckless pace of their advance.

In Paris the French High Command finally awoke to the desperate peril facing the Allied armies north of the Somme. On the 19th, General Gamelin, the Allied Commander in Chief, ordered them to retreat across the river before the Panzers reached the coast. That night Reynaud fired him. General Weygandt, the new commander, rescinded the order, visited the front lines, then gave the same orders himself. Precious days were lost. Meanwhile, Lord Gort suggested to London that he take the BEF to Dunkirk for evacuation by sea. The British government told him to retreat to the Somme. A day later it reconsidered. Churchill began to gather a fleet of small ships, motorboats, pleasure craft—just about anything that would float— for possible evacuation duty. Planning for "Operation Dynamo" began none too soon, for Guderian had given his tanks no rest, at times even defying orders from above to stop. But he knew that his advance had become more of a race than a fight. His Panzers drove through the countryside with hatches and throttles wide open. Tank commanders stood in full view and waved to the French peasants they passed, worried more about gasoline supplies and keeping their engines in good running order than about French opposition.

At midnight on the 19th, Guderian sent one of his divisions charging from Peronne to Amiens while the second sped to Abbeville at the mouth of the Somme. At noon on the 20th, Guderian had captured Amiens, and that night his forces were on the coast. He had built an armored corridor 55 miles wide across the fields of Picardy and clanked shut the trap that the general staff had devised weeks earlier. In Germany, Hitler was delighted.

Nevertheless, the Allies still had hope. The armies in Belgium would simply have to fight their way across the Somme and meet counterattacking forces coming up from the south. The plan looked plausible on paper, but the French were too disheartened, discouraged and confused to carry it out. Only the British responded with any action. On the 20th, Gort told the French he planned to drive south from Arras with a force of two divisions and an armored brigade under command of General Franklyn. The French promised to send in two divisions from the south to help, but the help never came. Franklyn attacked anyway. At two o'clock in the afternoon of the 21st, his 80-odd tanks rolled out of Arras and moved briskly towards Baupane. Initial progress was good. The British took 400 prisoners in the first few hours of combat, but then they ran into Rommel's division, bent on attacking Arras. A fierce tank battle ensued. The British held their own and did severe damage to Rommel's tanks, but they were too weak afterwards to continue advancing. On the 22nd, Franklyn fell back to Arras. The next night he quit town and joined the general Allied retreat to the coast. It was the only significant allied counterattack of the blitzkrieg.

By the 24th the Germans had hammered the Allies into a rough, irregular anvil of land that ran from Zeebrugge, on the Belgian coast, about 70 miles inland to the area of Valenciennes and then back down to the coast at Gravelines, a small port below Dunkirk. Guderian did not stop at Abbeville. He quickly took Boulogne, raced past Calais, which he besieged, and reached the southern border of the Dunkirk perimeter. In the north, von Bock's army group B (part of the Eighteenth Army had now joined the Sixth) proceeded to smash the Belgian army to bits while Kluge's Twelfth Army (part of Rundstedt's Group A) attacked the anvil's top in Valenciennes. Allied prospects were dismal indeed.

Then it seemed as if the hand of fate intervened. At 11:42 on the morning of the 24th orders went out to Guderian: Stop your tanks. The Panzers stood on the Aa canal, which runs from the coast inland to St. Omer. Admittedly it was bad tank country, the terrain crisscrossed with canals. But few doubted the Panzer commander's ability to crash through the remaining miles to Dunkirk. Yet for two days German armor stayed where it was—and gave the British 48 precious hours to prepare their escape. It was a major German blunder. How did it happen with victory so close? Apparently Hitler and Rundstedt got cold feet together, worried that their precious Panzers might yet be destroyed or damaged too badly to provide the punch needed for the sweep across the rest of France, already in preparation. Moreover, Franklyn's attack at Arras had frightened Hitler. And his generals still could not quite believe that the French army was as impotent as it had so far shown itself. Perhaps that attack from the south would come after all. Indeed, military logic dictated that it had to. Finally, Goering's foolish pride in the Luftwaffe was tossed on the scale of German decision: air power, the fat Marshal told Hitler, could finish the encircled allies without endangering the tanks.

Whatever the reason for the delay, the British used the time well. Churchill ordered the troops at Calais to fight to the death, tying up German armor for three days there. Three divisions dug in along the Aa canal, so that when Guderian resumed his advance on May 26 he ran into a wall of fire. And that night Operation Dynamo swung into action. The first ships chugged across the 30-mile-wide English Channel to begin the evacuation. In the field, Allied troops began to retreat from the northern and central edges of the perimeter towards Dunkirk.

The Belgian position had now grown hopeless, with the flank they guarded pushed ever closer to the sea and their soldiers near exhaustion. On the 26th the Belgians told their allies they did not know how much longer they could hold out. The next day King Leopold opened talks with the Germans. At midnight he surrendered. The Allies were furious and charged Leopold with betraying the cause of freedom. But in the light of history the accusation is unfair: Leopold had little choice but to quit. Quite simply, his soldiers couldn't fight anymore. They had waged a skillful and courageous campaign against overwhelming odds. And in the end much of the blame for their defeat lay with the French collapse in the south.

Still, Leopold's surrender vastly increased the Allied peril around Dunkirk. Von Bock quickly lunged to the coast and on the 28th stood only 17 miles from the northern anchor of the allied perimeter. Gort quickly rushed up every piece of artillery he had, and his gunners laid down so murderous a barrage that the German advance stalled. Thousands were thus able to stream into the Dunkirk shield. And now French heroism helped too. Rommel had trapped 50,000 French soldiers in a pocket around Lille. They fought with the courage of utter despair for three days and kept Rommel's tanks from joining the assault on Dunkirk.

Operation Dynamo, meanwhile, continued apace despite savage aerial bombardment. On the 27th the Germans had destroyed Dunkirk's port installations. Bad weather had kept them away the next day. When they returned, an angry beehive of British fighters awaited them, and the fights that laced the sky were a foretaste of the Battle of Britain to come. Down below, resourceful British sailors had found another way to pluck the men of the BEF from shore. Motorboats, rowboats, yachts, Dutch skoots, fishing boats, river barges and tugboats, even sailboats, edged onto the beaches and brought the soldiers to ships waiting offshore. Some of them were sunk by German bombs, but most of the enemy explosives thudded harmlessly into the beach. By May 30 the fleet of 850 ships and boats had taken 120,000 men to safety.

The German field commanders woke up to the fact that Goering could not make good his boast. Airpower alone could not stop the exodus. The fury of the Wehrmacht's assault increased. Artillery shells began to plaster town and beach. But still the pace of evacuation stepped up. On May 31 and June 1 a total of 110,000 men were rescued, many slogging through the water to reach boats and ships. Gradually the Germans shrank the perimeter with mighty hammer blows, and on June 2 it reached only six miles inland. That day, too, a fierce air battle raged in the cloudy skies above. Each side lost 30 planes, a stand-off. But again the British won valuable time. Dunkirk had now become an inferno. The town burned fiercely, and the shells and bombs never stopped coming. Evacuation could continue only at night.

Time began to run short. The perimeter had become a pocket. Still the Allies fought on and held on. In the last three days of Operation Dynamo—June 2, 3 and 4—another 75,000 soldiers were rescued, most of them Frenchmen. Finally, on June 4, it was all over. Kluge's men entered the shattered port. But the prize had slipped out of German hands, and the British had written one of the great epics of the war.

It can't have seemed much of a prize—350,000 exhausted and dispirited men without rifles and artillery or equipment of any kind. But they were alive and ready to fight on another day, fight with the experience of battle-hardened veterans. Moreover no one—not Germans, not French, perhaps not even the British—had thought an evacuation of such scope possible. Churchill himself had only hoped for the escape of 50,000 men. For the Germans there was a bitter note of irony: not one Nazi ship was in the Channel to harass the evacuation. The few vessels Admiral Raeder still had intact were off Narvik. The price for Norway had indeed been a high one.

In London, Churchill went before the House of Commons. He called the evacuation a deliverance, and a victory for the air force. "We got the army away . . . and [the Germans] have paid fourfold for any losses which they have inflicted." And then the Prime Minister hurled these words of defiance at the enemy:

"We shall not flag or fail. We shall defend our island whatever the cost may be, we shall fight on the beaches, we shall fight on the landing grounds, we shall fight in the fields and in the streets, we shall fight in the hills; we shall never surrender."

The night Dunkirk fell, the Germans finished regrouping. Von Bock now held the western section of the front, Rundstedt the eastern. On June 5 von Bock's tanks raced for the Seine. Slowed for the first two days, the Panzers picked up speed on the 7th. On the 8th, Rommel's divisions crashed up to the Seine at Rouen; that night his tanks were in the city. General Kleist's two Panzer corps hit the river a day later and captured Vernon on June 9. Further east his tanks reached Compiegne on the Oise, and Rundstedt crossed the Aisne. On June 12 the Germans were across the Marne—and this time there would be no "miracle of the Marne" like the one that had saved France in World War I. The capture of Paris was near.

The French government thought so too. On June 10 it fled to Tours. The roads leading out of Paris were already awash with refugees, and overhead the Germans bombed and machine-gunned the terrified civilians unmercifully, a "sport" they practiced all through the campaign. And there was grim news from Rome: Mussolini ended weeks of indecision and dealt himself into the war. Italian troops moved into France intent on collecting some of the spoils that German armor had won. When Churchill arrived in Orleans on the 11th for a conference with Premier Reynaud, Defense Minister Marshal Henri Pétain had already urged the government to ask the Germans for an armistice. Churchill quickly tried to steel the French will to resist. They must fight for every house, every street of Paris. But here the Churchillian eloquence failed. On June 12 the French declared Paris an "open city" and decided not to defend it. The next night the Reynaud government moved to Bordeaux.

The first German jackboot slammed sparks off the cobblestones of Paris at nine on the morning of June 14. The triumphant Wehrmacht goose-stepped down the Champs Elysées as thousands of despairing Frenchmen watched the Nazis strut past. The picture of a nameless Frenchman, tears streaming down his face, flashed round the world—a symbol of defeated and downtrodden France.

For the Germans, Paris was only a waystation. On the 15th the Panzers clattered into Burgundy to the gates of Dijon. Far to the east, Leeb's Army Group C attacked the Maginot Line and broke through at Saarbruecken. It was no longer a battle but a chase.

In Bordeaux differences between Reynaud and Pétain sharpened into a cabinet crisis. A dramatic meeting on the afternoon of the 15th found Reynaud almost isolated. Most of his government colleagues leaned to the defeatist side of Pétain and Weygandt. It was no longer a question of whether but of how to surrender. Weygandt insisted the government do it, not the army, in order to preserve the honor of French arms. Reynaud's proposals for setting up a government-in-exile in North Africa won little support. The next day, June 16, Reynaud resigned and Pétain took what was left of French power. On the 17th he asked the Germans for an armistice.

That morning a gangling, 50-year-old Brigadier General with a small moustache went to his office in Bordeaux to arrange his day's schedule. Charles de Gaulle had only recently joined the government as Under Secretary of Defense after proving his theories of armored warfare on the battlefield: in May his tanks had managed, however briefly, to delay the German dash to the sea. Later de Gaulle drove to the airport to see off a friend flying home to Britain. As the plane began to taxi down the runway, de Gaulle stepped casually out on the tarmac, ripped open the door, jumped inside and slammed it shut behind him. The officials on the ground were left to stare openmouthed. That night de Gaulle planted the flag of Free France in London and 24 hours later broadcast a ringing plea to his countrymen: "Whatever happens, the flame of French resistance must not and shall not die." But that night it was still a very small flame. And years would pass before de Gaulle's Free French movement became the authentic voice of France. Efforts to rally North Africa collapsed. An attack on Dakar failed. Only French colonies in Africa south of the Sahara joined the Gaullist cause.

Hitler took his time answering Pétain's request for an armistice.

First he met Mussolini and, to the strutting dictator's crushing disappointment, refused Italian demands for vast spoils they had not won. (Il Duce's 36 divisions had been stopped cold in the Alps by a small French force.) Then the Fuehrer worked out the terms of French surrender and chose the stage where France would sign an armistice. It would complete the degradation of a great people. For Hitler selected the very same spot where the Allies had dictated the conditions of peace to the Kaiser—a clearing in the woods near Compiegne. And he took from a nearby museum the railroad car in which that document had been signed. Negotiations were set to open in the afternoon of June 21, 1940.

A warm June sun filtered into the clearing as Hitler's big Mercedes and a caravan of German limousines pulled up. Hitler, Goering, Rudolf Hess (the Fuehrer's deputy), Ribbentrop, Army Commander Brauchitsch and Wehrmacht chief Keitel all got out and walked across the clearing to the carriage. They passed a slab of granite commemorating the World War I armistice. Hitler stopped to read the text carved on the stone. An eyewitness saw his face "afire with scorn, anger, hate, revenge, triumph." Inside the coach Hitler sat in the same chair used in 1918 by the French commander, Marshal Foch, and waited for the French delegation. It arrived a few minutes later, shock etched sharply in every face. They had not been prepared for this final humiliation. Hitler sat impassive as Keitel read out the introduction to the German terms. Then he left.

Talks continued for two days. The desperate French argued bitterly against conditions they considered harsher than those they had imposed on the Germans in 1918. And they pleaded that they had no authority to sign anything. Finally the Germans issued a one-hour ultimatum. Weygandt promptly telephoned his acceptance. The armistice left half of France unoccupied and under the administration of the Pétain government. Moreover, the Germans "promised" not to use the large French fleet against Britain as long as the ships were disarmed and laid up in French ports.

The French signed. It was 6:50 P.M., June 22. A light rain fell as the two delegations left the railroad car. Through the trees endless columns of refugees could be seen marching—nowhere. On the 24th an armistice was concluded with Italy. And on June 25 the last gun fell silent in France.

But one prize had eluded Hitler's grasp: the large French fleet. In London, Churchill moved purposefully and swiftly to make sure that the Germans would never get it. On July 3 he seized the powerful squadron docked in British ports. In British-occupied Alexandria, watchful gunners kept a battleship and four cruisers berthed at their piers. And off Gibraltar that morning an aircraft carrier and three battleships led a strong task force to Oran. The French were given a choice: join the British and continue the war, or give up to the British, or scuttle their ships. The French admiral refused. He would meet force with force. Talks continued all day as agonized British captains tried to avoid a showdown with men who had been their comrades in arms only days before. The French wouldn't budge, and Churchill was adamant. Too much was at stake. Once Hitler had the French fleet he could protect a seaborne invasion of England. Late that afternoon the British opened fire. Only the battle cruiser *Strasbourg* escaped and, heavily damaged, limped into Toulon. Pétain, who had set up a government for rump France in Vichy, retaliated with an air raid against Gibraltar and on July 5 broke diplomatic relations with Britain. It was one of those swift changes of sides that would prove so common in this war.

Loss of the French fleet was a severe blow to the Germans. But in the euphoria of victory the Nazis paid it little heed. Hitler was convinced that Britain would quickly sue for peace, that the island nation could not possibly fight on alone. Churchill's defiant oratory was dismissed as just so many words. The Germans even sent out peace feelers through the Vatican and neutral Sweden. And for weeks they failed to make any serious preparations for invading England. In mid-July, Hitler told his generals to work out a plan of attack, but he didn't think he'd really have to go through with it. Admiral Raeder opposed the whole business. He didn't have the ships to protect an invasion and urged the Fuehrer to rely on Luftwaffe bombardment to bring England to her knees.

On July 19, Hitler staged a monster victory celebration in Berlin's Kroll Opera House. The whole Prussian Officers Corps attended to honor the Austrian corporal. When he mounted the rostrum to speak, Adolf Hitler was at the summit of his glory, master of an empire that stretched across Europe from Russia to Spain. And now he offered Britain the peace of the victor: "I feel it is my duty to appeal once more to reason and common sense in Britain. . . . I can see no reason why this war must go on."

When the German generals filed out after the speech, they were convinced that England couldn't help but accept the Fuehrer's magnanimous offer. An hour later the British broadcast Churchill's scornful rejection. Shocked, Hitler and the generals buckled down to plans for "Operation Sea Lion"—the invasion of Britain.

Brauchitsch for one was confident that the attack would take only a month to complete. Rundstedt moved 13 of his crack divisions to jump-off points along the Channel to spearhead the assault against a 200-mile stretch of coast in southern England. Hitler prepared to commit 40 divisions to the first wave of attacks alone. But Admiral Raeder intervened. The navy simply didn't have enough ships to protect so large a force. He urged postponement of the invasion until the following May. Hitler refused. But he did agree to let Goering's Luftwaffe bomb Britain first. Orders to step up the air war—largely limited in July to attacks on shipping off the coast—went out on August 1. For the next ten days probing attacks increased; on the 12th, Goering was ready to start the major assault, "Operation Eagle."

This time, however, the Germans did not have surprise on their side. For two months the British had strained every nerve to build up their defenses. The coastline bristled with heavy naval guns. A million men joined the home guard. In July the first American rifles and field guns began to arrive in British ports. Churchill opened negotiations for lease of 50 over-age American destroyers. British factories turned out 250 new tanks. And most important, hundreds of Hurricane and Spitfire fighters swelled the ranks of the RAF. On June 4, Fighter Command had only 446 planes left. On August 11, it had 704, with another 289 in reserve. A network of the then revolutionary radar screens threw an invisible curtain around the island.

Goering had committed a force of 1,900 bombers and 1,100 fighters to Operation Eagle, which began on August 12 when several hundred planes ranged over the southern coast bombing radar stations, airfields and shipping. The British challenge was strong and effective: they downed 31 enemy planes and lost 22 of their own. The next day the Luftwaffe flew nearly 1500 sorties. The score: 45

to 13 for Britain. On the 14th the Germans eased up with a limited bombardment of rail installations. Then, on the 15th, Goering threw a haymaker. It missed. His bombers pounded targets across Britain far into the night, but again the RAF shot down twice as many planes as it lost, 75 to 34. And a German attempt to bomb industrial sites in the northeast was a dismal failure. Goering never again ventured that far north. On the 16th the RAF again outshot the Luftwaffe, 45 to 21. Two days later it was the same story: RAF pilots blasted 71 German planes from the skies and lost only 27.

Clearly the RAF had won a round. Between August 8 and 18 it had destroyed 363 German planes, against a loss of 181 British fighters. The Germans were forced to withdraw the slow Stukas, the terror of the European continent. Spitfires popped them out of the sky as if they were balloons. Moreover, the superiority of British fighters had been clearly demonstrated. Both Hurricanes and Spitfires were more heavily armed and more maneuverable than the Messerschmidts. The Spitfire could climb higher. Radar spotted enemy planes still many miles away, so that the RAF was always airborne to meet attack and could often intercept the Germans over water. Ground-based sector stations fed late battle information to fighters already in the air. Britain's pilots had trained two years for just this kind of war, and they fought it magnificently.

Now the Germans decided to strike further inland to maul fighter command fields wherever they were, not merely bases near the coast, and to renew bombing of radar and sector stations. On August 24 they resumed the offensive. More planes and more fighters were thrown into the battle. Fighter command bases were soon pockmarked with bomb craters. Slowly the Germans disrupted the vital communications network. And British losses in the air grew alarmingly. By September 6, the RAF had lost 466 fighters, the Luftwaffe 385. Even more serious, 231 British pilots were either killed or wounded. At this rate the Germans might well disrupt Britain enough to allow a successful invasion. Indeed, there was mounting evidence that Hitler was at last ready to strike. RAF planes noticed an alarming buildup of boats and barges in Channel ports. On August 31 only 18 barges were berthed in Ostend; on September 6 there were 218. The RAF, which had never been content with a purely defensive role, increased day and night bombardment of the French and Belgian coast.

Their guess as to German intentions, it turned out, had been a good one. After repeatedly postponing Sea Lion in August, Hitler decided at the end of the month to strike on September 21. In order to meet the deadline the German navy had to be ready on September 11. The fighter command would have to be destroyed before then. But now the Germans made a fatal change in tactics. They abandoned the highly successful attacks on fighter command bases and chose a new target: London.

There were two major reasons behind this decision. First, Luftwaffe generals thought an attack on London would concentrate Britain's fighter strength in one place and make it easier to destroy. And second, Hitler thirsted for revenge. On August 25, German planes had accidentally bombed London. Churchill ordered immediate retaliation, and the RAF flew several successful night raids against Berlin. The Fuehrer was outraged, and the German people suddenly turned jittery. Had not Goering himself promised that such a thing could never happen? The Fuehrer vowed to smash the British capital.

In the late afternoon of September 7 hundreds of planes flew up the Thames and dumped their bombs on gas works, power stations and the waterfront docks. Huge fires spread across the sky and served as beacons for a second wave of attackers, who came at night and stayed till dawn. It was the first taste of what Londoners would come to call the Blitz.

That night, however, it merely served to confirm fears that invasion was imminent. Maximum alerts flashed across the country. The home guard took up battle positions. The navy manned action stations. And the bomber command intensified raids on the concentration of enemy shipping at Channel ports. Britain was about as ready for the worst as it would ever be.

The Luftwaffe sent 200 bombers against London on the 9th and ran into a buzz saw. Only half the force reached the capital, and their bombs fell on the outskirts. The Germans lost 28 planes, the RAF 19. Raids continued that night and the next day. Then it was September 11, and Hitler again had to postpone Sea Lion: fighter command was still very much in action. Three days later there was another postponement. The navy would go on the 17th; the invasion would be on the 27th. It was the last possible date before bad weather set in. Nightly raids against London had burnished the sky but not brought a decision. Hitler and Goering decided to go for broke—one massive daylight raid to destroy London on Sunday, September 15.

Wave after wave of German planes flew across the Channel that day, and each one got its own escort of British fighters. Again and again the Luftwaffe had to dump bombs without aiming them, usually on the outskirts of London. Dogfights crisscrossed the sky as tired British pilots scrambled into the air on countless missions. At one point during the day every Hurricane and Spitfire the RAF had was aloft. When it was all over, the British claimed 185 "kills" against a loss of 26. A "recount" later showed that only 60 enemy craft had been shot down. But the impact was the same. After a month of bitter air war the Germans did not have the power to stage a successful daylight raid on Britain. That night the British drove home the point: they subjected invasion boats gathered in ports from Antwerp to Boulogne to the worst bombardment yet.

For the Germans too the message was clear. On September 17 Hitler postponed Sea Lion once again and on October 12 put it off until the following spring. After that it was only talk, and it was scrapped altogether in February, 1942.

But the Battle of Britain continued. Through November the Germans sent an average 200 bombers against London every night in a systematic attempt to break a people's will to resist. Much of London lay in rubble, but Goering's bombs bounced off the great British heart like rubber balls. Soon the capital was ringed by anti-aircraft guns. The RAF developed effective night fighter techniques. And gradually Londoners adapted to life under a hail of bombs. Each night they crowded underground shelters in church cellars or slept in the deep shafts of London's subways. Others manned rooftops to watch for fires and help fight them. The blazing skyline became a part of nighttime living.

On November 3 an eerie stillness fell over the city. For the first time in two months air raid sirens remained silent. It was a watershed. The Luftwaffe would continue to blitz London and bomb major British towns and cities until far into 1941, but the Battle of Britain as such was over. It had cost the Germans 1,733 planes; the RAF had lost 915. The two-to-one ratio told the story of Hitler's first, and perhaps decisive, defeat. Goering had not come close to winning control of the skies, the key prerequisite to invasion, and in trying to get it he had crippled the Luftwaffe. Germany would never make up the loss. British factories began to outproduce the Germans during the Blitz, and Goering wasn't able to catch up. Moreover, even if he had won the Battle of Britain, it is doubtful if the invasion could have succeeded. For the German navy continued to pay the price for victory in Norway. Raeder didn't have the ships needed to protect the barges or the guns to fight off the British fleet.

Still, the lion's share of glory went to the RAF's fighter pilots—less than a thousand daredevil young men who flew into combat the way knights used to ride into battle. As Churchill said of them: "Never . . . have so many owed so much to so few."

Chapter

☆ 4 ☆

With Italy's entry into the war, fighting spilled beyond the borders of Europe into Africa and the Middle East. Here chance gleamed brightly for the Axis powers. Mussolini had a large army in the Italian colonies; a fast strike from Libya could have pushed the British out of Egypt, cut the lifeline of her empire, the Suez Canal, and laid bare the oil-rich Middle East. England could not have long survived such a blow to her economy and would have strangled to death. But the Italian soldiers had no stomach for this war, and Hitler did not supply them with enough German steel for victory.

Certainly Grand Admiral Raeder tried hard to convince Hitler to put it there. A thrust across Suez, he told him, could win the oil fields of Arabia, bring German armor all the way to the borders of Turkey and allow a strike against the Caucasus of Russia. But the Fuehrer's mind was landlocked, incapable of grasping a wider strategy based on ships and the far reach of naval power. Once he had abandoned Sea Lion, he thought only of an overland attack against the Soviet Union; a repetition of the French blitzkrieg across the wide steppes of Russia that would at last make the dream of *Mein Kampf* for more *lebensraum* in the east come true. The Italians were left to bungle the chances of victory by themselves.

On paper, at least, Mussolini's forces shouldn't have failed; they were strong enough that June of 1940 to win a victory in Egypt many times over. Italy had an army of 215,000 in Libya, and ample tanks, guns and planes. General Wavell had 36,000 men and very little armor. But the British had a few extras the Italians lacked: good leadership, courage and the will to fight. It proved enough.

The long and bloody desert war began 24 hours after Italy had stabbed France in the back. A light British force attacked much stronger Italian troop concentrations and inflicted heavy casualties. For the next month desultory fighting continued without much territory changing hands. Then it died down. Only in September did Mussolini succeed in goading the frightened Marshal Graziani into an attack across the Egyptian border. It was more of a farce than a battle. It opened with a thunderous Italian artillery barrage that did little damage. When the smoke cleared, the incredulous British faced a neat line of Italian soldiers mounted on motorcycles, with row upon row of tanks, armored cars and trucks arrayed just as neatly behind. British gunners quickly shot this parade-ground formation to bits, and then fell back before the sheer weight of Italian men, guns and tanks. Graziani proceeded to lumber across 60 miles of undefended Egyptian desert in four days and sat there until December, when Wavell was ready to launch his first offensive.

Stymied in Libya, Il Duce now sought glory elsewhere. As he told Hitler on the morning of October 28, 1940, when they met in Florence, "Fuehrer, we are on the march. Victorious Italian troops crossed the Greek-Albanian frontier at dawn today." (Italy had conquered Albania in 1939.) Hitler was appalled at this latest bit of mock heroics. It was already late fall when bad weather favored strongly entrenched defenders. And Italy's performance in Africa had not inspired any confidence in the prowess of her arms.

Hitler's fears were quickly justified. The Greeks gave the peaceloving Italian army a fearful licking. They had not expected to. They had only meant to show the flag and protect the nation's honor. Instead, the Greek high command suddenly found itself winning a war it had made no plans to conduct. Young second lieutenants and their platoons chased the Italians back into Albania with no orders from their superiors and no over-all plan of attack. Italy was quickly mired in a frustrating and indecisive campaign.

Britain at once rallied to the Greek side. Churchill didn't have much to spare in the way of men and equipment, but he sent a squadron of bombers and a few soldiers he bullied Wavell into letting go. Greece didn't want much more, fearful that Hitler might then join the war against her. Certainly the Germans thought about intervention, for Hitler and his generals realized very soon that they would probably have to help Mussolini in Greece and Africa. An army of ten divisions was readied for service in the Balkans. A small armored force was tentatively committed to Libya; it was the genesis of the famed Afrikakorps.

Unlike Hitler, Churchill had no doubts about the importance of the Middle East. Even during the Battle of Britain and the blitz that followed he sent whatever he could beg, borrow and scrape together to bolster Wavell's strength. Slowly troops from the British Commonwealth moved into Egypt—Australians, Indians, South Africans, New Zealanders. As British factories increased production, more heavy equipment was sent out. For months Churchill badgered Wavell (as he would all his Mideast commanders; he tried to run the desert war from London) to drive the Italians out of Egypt. At last, on December 9, Wavell felt he was ready. He had planned a modest campaign of about five days that would shove the Italians back into Cyrenaica, the eastern half of modern Libya. Instead, Wavell found himself waging a two months' blitzkrieg that took him to the frontier of Tripolitania, the other half of Libya.

The British quickly raced through miles of desert no-man's-land and, at dawn on the 9th, swept through a gap in Italian lines south of Sidi Baranti. The Italians fell back at once before the weight of British armor. Sidi Baranti was taken on the 10th. The jubilant British claimed capture of "five acres" of officers and "200 acres" of soldiers. On the 11th they were near Sollum on the Egyptian border. Their haul: 38,000 prisoners, 400 guns and 50 tanks at a cost of 133 British dead. Four days later the Italians were back in Libya preparing the defenses of the important coastal towns of Bardia and Tobruk. They didn't prepare them very well. Bardia fell on January 4, 1941, Tobruk on January 22. The British took 75,000 prisoners. The glittering Italian army of six months ago had been smashed, and Wavell had won a stunning victory. But he had to take a breather. His lines of communication were too long and stretched too thin (a recurrent ill all through the desert war), and his armor ran into mechanical trouble.

Once they had regrouped, the British sent one column down the coastal road towards Benghazi, which fell on February 6. A second armored spearhead drove straight across the desert to the coast below the city, where it trapped and cut up an Italian division. On the

7th all of Cyrenaica was in British hands. Wavell's "Army of the Nile" had covered 500 miles of scorching desert in two months, taking 130,000 prisoners, 400 tanks and almost 1300 guns. The British lost 500 men in the whole campaign.

Wavell was not allowed to push on any further. Greece haunted the sleep of British planners and Churchill wanted men and supplies in the Mideast transferred to the Greek theater. He was sure that Hitler would soon come to the aid of his beleaguered Italian ally, and by mid-March the British had built up a 50,000-man force there. Moreover, Wavell had to mastermind three campaigns designed to sweep the Italians out of their East African Empire (a task completed in May, 1941, when Haile Selassie returned to Addis Ababa, five years to the day after he had fled Ethiopia).

In Berlin, meanwhile, Hitler took a second look at the Libyan situation and decided German intervention was now necessary. On February 12, 1941, a supremely confident Erwin Rommel landed in Tripoli to set up headquarters for the fledgling Afrikakorps. For six weeks Rommel methodically built up German armored strength in Tripolitania and set up a command structure that would leave him independent of Italian interference.

German activity worried the British, but there was little Wavell could do to counter it. His forces west of Benghazi were weak and depleted because he had sent so many of them to Greece. He didn't have enough fighters to protect Benghazi from German air attack, so supplies had to be trucked in from Tobruk. And Wavell knew that the flat salt pans between Benghazi and the Tripolitanian border were ideal tank country, with victory sure to go to the stronger armored force.

Rommel knew it too. On March 31 he was ready to attack with two armored divisions backed up by motorized infantry. It would be the first of Rommel's many spectacular African campaigns: in 12 days he wiped out all the gains it had taken Wavell two months to make. Still, the German paid his enemy the supreme compliment— he copied exactly Wavell's last attack. Rommel sent one column down the coastal road to Benghazi, the other across the desert. On April 3 his tanks clattered into the port after the British had abandoned it. Air power was a key to the German success. Rommel had 100 bombers and 100 fighters. The British fought with very little air support. Rommel used the advantage well. On the 7th his troops were outside Tobruk.

The port was chock-full of supplies. If Rommel captured them, especially the large quantities of gasoline stored there, he would have himself virtually a brand new army. Wavell quickly loaded an Australian division onto ships and sent it to Tobruk. It arrived on April 8. The Germans probed the city's defenses, found them too strong and decided to dash for the Egyptian border instead. Their tanks got there on April 12, when they captured Bardia and lunged beyond the frontier into Egypt itself. But Rommel had to call a halt. He wasn't strong enough to besiege Tobruk and continue his advance —at least, not without substantial reinforcements.

A pause set in as both sides sought to replenish armor lost in the fighting. By April 20 the Germans had begun unloading tanks at Tripoli in some quantity. The next day British ships were offshore, and their guns crippled harbor installations. The raid helped slow the flow of German supplies. The problem of reinforcing Wavell, however, remained. Churchill managed to find 300 tanks and was able to persuade his generals and admirals to let him ship them to Alexandria. It took half the British fleet to protect the convoy, which made it safely into port on May 10 after a hair-raising voyage. Unfortunately the armor arrived too late to find prompt use. When the ships docked, the whole Mideast threatened to explode. Hitler had conquered Greece and prepared to invade Crete, whence German planes could easily bomb Suez. A pro-German revolt shook Iraq, and Vichy authorities in Syria had allowed substantial Nazi infiltration. Before Wavell could again turn his attention to the western desert, he had to deal with the situation in the two Arab countries. In the meantime, Rommel's strength was increased by a full division.

A Nazi sympathizer, Rashid Ali, seized power in Iraq on March 30. The coup worried Churchill enough to move a brigade from India to the Iraqi port of Basra. Fighting broke out in May. A cautious Hitler sent a few planes in to help his man, but the RAF promptly disposed of them. A British army was quickly patched together and defeated Rashid Ali's troops. Once again Hitler had lost a golden opportunity: had he moved in boldly and in force, his tanks would soon have rolled towards India. Instead, Rashid Ali saw the handwriting of defeat and on May 30 fled to neighboring Persia.

Even before the Iraqi fires were banked, the British realized they would have to take next door Syria before it, too, became a Nazi base. Charles de Gaulle's Free French forces were assigned the task— by persuasion if possible, by force if necessary. Wavell again had to send British troops to support the Gaullist effort. As at Oran and Dakar in the previous year, Vichy troops offered stiff resistance and the conquest of Syria took most of June.

This campaign was of more than military and strategic importance. It served to sharpen a brewing conflict between de Gaulle and the British which was never fully resolved and whose effect lingered into the 1960s. For the Free French leader feared that Britain would never return Syria to France. His suspicions turned to certainty when the British evaded demands for French control of the country, and he won his point only after threatening to break Free French relations with London. The incident left a bitter taste. De Gaulle never trusted the British or the Americans after that, and his distrust shaped the policies he followed as French President from 1958 on.

Operations in Iraq and Syria, as well as mechanical difficulties with the new tanks, delayed Wavell's attack into Libya until June 15, 1941. And when he struck, Rommel was ready for him. Fighting raged inconclusively for three days. Then, on the 17th, Wavell had to break off his offensive, which had gained him nothing. He had lost 90 tanks, Rommel about 100. The two sides were back where they started. Still, the Germans did not pursue Wavell's forces. The Desert Fox was under strict orders to stay put until he could be reinforced again en masse. Since Hitler was about to attack Russia, this would take some time. And indeed a major battle in the western desert did not flare again until late in the fall of 1941.

This attitude of Hitler's was typical of his whole approach to the vital Middle East. For him it was never more than a sideshow, an Italian responsibility that Il Duce continually failed to meet, so that German arms had to rescue him. Hitler's blindness to the glittering chance of conquest open here would in the end help Germany lose the war. So, of course, would the decision to invade Russia.

The Fuehrer had begun planning an attack on the Soviet Union right after the fall of France. His generals had cranked out a quick plan in the summer of 1940: a hundred divisions could defeat the Red Army in four to six weeks. Hitler even picked a date, the spring of 1941. Then Britain's refusal to quit or make peace derailed German plans for a while. But on December 18, 1940, Hitler issued his now-famous directive 21 on the conduct of the war—the blueprint for "Operation Barbarossa." Armored blitzkrieg would sweep across Russia from Finland in the north to Rumania in the south. The aim of the drive was twofold: capture the rich industrial Donets basin and conquer Moscow, the transportation hub of the Soviet Union.

The Germans had consolidated their hold on most of the Balkans that fall. Hitler had installed a fascist government in Rumania, the continent's largest oil producer, and sent a strong military mission to Bucharest. Rumania, Hungary and Slovakia had signed the Axis Pact (concluded in September among Germany, Italy and Japan). Bulgaria leaned strongly towards Berlin and, in February, joined up. On March 1, German troops crossed from Rumania into Bulgaria to prepare the invasion of Greece. Italy's situation there had not improved. The Greeks, recovered from their own surprise at winning, had driven the invaders far back into Albania and held about a quarter of that country. And after the Germans moved into Bulgaria, Churchill finally persuaded Athens to let him send more British troops and equipment into the Greek theater.

Hitler stepped up pressure on the lone Balkan holdout, Yugoslavia. So far repeated efforts to browbeat Belgrade into the Axis had failed. The wily Serbs had always managed to avoid any firm commitment. On March 18 Hitler met Prince Paul, the regent, in Berchtesgaden. It was another replay of the record he had first put on for Schuschnigg of Austria three years earlier. Impressed and frightened, Paul told his government to join. On March 24 the Yugoslavs signed up at a secret meeting in Vienna. Two days later a rebellious general staged a successful coup in the name of 18-year-old King Peter (who shimmied down a water pipe of the royal palace to escape the regent's detection). The Balkan powder keg was about to go off.

When Hitler heard of the coup, he threw one of the great temper tantrums of his rage-filled career. He called in his generals: Yugoslavia was to be smashed "with merciless brutality . . . in a lightning operation." Rumania, Hungary and Italy would join the attack. The Yugoslav campaign would be coordinated with the planned German drive into Greece. The decision to "punish" Yugoslavia, made in the white heat of anger, was one of the most fateful of the war, for it forced Hitler to postpone his planned invasion of Russia from the end of April to June. As a result, German tanks bogged down in deep December snows outside Moscow instead of rolling into the capital in October across hard-crusted earth.

The German war machine now moved swiftly. Tanks already en route to Poland from Rumania were called back to the Balkans and the Hungarian and Rumanian armies were alerted. In Belgrade the new government mobilized, but refused to set up a joint defensive system with the Greeks and the British. Moreover, it determined to defend the whole vast country instead of opting for a selective defense in mountain and river strongholds. It was the mistake of Poland all over again.

Hitler, of course, stuck to his trusted techniques. At dawn on April 6 he sent the first wave of a thousand-plane air fleet winging towards Belgrade. The Yugoslavs knew little of air defenses, the Germans could fly in at rooftop level and pound the small simple houses of the city unmercifully. The raids lasted for three days. When they were over, 17,000 Belgraders were dead and bears and lions staggered dazedly through the streets. Bombs had destroyed the city zoo.

On the ground German troops poured into Yugoslavia from Austria, Rumania and Bulgaria. A Hungarian army moved against Zagreb. Striking from Bulgaria, General List's Twelfth Army quickly built an armored corridor across southern Yugoslavia and thus divided Greek and Yugoslav troops. At the same time, List's tanks pounded south; on the 8th they entered the Greek port of Salonika. Further north, Hungarian and German troops entered the ruins of Belgrade on April 13. For all intents and purposes, the Yugoslav campaign was over. Nowhere had the Yugoslavs concentrated enough forces to make a significant stand. On April 17, Peter II, King of Yugoslavia for only 22 days, went into exile.

The story was much the same in Greece. Again the high command had decided to hold the entire front, from Albania to the sea. And again defense forces were strung too thinly to resist the weight of List's four armored divisions. The presence of 50,000 British troops in Greece prolonged the campaign a little, but could not change the outcome. Once more the Germans dominated the skies, and the few British fighters in the area were no effective challenge to the Luftwaffe. Moreover, List was able to separate Greek and British forces and thus destroy them separately. Greek armies in the north surrendered on April 23. On the 27th the swastika flew from the Acropolis in Athens. The British had already retreated below the capital and, despite murderous German air attack, had begun yet another evacuation. Nights were moonless, and the navy was able to pick off the bulk of the British force. Still, losses were heavy: 15,000 men, a dozen ships and much heavy equipment. It was another Dunkirk and for all the heroism displayed, proved again that wars are not won by successful evacuations.

Next came the German conquest of Crete, the most prophetic and futuristic campaign of the war. Churchill had moved British troops to the island in November, 1940, well aware that German planes could threaten Egypt and Suez from Cretan fields only a few hundred miles away. At the end of April most of the men picked off the Greek beaches were landed on Crete to swell the number of defenders. Thus, in May, General Bernard Freyberg, the New Zealander in command, had a large if ill-equipped army. Air support, for example, was woefully inadequate. Still, Freyberg felt confident he could repell a conventional attack from the sea. But Crete was, instead, destined to suffer the first full-fledged airborne invasion in history.

It came early in the morning of May 20 with a traditional aerial bombardment. Unchallenged in the skies, the Luftwaffe bombed anything that moved on the ground and all but knocked out anti-aircraft defenses. Then a fleet of transports lumbered overhead, and hundreds of paratroopers jumped. Few made it safely to the ground. Sharpshooters picked them off like skeets. But the air assault had only begun. Old cargo planes came next, flying at speeds of only a hundred miles and dragging a dozen gliders behind them.

The Germans had selected their major targets: the airfields at Heraklion, Retimo and Maleme, and the neighboring towns of Canea and Suda. The landings were not an unqualified success. Wherever the gliders or paratroopers landed, they met heavy fire. At dusk on

May 20 the invaders had not captured a single target. At Maleme a lone battalion of New Zealanders held off an enemy three times its size. The whole Nazi attack was in danger of collapse. General Student, the German commander, decided to go for broke at Maleme. On the 21st he sent his last two companies of paratroopers against the field and flew in several detachments of mountain troops on transports. The big planes crash-landed on the field under heavy artillery fire, but the soldiers got out safely and that afternoon Maleme was in German hands. That stroke effectively settled the fate of Crete, for now Student could get more men and supplies onto the island and was not dependent on the sea lanes. The British, meanwhile, had decisively defeated two German attempts at a seaborne landing.

It took troops at Maleme five days to link up with their comrades at Canea. When they did, Freyberg had decided on another evacuation. The British fleet again lost a dozen ships to German airpower, but got 18,000 men off safely. All Crete was in German hands by May 30, 1941.

The battle for the island was unique. It was the first and only time in the war that so large a force—more than 15,000 men—were taken across a body of water by air. And the implications were more than ominous. If the RAF had not won the battle of Britain, Goering may have been able to launch a successful airborne invasion of England. And he could still have repeated the attack—for example, against Malta or Cyprus. Indeed, General Student had planned an island-hopping campaign that would have taken him to Suez. However, German losses in the Cretan campaign had been too heavy to allow any repetition. They had committed their entire airborne force to the struggle and suffered 6,000 casualties. A total of 170 transport planes had been destroyed. Not until our day, in the Vietnam war, have Crete-style operations become the commonplace of battle. Helicopters now transport large land forces quickly across impassable terrain.

A year had passed since the fall of France. Britain had survived at home and held on to her lifeline in the Middle East. The sea lanes of the Atlantic were under fierce attack, but they were still open. Hitler had conquered the Balkans, brought his troops to the borders of Egypt and readied an attack on Russia. In so doing he had turned his back on a cherished principle: never fight a two-front war. It would prove his undoing.

Signs of German intentions multiplied all through the spring of 1941. Allied intelligence quickly detected indications of a massive buildup in the east. An American diplomat in Berlin learned of the German plans, and in March the State Department told Russia about it. But Stalin refused to heed this or a host of other warnings. Suddenly he became desperate to believe in Hitler's peaceful intentions, no matter what the evidence.

Division after German division moved east. Hitler's generals pored over maps and studied battle plans. Three Wehrmacht army groups, a Finnish and a Rumanian army and the greatest concentration of armor ever gathered would attack along a 1500-mile front. Hitler was convinced of victory. And he was not about to let the generals tell him how to run this war against the "subhumans" in the east. Ordinary rules of war would not apply, he told them. The army was to take few prisoners. Summary executions were to be part of the battle. Grain-rich areas in the southeast would become German breadbaskets. The local population would starve to death. It was a blueprint for mass murder.

As so often in the past, this German attack was a complete tactical surprise. On June 22, 1941, German planes streaked east before dawn, 3000 of them, and bombed Russian installations behind the front. A heavy artillery barrage shook Soviet forward positions. A wall of armor splintered through towns and villages. At first the Russians simply refused to believe they were under attack. A Russian soldier who radioed "We are being attacked—what should we do?" was told "You must be drunk." Defense Minister Timoshenko told a startled colonel at Brest-Litovsk that "Comrade Stalin has forbidden opening artillery fire against the Germans."

At dawn the German ambassador drove up to the Kremlin to see Molotov and charged Russia with acts of sabotage, terrorism and spying. Molotov looked at the envoy with expressionless eyes: "It is war. Your planes have just bombed ten undefended villages. Do you think we deserved that?" It was midmorning before Molotov went on the air and in a cracking and stuttery voice called the blitzkrieg attack "an unparalleled act of perfidy." But even as he spoke Molotov seemed more shaken than defiant. That night Russians heard more inspiring words. They came from London, where Churchill offered immediate British support against the "dull, drilled, docile, brutish masses of Hun soldiery."

Meanwhile, the invasion ground forward with smooth German precision. Field Marshal Leeb's army group struck for Leningrad while a Finnish army rapped down the Karelian Isthmus. In the center von Bock's 50 divisions, including Guderian's and Hoth's Panzer groups, aimed for Minsk, Smolensk and Moscow. Rundstedt pushed four armies through southern Poland into the Ukraine and on to the Caucasus. Rumanian troops manned a line along the river Pruth in the extreme south. Another 26 divisions were held in reserve.

Von Bock's and Leeb's troops advanced with dazzling speed. On June 26 they had annihilated two Russian armies. Leeb was in Riga on the 30th and had swept through most of the Baltic States. Von Bock captured Brest-Litovsk and Minsk. Ten days after the invasion began, the Germans had taken 150,000 prisoners and destroyed 1200 tanks. On July 10 von Bock's infantry pushed through the outskirts of Smolensk. The Germans were 500 miles east of Warsaw and two-thirds of the way to Moscow. In the south, Rundstedt advanced more slowly, but his tanks had begun to close in on Kiev.

Yet, for all its startling success, this blitzkrieg was different from the others: the Red Army refused to collapse. Russian generals failed to panic as the French had. Soviet soldiers fought with utter contempt of death. They kept on shooting long after they were surrounded and cut off without hope of escape. Red Army casualties mounted into the hundreds of thousands, but the reckless expenditure of manpower did gradually slow down the Nazi blitzkrieg. By July 19 the German generals grew worried and were no longer sure that they could really finish this campaign before winter.

Von Bock's tanks could not get through the outskirts of Smolensk, and for three weeks one of the fiercest armored battles of the war raged for control of the city. Von Bock finally took it on August 7, but he could not push far beyond. Marshal Voroshilov had built strong defenses 25 miles to the east which the Germans were unable to crack for many weeks. In the north, Manstein's and Reinhardt's tanks had indeed cleared the Baltic states in one swift stroke—only to stall at the hastily erected River Luba line. They needed another six weeks to cover the remaining 125 miles to the outskirts of Leningrad, and it was not until September that Russia's second city was shelled and cut off from the outside. Rundstedt scored only limited gains in the Ukraine.

To make matters worse, Hitler now began a bitter quarrel with his generals on what to do next. No firm decision was reached for weeks and only on August 23 did the Fuehrer finally reject plans put forward by Brauchitsch, von Bock and Guderian for a concerted strike against Moscow in the center of the front. Instead, he proposed diverting von Bock's armor. Some reinforcements would go north to help the advance on Leningrad; Guderian's group would swing over to Rundstedt's front for a drive into the Ukraine and beyond it to the Crimea. "My generals know nothing about economics," Hitler snorted, explaining that he needed the breadbasket of the Ukraine and the industries of the Donets basin. As for Moscow, it was only "a geographic expression."

Accordingly, Rundstedt launched a giant pincer attack in the Ukraine designed to envelop its capital, Kiev. And the Fuehrer's judgment seemed quickly vindicated. By the end of August, Guderian had crossed the Dnieper above Kiev, Kleist below it. On September 10 Kleist had moved many miles beyond Kiev along the Dnieper, while Guderian stood 700 miles northeast of the city. Both generals now wheeled their tanks sharply and began to close the pincer behind four Russian armies. On the 13th they were only 20 miles apart, and on the 16th the trap clanked shut at Lokhvitsa. Several days later the stubborn defenders of Kiev were annihilated and the Germans entered the city. They took more than 400,000 prisoners.

But it was now late September. The Red Army had not been defeated. Only a quick and massive knockout blow could prevent a winter campaign, for which the Wehrmacht was not prepared. Thus, for all its splendor, the victory at Kiev was a tactical blunder. Moreover, Hitler's hopes of quickly taking Leningrad were also dashed. Leeb besieged the town but could not capture it; the Germans never would, despite an unparalleled siege of two and a half years.

The Fuehrer changed signals. He would attack Moscow after all. Guderian's battered tanks were transferred once again to von Bock's front in the center. On October 2, 1941, "Operation Typhoon" began as von Bock hurled a million and a half men and Guderian's Panzer army against Moscow. Still, Hitler had not committed everything to this drive as his generals had wanted him to. Leeb was to keep up the pressure on Leningrad, and Rundstedt was ordered to strike into the Crimea, the Donets basin and the Caucasus, targets 400 miles beyond the Dnieper. Rundstedt said later he had "laughed aloud" at such orders. Nonetheless, he carried them out. On November 21 he pushed his men into Rostov, and on the 22nd the Russians pushed them out again.

At first von Bock's offensive prospered. His armies covered 130 miles in two weeks. On October 15 they stood only 65 miles from Moscow. Von Bock sent one spearhead towards Kalinin, northwest of Moscow, in an attempt to outflank the capital. Two armies punched down the middle, along a straight line from Smolensk to Moscow. A fourth column drove up from the south for Tula. The Russians fell back everywhere. Panic gripped the capital. Thousands fled. Whole industries were moved east and government departments and embassies evacuated.

They might have stayed, for von Bock's soldiers quickly ran out of breath and his tanks ran out of gas. The Wehrmacht drive had lost its deadly sting. And slowly, day after day, a new general led a new army into the field. His name was winter, his weapons mud, rain, sleet, snow, ice and bitter cold. Tank tracks slithered in the mud. Armored car drivers could not see through their snow-clogged windshields. Slowly the Panzers ground out the mileage. On October 20 they were 40 miles from Moscow; at the end of the month they were even closer. Now cold replaced mud. On November 8 the mercury was down to eight below zero. Fuel began to freeze in tank engines. Oil wouldn't pour properly. Fires had to be lit under tanks to start them. And German soldiers, still shod in summer boots and without warm socks, suffered the first cases of frostbite. No winter clothing had reached them yet—no heavy coats, sweaters, gloves or even food. Hitler had been so sure of a summer victory that he had not equipped his troops for a winter campaign. For the first time in this war, cold and hungry German soldiers became afraid. The Russians, their feet stuck in fur-lined boots and their ears snugly covered by heavy hats, fought like demons.

Yet German firepower remained overwhelming. Red Army losses had been mammoth, and Stalin began feeding his last reserves to

Moscow's defenders. Bit by bit, they fell back. The Germans still had hope, but Hitler stubbornly refused his generals' plea to take up winter quarters now and attack again in the spring. Slowly the miles fell away—29 miles to go, 22 miles. Von Bock's long reddish face contorted with pain as he fought down his vicious stomach cramps. Like a tottering prizefighter with only one punch left, he lurched forward on December 1 and pushed through the snow-covered forests that gird Moscow. And on the morning of the 2nd, soldiers of the 258th infantry division stumbled out of the woods and into Khimki, a Moscow suburb. The Germans could see the tall towers of the Kremlin brooding against a snow-laden gray sky. In Berlin, Goebbels ordered all newspapers to stop the presses and leave space for news of Moscow's capture. But that headline would never grace a front page. German troops got no closer for the rest of the war.

The next day a Russian counterattack drove the Germans out of Khimki. On the 4th, Bock told Berlin that spearheads of his Fourth Army had pulled back. On December 5, Guderian's Panzers stopped their advance from the south. The mercury slumped to 31 below zero, and the tanks literally froze to the ground. That day the Wehrmacht assault all along the 200-mile perimeter around Moscow finally ground to a halt.

On December 6, Marshal Zhukov struck a massive counterblow and the vaunted Wehrmacht reeled like an exhausted drunk back across the winter wasteland. The myth of German invincibility in land warfare lay shattered.

EASTERN FRONT
0   miles 200   400
Boundaries and names are those of Sept. 1939.
Axis Powers
Area controlled by Axis Powers in late 1942.
Arrows indicate direction of major Allied offensive campaigns.
ATLANTIC OCEAN
Barents Sea
Murmansk
White Sea
Archangel
NORWAY
SWEDEN
FINLAND
Helsinki
Stockholm
Leningrad
Baltic Sea
ESTONIA
SOVIET UNION
Riga
LATVIA
Moscow
LITHUANIA
Smolensk
E. PRUSSIA
Minsk
Orel
Berlin
Warsaw
POLAND
Pinsk
GERMANY
Kiev
Kharkov
Stalin (Volgo
Prague
Lvov
SLOVAKIA
Rostov (on Don)
Vienna
Budapest
HUNGARY
Odessa
RUMANIA
Maikop
M
Belgrade
Bucharest
Sevastopol
Yalta
YUGOSLAVIA
BLACK SEA
Adriatic Sea
BULGARIA
Sofia
ITALY
TURKEY
ALBANIA
GREECE
Aegean Sea
Map by William Jabe

Chapter ☆ 5 ☆

On December 7, a day after Zhukov began his winter offensive, Japanese bombers attacked Pearl Harbor and sank most of the U.S. fleet berthed there. Three days later America was at war with Japan and its European allies, Germany and Italy, and had become an ally of Russia. For Moscow this meant assurance of a continued flow of U.S. military supplies.

The groundwork had been laid some months earlier when President Roosevelt promised to give Russia $1 billion in military aid so she could survive the German invasion. Over the next three years U.S. supplies flooded the Soviet Union: 210,000 cars, 1,200,000 tons of steel, 3000 anti-aircraft guns, more than 6000 planes, 5,000,000 pairs of army boots and 23,000,000 yards of cloth.

The prospect must have heartened Red Army soldiers as they stormed across the snowy waste to drive the Wehrmacht from the gates of Moscow. Zhukov had gathered a hundred divisions and struck along a 560-mile front from Kalinin in the north to Yelets in the south. The Germans fell back everywhere. Trucks, tanks and guns were abandoned in the snow. By December 13, Soviet troops had advanced as much as 40 miles, and that day Radio Moscow announced that the siege of the capital had been lifted.

Once again Hitler's generals urged a broad withdrawal of their forces to more easily defensible positions. But the Fuehrer would not hear of it. He began a wholesale replacement of his field commanders (Rundstedt, von Bock, Leeb and even Guderian and Hoeppner), and on December 18 he took over personal command of the army from Brauchitsch. From now on his "intuition" would shape the conduct of the war. And indeed his iron determination to stand fast prevented the retreat from turning into a rout. Nowhere did the Red Army advance more than 200 miles that winter, and in the center of the front the Germans dug in barely 100 miles from Moscow and could not be dislodged. Hitler had devised an ingenious strategy. In the summer and fall the Germans had put supply depots into towns with good rail communications. Now he turned Kharkov, Kursk, Orel, Bryansk, Viazma, Gzhatsk, Rzhev and other towns into so-called hedgehogs that bristled with guns and armor and were modeled on the square-shaped formation that medieval Swiss pikemen had adopted to fight off cavalry. The Russians only managed to overrun a few of them and to push within about 20 miles of Kursk, Orel and Kharkov. Striking from positions north of Kalinin, the Red Army had driven southwest to within 50 miles of Smolensk, but it got no closer. At the extreme southern end of the front the Russians leap-frogged across the mouth of the Sea of Azov to capture the Kerch peninsula on the Crimea and ease some of the pressure on the port of Sebastapol, which had been under siege since September. Finally, in the far north the Red Army had managed to establish contact with besieged Leningrad.

By mid-January, however, a good deal of the steam had gone out of the Russian drive and much of the euphoria had left the Red Army's general staff. On January 25, 1942, the Germans launched their first counterattacks, and for the next two months Soviet advances were sporadic and uneven. There were other troubles too. The offensive had doubled the front lines; as a result, communications and supplies became harder to maintain. Advance units didn't have much air support. Finally, the Red Army was every bit as exhausted as the Wehrmacht. When the spring thaws began late in March and turned the vast steppes into a soggy mass of snow, broken ice and black mud, the winter offensive petered out. A six-week lull descended on the Russian front. Both sides licked their wounds, took stock and made plans for the summer.

Even though the Red Army had not gained all it had hoped to, the Wehrmacht's defeat at the gates of Moscow had enormous impact. Hitler would have to fight the long war of attrition he had desperately wanted to avoid, and do it with an inferior army. The Germans had suffered nearly a million casualties in the long winter campaign, and the 52 Italian, Rumanian and Hungarian divisions Hitler had collected as replacements were not up to Wehrmacht standards.

Equally important, hope flashed anew across occupied Europe. Partisan movements sprang up in the Balkans. In Yugoslavia the Axis were soon fighting a full-scale guerrilla war. Even the Germans themselves began to doubt the possibility of final Nazi victory. Moreover, German strategy would have to undergo some fundamental revisions. Hitler could no longer hope to destroy the Red Army. Instead he would have to smash Russia's economic base by depriving her of oil, wheat and industry. Policy had to dictate choice of targets: the oil fields were in the Caucasus, the wheat in the Kuban, industry in the Donets basin between Kharkov and Stalingrad. The major German thrust that summer, therefore, would have to be in the south, not directly against Moscow.

First, Hitler planned to clean up the Crimea with the conquest of Sebastopol and the Kerch peninsula. Then the Panzers would drive from Kursk to Voronezh, thus threatening both the railhead of Satarov, southeast of Moscow, and Stalingrad. Next, the Wehrmacht would strike from Taganrog to recapture Rostov and push northeast to the Volga, to attack Stalingrad from two sides. Finally, after either destruction or capture of Stalingrad (pinching off oil supplies barged up the Volga), the Germans would wheel south into the Caucasus and head for the oil fields of Baku. Once in the Caucasus, the Wehrmacht could drive through the Middle East to meet Rommel coming up from Egypt. (While Hitler drew up these plans for his 1942 summer offensive in Russia, the Desert Fox was preparing his drive to El Alamein.)

Fighting resumed on the Russian front in May with a preview of the German summer offensive. Action centered on Kerch, Kharkov and Sebastopol. Manstein jumped off in the Crimea on May 8 with an attack on the Kerch peninsula, which the Russians had neglected to fortify properly after recapturing it. Thanks to heavy air support, Manstein quickly pushed the Red Army back into the town of Kerch itself and overran it on May 13. About 40,000 Russians escaped across the Strait of Kerch but left most of their equipment behind. Two weeks later the Germans would use guns captured here against Sebastopol.

In an effort to relieve the pressure on Kerch the Russians began a planned drive on Kharkov a little early, on May 12. Initial progress was rapid because Marshal Timoshenko had caught the Wehrmacht by surprise. But his offensive was part of a sweep planned the previous winter, when the Red Army had expected to stampede the Germans out of Russia. For conditions that spring it was hopelessly overambitious. Timoshenko managed to shoulder his way into a Kharkov suburb on May 19, but in the meantime the Germans had brought up strong formations to the north and south and proceeded to fashion a deadly trap. The Russians lost 200,000 prisoners. The disasterous Kharkov battle was over on June 1.

Four days later Manstein began to storm the beleaguered port of Sebastopol. It took him a month to reduce the fortress. When he finally took it early in July, only a heap of rubble was left. The Germans began with a six-day artillery bombardment. Planes dropped 50,000 explosive and fire bombs. Inch by inch the German and Rumanian armies ground forward. Soon the Russians were fighting out of caves and from behind heaps of rubble. The stench of corpses rotting in the July sun became overpowering. Hunger and famine stalked the defenders. Finally, in early July, after a siege of 250 days, Manstein entered the ruined city.

Hitler's major summer drive began on June 28, when Hoth's Fourth Panzer Army spearheaded a drive from Kursk towards Voronezh. Within a week the Germans had crossed the Don just a few miles from that industrial city, and on July 7 fought in its suburbs. But the Russians had piled huge forces behind Voronezh, determined to prevent a breakthrough that could imperil Moscow and the vital rail links that brought oil up from the Caucasus. The Wehrmacht tried for ten days to capture Voronezh, but then gave up the attempt as Hoth's tanks flowed south down the western bank of the Don towards Stalingrad.

Meanwhile, the German Sixth Army had begun to move down the Donets corridor between the Don and Donets rivers and it met almost no Russian resistance. Further south, Kleist's tanks had crossed the Donets going north, then wheeled southeast. By July 12 they had outflanked Voroshilovgrad and captured Millerovo. Kleist now changed directions once more, recrossed the Donets and headed south towards Rostov. The Germans were about to flood across the whole Don Bend. (The Don flows southeast from Voronezh to within 25 miles of the Volga at Stalingrad, then turns south for about a hundred miles before changing direction again to flow southwest into the Sea of Azov below Rostov; the area in between is called the Don Bend of Donbas.)

Then Hitler committed a critical blunder: he sent Hoth's Fourth Panzer Army charging south to help Kleist cross the lower Don and sweep into the Kuban and the Caucasus. The Sixth Army was left to advance on Stalingrad alone. Instead of capturing Stalingrad first and then pushing for the oil fields, as his original and logical plan had envisaged, Hitler now hoped to do both simultaneously. Predictably, he failed to do either.

For Kleist did not need Hoth's help against Rostov. Indeed the number of tanks on the lower Don led to a traffic jam that if anything slowed the Panzer armies' advance. Had Hoth stayed north, he could have streaked to Stalingrad and captured it in short order. The Red Army was handed a most precious gift: time to prepare the city's defenses.

By July 22, Kleist's and Hoth's tanks stood along the northern shore of the Don from Tsymlianskaya to Rostov, which fell on July 23. Kleist got his first tanks across on the 25th, and the bulk of his forces two days later. Hoth did not cross until the 29th. Shortly thereafter Hitler again changed his mind. Hoth was ordered to leave one Panzer division to screen Kleist's blitzkrieg drive into the Caucasus while he wheeled the bulk of his army northeast to help Paulus advance on Stalingrad. This would prove to be Hitler's second major mistake of the campaign. It is true that Kleist stormed through the Kuban and the Caucasus at breakneck speed: he reached the Maikop oil wells (which the Russians burned) on August 9. By August 20 he had cleared the grain-rich Kuban and stood less than a hundred miles from the Caspian Sea. But without Hoth's added armored punch he could not break beyond Mozdok to Grozny and the rich oil fields of Baku beyond it. Stalin, meanwhile, built a bristling line of fortifications across the Caucasian mountains and found a huge army to man them.

In the meantime, Paulus had pushed forward to the Middle Don. By the second week in August he was across the river, although he left several bridgeheads in Russian hands, which he screened with weak Rumanian forces. Hoth had smashed north beyond Kotelnikovo. By August 19 the Germans were fighting between the Don and the Volga; on August 23, Sixth Army columns lunged to the Volga above Stalingrad. That night the Luftwaffe flew one of its now traditional terror raids: 600 planes turned the city into a furnace with fire bombs and killed 40,000 people. Thousands of refugees crowded the Volga ferries to escape from the burning town. Inexorably the Panzers moved closer. German artillery began shelling river traffic before the end of August.

The Soviet High Command had committed two armies to the defense of Stalingrad: the 62nd under General Chuikov was to hold the city itself, the 64th the southern suburbs. For the next two weeks Red Army resistance outside Stalingrad stiffened, but the Russians could not halt the German advance. On September 12 the Wehrmacht scored a major breakthrough when Hoth's tanks battered into the Kuporosnoye suburb and reached the Volga south of the city. The blow separated the 64th from the 62nd army and clanked shut a steel chain around Stalingrad. Chuikov was reduced to holding a horseshoe-shaped enclave 25 miles wide. Blackened and exhausted by retreat and fighting with their backs to the wide river, his troops were low in morale. But Chuikov was a remarkable general, perhaps the most remarkable the Russians produced in the war, and he was able to fire up his men in most extraordinary fashion. His efforts were helped along by a famous directive issued by the Soviet War Council: "The enemy must be smashed at Stalingrad." Gradually the men of the 62nd Army came to believe he just might be.

On September 13, German tanks breached the city line as armored spearheads drove for the center of town and the main river docks. Hitler and Paulus were confident that Stalingrad would now fall quickly. But their optimism was ill founded. The Red Army would fight to the last man for every pile of rubble. And throughout the battle the Germans singlemindedly concentrated on the shattered buildings and streets in which the 62nd Army fought and died, and not on the Russian artillery and supply depots on the eastern bank of the Volga which sustained and buoyed the defenders.

Thus Chuikov was able to stop the September 13 drive by ferrying the 10,000-man Rudintsev division across the Volga during the night of the 14th and throwing the fresh soldiers into the battle for the shell of the central railroad station and for Mamai Hill in the middle of town. Moreover, fighting soon turned into hand-to-hand combat which artillery and bombs could not decide. What the German generals had overlooked was the simple fact that a pile of bricks and mortar offered better protection than an exposed house. Soon Stalingrad had been turned into a vast fortress of pillboxes and anti-tank obstacles—almost a miniature Maginot Line built by German shells and bombs. And the Nazis simply could not overcome the Russian will to resist.

But they did gobble up territory: street by street, they shrank the Russian perimeter. On September 21 the business district was in German hands. The Panzers now drove hard for the central docks. They made it on the 22nd, and split the 62nd Army into two pockets. But once again Chuikov ferried reinforcements across the river and counterattacked incessantly. He was never far from the front. One day he watched German patrols push to within a few hundred yards of his command post. He had already slipped his revolver into his hand when they were driven off. Another time, flaming oil poured past his headquarters and soon encircled the building. Grimly Chuikov continued giving orders to his troops over the radio until the flames were put out. Fighting grew so heavy and so close that no-man's-land shrank to the distance a soldier could toss a hand grenade. Progress was measured in yards. A city block was a major battlefield, a house a fortress.

On September 27, Paulus began a drive against the industrial area of Stalingrad. Hundreds of Stukas pounded Russian lines. German infantry cut through heavy mine fields and advanced as much as three thousand yards, a blitzkrieg strike for this battle. Red Army troops were knocked off Mamai Hill. "One more such day and we would have been thrown into the Volga," Chuikov commented, and he sent an urgent SOS to headquarters for more troops. That night two infantry regiments made it across. On the 28th the Germans resumed attacking with a massed force of infantry and armor—here an absolutely disasterous tactic. Gratefully, Russian artillery shot the attackers to bits. But the fury of the battle did not abate. In October, Stalingrad had become an obsession for Hitler. Nothing else mattered. The Wehrmacht had to conquer those few square miles of rubble, even though the Fuehrer's main objective had already been achieved; the Russians could no longer ferry oil up the Volga from the Caspian Sea because ships and barges were shelled constantly.

October was the cruelest month for the Russians. Bit by bit the Wehrmacht nibbled away at Soviet-held territory. On October 7 the Wehrmacht took part of the big tractor plant "Garden City." Heavy fighting ripped the Red October plant. On the 9th something of a lull fell on the front. It lasted through the 13th, while Paulus prepared an all-out offensive. Meanwhile, German planes showered leaflets on the defenders, urging them to surrender.

The Wehrmacht struck on October 14 with savage fury. Said a Russian general later: "I would not have believed such an inferno could open up on earth." Two Panzer and three infantry divisions battered the Russian lines along a three-mile front. "There were three thousand air sorties that day," Chuikov would write later. "They bombed and stormed our troops without a moment's respite." It was a sunny day, but smoke and soot reduced visibility to 100 yards. "Our dugouts were shaking and crumbling up like a house of cards." But German losses were devastating: 3000 dead around the tractor plant alone, and at least 40 tanks destroyed. Fierce German attacks continued through the 15th. For Chuikov the situation had grown desperate. A regiment made it across that night, two more before dawn on the 17th. But the handful of troops could not have stemmed the German tide had not Russian guns and *katyushas* (powerful multiple-firing mortars) on the other side of the Volga kept up a sustained bombardment.

Gradually the fury of Paulus' attack weakened, and by the 20th it was apparent that some of the punch had gone from the German assault. On the 23rd both sides were near exhaustion. On October 27, the Russians managed to put half a division into Stalingrad. By the 30th the pace of battle had definitely slowed. Chuikov's men were now pinned into several bridgeheads, none deeper than a few hundred yards. For the first ten days of November they attacked often in a vain attempt to widen their perimeter. Then, on the 11th, von Paulus struck for the last time.

Again he sent five divisions with armor and air support crashing against the well-entrenched defenders in yet another effort finally, at long last, to crash through the Volga and end the Russian resistance. But the Germans came no closer than a hundred yards of the river. On the 12th the offensive fizzled. For the next week Chuikov tried to break out of a small salient in the north but failed. Then, at 7:30 A.M. on November 19, the quietest hour of the day, the weary defenders heard distant gunfire in the north. The men of the 62nd Army poked heads out of their dugouts and shelters into the gray, wet, cold dawn to listen with growing delight. For the boom of far-off cannon signaled the start of a great Russian counteroffensive many months in the making. No longer would Stalingrad's defenders have to fight alone. Help was on the way, and the spark of victory seemed to flash through the gray skies even though the battle for the city was far from over and would drag on for another two and a half months.

Marshal Zhukov had prepared the Russian attack with great care. He had posted Marshal Rokossovsky's Don Front group from the Volga to beyond the Donbas and Vatutin's Southwest Front adjacent to it almost to Vershenskaya. Both groups occupied ground on the western banks of the Don—the bridgeheads Paulus had not bothered to clear the previous August. To the south of the Volga below the beleaguered city stood Marshal Yeremenko's three-army Stalingrad Front. Vatutin and Rokossovsky were to smash south and southeast across the Donbas while Yeremenko raced north. The armies were to meet at Kalach on the Don and trap the Germans inside the Stalingrad pocket. Russian forces on the three fronts totaled a million men, 13,000 guns, 900 tanks and 1100 planes. Paulus' forces— the Sixth Army, the Fourth Panzer Army and two Rumanian armies —were about as strong, but Russian superiority at key points was crushing.

The offensive began with thunderous artillery barrage by 3500 guns that lasted for two hours. Then Vatutin and Rokossovsky crashed into the Third Rumanian Army like a dozen bolts of thunder. Vatutin's tanks raced across 75 miles of open country in three days and reached Kalach on November 22. Yeremenko had moved out on the 20th and fought his way to the Don in two days against less stiff resistance. The Russians took 30,000 prisoners in the drive and all but shattered both the Rumanian armies. On November 24 the Red Army had bolted the trap, and the Germans were cut off. But the bolt was not yet very thick—no more than 40 miles—and for the next week the Red Army concentrated on widening it before Paulus did the logical thing and attempted to break out.

But of course logic was not part of Hitler's strategic arsenal. A breakout would mean abandoning the Stalingrad position. "I will not leave the Volga," the Fuehrer screeched when his generals suggested the obvious. So Paulus stayed and set up a hedgehog defense inside his perimeter. Goering promised to fly in 750 tons of supplies every day. As usual he couldn't deliver, for the Russians quickly established fighter superiority over the "cauldron." However, Zhukov was wary of opening an all-out attack against Paulus' hedgehog at least until he had built up a crushing superiority on Rokossovsky's front.

After the Red Air Force had shot down 50 transports on November 30, 1942, the Germans decided on a rescue expedition. Manstein was called in to command the newly formed Army Group Don, which included an armored division sent east from France, and on December 12 he marshaled his forces at Kotelnikovo, 25 miles southeast of the Don and 100 miles south of Stalingrad. He planned to advance up the Caucasus railroad and open a corridor to the trapped Germans inside the Stalingrad pocket. In three days Manstein advanced 30 miles. It was tough going. Winter had come to the Volga country and, as usual, ice and snow aided the Russians more than they did the Germans. Still, Manstein pushed his troops across the Aksay river on the 15th against stiffening Soviet resistance. Hundreds of German bombers were thrown in to fly close support for the ground troops, and on the 19th the relief force had reached the Myshkova river, the last natural barrier before Stalingrad. Manstein pushed a few tank formations across this river too and "could already see the glow in the Stalingrad sky." The rim of the German pocket was only 25 miles away.

For the next four days Paulus could have attempted a breakout. He did not because of Hitler's insane insistance that the swastika stay on the Volga. In the meantime, the Russians had rushed reinforcements to the Myshkova. On the 24th, Malinovsky's Second Guards Army counterattacked and hurled Manstein back to the Aksay. The Germans were unable to make a stand there, and on December 29 they were again in Kotelnikovo. Before the new year, Manstein had been pushed back another 60 miles into the Caucasus. Further northwest, Vatutin had cleared the Donbas to the Chir river and by December 31 was advancing towards the Donets basin on a broad front.

With the dawn of 1943 the Russians were ready to crush the Germans still inside the "cauldron." Paulus' situation had grown steadily worse. His airborne supplies had dwindled to 100 tons a day for 22 divisions, and soon was even less than that. The Germans began eating the horses of the Rumanian cavalry trapped with them. On January 8, when Rokossovsky had completed his buildup, he handed the Germans an ultimatum that promised them good treatment. Paulus was tempted to accept. Hitler refused.

Rokossovsky started his attack on the 10th with a 7000-gun and *katyusha* barrage and that very day advanced as much as five miles. Three days later the Red Army had cut a 250-square-mile chunk of land from the Germans. On January 17, Rokossovsky took the enemy's biggest airfield. Again he asked Paulus to surrender, and again Hitler forced him to refuse. Yet the Wehrmacht continued to fight with a fierce kind of despair. Every truck that had run out of fuel was turned into a pillbox. On the 24th the Germans were back inside the Stalingrad city limits.

That day the Rumanians began to surrender in larger numbers. Some had not eaten since January 20. Then the Germans started to give up. Officers paid huge bribes to anyone willing to fly them out. On the 28th the Germans were cut into three pockets, just as Chuikov's men had been the previous October.

In a dark room underneath what had once been a department store, Paulus sat on a field bed and waited for the end. In Berlin, Hitler was determined that every last German at Stalingrad should die rather than surrender. If this be defeat, let it be a Twilight of the Gods, with all the splendor of a Wagner opera. Goering likened the Sixth Army's stand to that of the Greeks at Thermopylae. ("When you come to Germany, say you have seen us lie at Stalingrad.") Hitler sent Paulus a Field Marshal's baton. It was tantamount to an order of suicide: no German Field Marshal had ever been captured. It was one order Paulus would ignore.

On January 31, 1943, a Nazi officer climbed out of the rubble and walked over to Fedya Yelchenko, a young lieutenant with a turned-up nose. Paulus was ready to surrender. Yelchenko found the Field Marshal lying on a cot, unshaven and miserable. Would he take him to Rokossovsky in a car and protect him from harm? Fedya Yelchenko laughed and said he would. By February 3 the last German had crawled out from under the rubble. The battle was over.

In the Third Reich a roll of muffled drums filled the airwaves while a mournful announcer admitted defeat. As the stirring chorus of Beethoven's Fifth Symphony blared out of every loudspeaker, millions of Germans saw the specter of another lost war sharply and clearly for the first time.

Chapter
☆ 6 ☆

One day in October, 1942, a German engineer named Hermann Graebe heard rifle fire coming from the outskirts of the town of Dubino in the Ukraine, where he managed a German construction firm. Graebe and his foreman walked quickly in the direction of the noise. They found a truck convoy guarded by SS men standing near some freshly dug pits. A group of men, women and children were being unloaded from the trucks. An SS guard, a horsewhip in one hand, made them strip nude and place shoes, underwear and top clothing in separate heaps. The people were calm and joked among themselves. An old white-haired woman chucked a baby under the chin until it gurgled with delight. A father talked soothingly to his ten-year-old boy, who fought to hold back his tears. As Graebe watched, a slim girl with black hair standing near him pointed to herself and said, "Twenty-three years old." A guard counted off a group of about 20 persons and made them walk to the pit. Graebe followed and found a mass grave, about two-thirds full of blood-smeared bodies, some still twitching; perhaps a thousand persons in all. A German with a tommygun across his knees sat on the edge of the pit smoking a cigarette. The SS directed the newest victims to walk into the ditch and to lie down in front of the dead and dying. At a signal the tommygunner opened fire. The shooting continued all day and far into the night. Next day Graebe came back for another look: the pit was full, and 30 Jews lay dying near the edge. Dubino's Jews had been exterminated.

The scene was typical for German-occupied Poland and Russia. In June, 1941, Hitler had decided to get serious about his long-cherished plan to eradicate Jews from Europe. He issued an edict, never put on paper, about "the final solution of the Jewish problem." The solution was simple enough: systematic mass murder. Until then killing Jews had been a haphazard business. Those in Poland had been herded into ghettoes, their property stolen and they themselves beaten, starved and sometimes murdered. But this was just a rougher version of how they had been handled in the German concentration camps. More efficient methods of destruction were needed. The SS first came up with proposals for Special Action Groups to do the job.

Four such groups goose-stepped into Russia right behind the conquering Wehrmacht and set to work with complete license to kill "Jews and commissars." (The generals were told to look the other way if they felt squeamish about it.) In a single year one action group killed 90,000 Jews. But shooting proved too cumbersome and too slow. Squads of SS gunners firing round the clock needed two days to murder 33,000 Jews outside Kiev—the infamous Babi Yar massacre. Extermination squads fired away all through the summer and fall of 1942 and by November had killed "only" about 360,000 people. Himmler figured that there must be about eleven million Jews in Europe, including England. At that rate they'd never be finished. Shooting just wasn't fast enough for the "final solution."

So they tried death vans: Jews were herded into closed trucks, engines switched on and the exhaust gas pumped inside. The prisoners died of carbon monoxide poison. But a single truck could hold only 25 people, so the efficiency experts of murder came up with the perfect answer, the death factory, where the largest number of people could be killed in the shortest possible time with a minimum of waste. The Nazis operated about 30 of them before the war was over, most of them in Poland, although some of the most infamous ones—Dachau, Buchenwald, Mauthausen—did their deadly business in Germany and Austria. Most of the six million Jews Hitler killed died there, as did millions of Slavs and other "inferior" people.

The largest and most efficient of the death factories was Auschwitz in Poland: anywhere from one to three million people died in the camp's four large gas chambers, and were then burned in attached crematoriums. The gas chambers were disguised as bath houses, and each one was large enough to accommodate 2000 persons. Crystallized prussic acid (known as Zyklon B) was dropped through the air vents and killed those inside within three to fifteen minutes. SS doctors selected the victims as the Jews climbed out of the freight cars that had brought them to the camp railroad siding. Those who looked as if they could work were assigned to the Krupp and I. G. Farben plants, built nearby to take advantage of the large pool of slave labor. The others, including children, who obviously couldn't do factory work, were taken to the gas chambers. None of them knew they were about to die: there had been riots at other camps where they did know. Instead, the victims were ordered to strip and told to prepare for a bath and delousing, which was common practice in all prisons. The setting was pretty enough to banish all thought of death: neat, well-kept lawns, flowers and hedges and an all-girl band playing music from Viennese operettas. Few suspected anything was amiss until they saw the crush of people inside, heard the doors clank shut and realized that the vents on the ceiling were not shower nozzles.

A half hour after the last Jew was dead, special SS squads opened the heavy metal doors and set to work breaking all the gold teeth and gold fillings out of the mouths of the victims. The gold was added to the pile of valuables the SS had collected beforehand. The Nazis wasted nothing. Even shoes and clothing were carefully stacked; some can be seen to this day in the Auschwitz museum. Then the corpses were dragged into the crematoriums. Camp commanders conceded that not even the most fragrant flowers could do much about the stench of death that often hung over Auschwitz and its surroundings. The gold, jewels and watches soon overflowed 42 vaults in the Berlin Reichsbank. Later they were sold, and the SS invested the money in stocks and bonds.

Life for the millions who spent some time alive in the camps, and for the handful who survived, was an endless nightmare. They faced beatings, solitary confinement or death at every turn for violations of a gelatinous spiderweb of rules. A Buchenwald inmate described some of them: a missing button, shoes not shined to a bright gloss despite ankle-deep mud, a visit to the latrine during working hours. Camp guards were omnipotent and free to use prisoners for their own profit. Some had inmates build and decorate villas for them. Ilse Koch, wife of a Buchenwald commander, had lampshades made of human skins with striking tatooes on them.

The old Jewish quarters in towns and cities soon became way stations to the death camps where Jews lived until there was room for them in the gas chambers, until new camps had been built or until enough transportation was made available. Most Polish ghettoes quickly burst at the seams. The one in Warsaw was the worst. By the fall of 1940 the Germans had forced half a million people into an area of two square miles where only 160,000 had lived before the war. Then the Nazis built a wall around the Jewish enclave, located a few industries there and put the inhabitants on starvation rations. At least 100,000 persons tried to survive on straw soup. Until Pearl Harbor a little American help was allowed to trickle into the ghetto and the Germans gave the Jews a measure of autonomy to run their own affairs so that some order emerged from the chaos of life behind the walls.

Once America entered the war, however, the conditions of the Jews grew rapidly worse. The Nazis now hoped to starve the Warsaw ghetto to death, but when the SS realized that the Jews wouldn't die fast enough, they decided on a great "resettlement" action. An SS brigade arrived on July 22, 1942, to begin transporting Warsaw Jews to the death camps. By the end of October about 300,000 had been moved, most of them to Treblinka. Only 60,000 Jews were left by January, 1943. Himmler then set a deadline: the ghetto must be cleared by February 15. Bitter cold and a desperate shortage of freight cars owing to the Stalingrad debacle forced postponement of the resettlement action until spring. The new deadline was April 19. The SS figured it would take three days.

But the Warsaw Jews, who for years had gone docilely to the slaughterhouses like so many lambs, had had enough of meekness. In the winter months they secretly gathered pistols, rifles, even machine guns, hoarded ammunition and manufactured Molotov cocktails. When the SS surrounded the ghetto with 2500 men, a tank and some armored cars, the Jews were ready. Suddenly heavy gunfire erupted from windows and street corners. Molotov cocktails rained down on the tank and armored cars. The astonished SS retreated in confusion. Resistance was the last thing they had expected. But resist the Jews did. When the Germans returned the next day, they were met again by gunfire that burst from every street corner. Women plucked revolvers from the folds of their long gowns and fired them with both hands or whipped hand grenades from their bloomers.

In Berlin, Himmler read reports of the fighting with unbelieving eyes. Furious, he ordered General Juergen Stroop to crush the uprising at once. Stroop tried, but even when he decided to burn down the ghetto the fighting did not end. Jews ran shooting from their burning homes to houses as yet untouched by flames. After a week of fighting, Stroop had killed or captured 27,000 Jews. The survivors kept on shooting. By May most of them lived down in the sewers. The SS turned on the water main and tried to drown them. The Jews managed to turn off the water. They even survived the smoke bombs the SS dropped down sewer gratings. But there is a limit to human endurance and courage. Finally, on May 16, 1943, Stroop was able to cable Berlin that the "Warsaw Ghetto is no more." He listed his losses as 16 dead, 90 wounded. They were much higher, but Himmler was sensitive about his casualties.

This act of Jewish defiance was never repeated on quite such a massive scale, and although there were camp rebellions, the Germans went on methodically murdering and torturing their prisoners, sometimes most horribly in the name of science. For Nazi doctors performed endless experiments on human beings—experiments that did not produce a single scrap of knowledge to advance the healing arts. For only sadists and quacks, men without talent or accomplishment, would engage in such pseudo-scientific research. They tested man's ability to withstand high-altitude pressure and cold. Their findings: men slowly went insane inside the high-pressure chambers until their lungs burst and they died. Those dumped into icy water had their body temperature drop to 80 degrees (from a normal 98.6) and died after being hauled out.

Traffic in death brought forth a new breed of "expert"—transportation specialists who shuffled freight trains full of human chattel through the Reich's railroads, file clerks who handled the index cards of murder, bureaucrats of slaughter who never sullied their own hands with Jewish blood. The most infamous among them was Adolf Eichmann, who escaped to South America after the war, and was found and captured by Israeli agents in 1960. He died on a Jewish gallows after trial in a court of law.

Yet for all the cold-blooded efficiency of terror the Nazi machine developed and perfected, it could not snuff out man's will to resist —to the death if need be. Two Czech exiles parachuted into Prague in mid-1942, waylaid SS hangman Reinhardt Heydrich, the "protector of Bohemia," on a street corner and shot him dead. The Nazi reprisal: 3000 Jews sent to concentration camps, 10,000 Czechs arrested, 1300 killed. A whole village, Lidice, was razed and its 172 men—including a 12-year-old boy—lined up and shot. The two assassins were caught and died in the retaliation sweep.

Yet similar acts of terrorism swept Europe. The Yugoslavs fought a partisan war. Underground movements erupted in all the occupied countries and even in Germany and Austria. Overworked Nazi firing squads could not crush them, though they tried. Every act of sabotage, every blown bridge or railroad station brought fierce retaliation. Lidice was not the only village wiped out. For the Germans a ratio of a hundred to one was just about right.

Nazi bestiality was not limited to Jews and underground fighters. It engulfed anyone unfortunate enough to fall into the Nazi net. Millions of slave laborers were shipped from all parts of Europe to work in German factories, and their treatment was worse than that given cattle. They had barely enough to eat, and most of them slept in latrines, wooden shacks, chicken coops or factory yards. Medical attention was all but nonexistent, and the slaves died like flies. But the supply was endless, and the slave labor population was distributed across Germany. Soon most farmers had a few to help till the fields or do the housework. The New Order Hitler was building in Europe would be a slave society with Germans the masters.

As Nazi cruelty brutalized the German people beyond the pale of common humanity, other barriers also fell. Prisoners of war, for example, whose treatment is regulated by international convention, were victimized and tortured. Russian POWs, as members of an "inferior race," were used for medical experiments. Thousands of others were simply murdered or starved to death or forced to work as slave laborers. Americans and Englishmen were given better treatment at first, but after Allied bombers devastated the Reich, downed pilots were often murdered on the spot or brutalized in POW camps. In late 1944 a group of 47 Allied pilots were fiendishly murdered at Mauthausen: they were made to carry huge blocks of granite up a hillside over and over again until they dropped and died.

In occupied Europe Nazi officials became common thieves. Hitler's government stole everything in sight, including the conquered nation's gold, art treasures, labor, grain, oil, meat, factory production, machinery—everything, in fact, that could be moved out and used to enrich and further the Nazi cause. In the course of 12 years Hitler and his supporters managed utterly to corrupt the vast majority of the German people. And it is this corruption that in the end made futile the many efforts by the "other" Germany, the good and decent and dedicated, or even simply those horrified by Nazi excesses, to overthrow the Hitlerites. Plots brewed through the whole history of the Third Reich, but the only time one bubbled into action, in the July 20th uprising, it failed, and was not able to ignite the mass of the German people. The generation of Germans that had borne Hitler to power stood behind him like a wall of steel and sustained his rule with all their might and blind obedience. History has judged that generation's complicity in Hitler's crimes harshly, despite the Germans' claims after the war that they had known nothing of death factories and slave labor, the murder of hostages and the plunder of conquered peoples—that only Hitler and his band of criminals were to blame. Murder on the Nazi scale, however, could never be practiced by only a small group. Its sheer size demanded active participation of many and the acquiescence of millions more. The stench of the gas ovens at Auschwitz and at the other death camps could not be hidden from those who smelled it; nor were their mouths and the mouths of the killers themselves sealed.

Not that men have not murdered each other before in history; the record of the human condition is filled with bloody massacre. But never before or since have so many millions been killed as deliberately as by the Nazi rulers of the Third Reich. Men like Adolf Eichmann killed with a stroke of the pen, committing mass murder with dull methodology. Millions died in Stalin's Russia and the terror he blanketed across the Soviet Union was as evil as Hitler's. But not even at his worst did Stalin resort to the deliberate bestiality of the Nazis or carry it out in such scope. The Germans murdered neatly, coldly, without passion or feeling, and they wasted nothing— not the gold in a man's mouth, which they could sell, nor the fat in his body, which they could manufacture into soap, nor his tattooed skin, which they could make into lampshades, not even children's shoes, now piled in great heaps in the showrooms of Auschwitz.

Chapter

☆ *7* ☆

Winston Churchill spent Sunday December 7, 1941, at Chequers, the country home of Britain's Prime Ministers. He had two Americans as guests, Ambassadors Averell Harriman and John Winant. After dinner Churchill switched on the radio. It was a few minutes after nine o'clock, and the evening news had already begun. "There were a number of items about the fighting on the Russian front and on the British front in Libya," Churchill later wrote in his memoirs, "at the end of which some few sentences regarding an attack by the Japanese on American shipping. . . ." Minutes later Churchill was on the transatlantic telephone. "It's quite true," FDR told him, "they've attacked us at Pearl Harbor. We're all in the same boat now."

Churchill all but wept for joy. Finally, finally, after months of doubt and despair, the United States was in the war "up to the neck and in to the death." The end was no longer in doubt. "Britain would live. . . . We should emerge safe and victorious." That night, "being saturated and satiated with emotion and sensation, I went to bed and slept the sleep of the saved and the thankful."

For all the tragic loss of life and ships at Pearl Harbor this was the moment Churchill had worked towards ever since the outbreak of hostilities. In hundreds of letters and cables to the president he had pleaded, cajoled, threatened and argued for U.S. entry into the war. FDR had been sympathetic but did not feel he had enough popular support to risk so momentous a step. The isolationist tide that flowed through the U.S. in the thirties and early forties was simply too strong. But Roosevelt had edged the U.S. closer to war month by month.

In 1937 he had begun trying to "educate the American people" about the dangers of the dictators, but had elicited only lukewarm public response. Initial efforts to lift a ban on arms shipment to any nation at war had failed. Congress did not repeal the embargo until November of 1939. Six months later that decision literally saved England, for it allowed her to buy U.S. guns to replace those lost at Dunkirk. In June, 1940, alone the United States sold Britain hardware worth $43 million. It equipped the home guard.

That year, too, FDR got a war budget through Congress. It provided for construction of a two-ocean navy, including eight 55,000 ton battleships, and laid down plans for production of 50,000 aircraft a year. The President also negotiated lease of the 50 destroyers to Britain (in exchange for British bases in the Caribbean) and pushed through a military draft law. And when Churchill wrote to him that the British treasury was empty and Britain could no longer pay for desperately needed U.S. equipment, FDR came up with an ingenious scheme—lend lease. America would lend Britain the tools of war. Payment would be made after the fighting was over. Congress allocated $7 billion for the plan. By the spring of 1941, therefore, the U.S. was committed to do "everything short of war" to help the Allies. U.S. ships began spotting enemy submarines for the British fleet, and even took over some convoy duty.

In July, Harry Hopkins, FDR's most trusted aide, went to Moscow to see whether Russia could survive and to find out what the U.S. could do for the Soviet Union in the way of material help. That visit led to the conclusion of an aid agreement in the fall.

In August of 1941, Roosevelt and Churchill met in Newfoundland to hammer out the principles on which the war was being fought. The Atlantic Charter that emerged from the meeting committed the Allies to the "four freedoms"—freedom of speech and religion, freedom from want and fear. It disclaimed all territorial ambitions and contained assurances of free trade and self-determination of peoples after the war. It was an unprecedented document for a neutral and a belligerent to sign; although it was not formally a treaty, it pushed the United States closer to the British side.

In September, U.S. ships were ordered to shoot U-boats on sight. All through the fall months coordination between the United States and Britain grew closer, but the mood of the country still was not ready for war. It would take a hail of Japanese bombs to effect such a change.

The day after Pearl Harbor, Churchill determined to hasten to Washington; a week later he was aboard ship. The need for a top-level strategy session with FDR was obvious. Churchill was confident the U.S. industrial power, her capacity to build guns, planes and tanks, had assured eventual victory. He considered Japan's stunning triumphs in the Pacific "merely a passing phase," believing that in good time the Japanese "would be ground to powder." But he was convinced that victory in Europe would have to come first, and he was determined to commit the Americans to that end with the bulk of all their strength. And more than anything else that determination was the reason for his hasty voyage. Churchill knew that U.S. generals and admirals had their eyes glued on Japanese victories in the Pacific. He would have to change their outlook, and he'd be able to do it only if he convinced the President on a Europe-first strategy.

Churchill's plans called for an initial Anglo-American assault against North Africa lest the Germans seize it from Vichy and thus make an ouster of the Wehrmacht from all Africa that much harder. Luckily the news from Libya had been good lately. After months of inaction in the desert the British had begun to score impressively against Rommel's tanks. For the impatient Churchill, it had been a long wait.

On July 2, 1941, Churchill had transferred Wavell to India and replaced him in the Middle East with Sir Claude Auchinlek, who he hoped would prove a more aggressive and daring commander. But to his dismay he found Auchinlek a stubborn and methodical man, unwilling to attack until he had enough men and equipment. Moreover, Auchinlek was inclined to downgrade the importance of the western desert. He figured a major German thrust was more likely to come from the north through Turkey, Syria and Palestine. That summer, therefore, he was more interested in mopping up Syria and Iraq than in attacking Rommel. A crisis in Iran brought additional delay. The Shah had allowed the Germans to build up a large mission in Teheran, and it took joint British and Russian military intervention in August, 1941, to depose the ruler and restore the situation.

Thus it was not until November that Auchinlek consented to battle German forces settled some miles inside Egypt. Luckily Rommel himself had not been able to attack. Busy with Russia, Hitler had not resupplied him in the summer, and in the fall British planes on Malta and the Royal Navy in the Mediterranean sank most of the Italian ships that tried to bring in supplies. Still, when the British struck on November 18, 1941, they only just beat Rommel to the punch. The Desert Fox had almost completed preparations for a smash of his own against Tobruk, which he had besieged since the previous April.

Auchinlek's plan was a simple one: Eighth Army troops would drive into Libya south of Sidi Omar and then dash to Tobruk to lift the siege. At the same time, the Tobruk defenders would break out of their perimeter and link up with the attacking force. The offensive got off to a good start, and on the evening of the first day the British were 30 miles inside Libya. The next morning one Eighth Army brigade skimmed across the desert to capture the airfield at Sidi Rezegh, within ten miles of the Tobruk perimeter.

But Rommel awoke to the danger of the British attack and moved swiftly to contain it. He sent a strong tank force against Sidi Rezegh. The battle there began early on November 21, at about the same time the British struck out of the Tobruk perimeter. Two days later the Afrikakorps had destroyed almost 100 Allied tanks and pushed the Eighth Army beyond the airfield. The breakout attempt at Tobruk halted. Next Rommel took two armored divisions on one of the wildest rides of the desert campaign. He simply slammed his tanks right through the British lines to the "frontier wire" on the Egyptian border. The bold stroke splintered enemy positions, but in the swirling dust and sand and gunsmoke German tanks got enmeshed with the British and confusion soon dominated the field. At one point a British brigade could not join the fight because gunners did not know where to shoot.

Amid this chaos Auchinlek flew to the front to take personal command of the Eighth Army. Resistance stiffened at the border. An Indian division far out in the desert began to slash Rommel's flank. Stymied at the border and in danger of having his lines of communication cut, the Desert Fox resorted to a maneuver only possible on the hard, flat terrain of the desert: his tanks simply made a sweeping U-turn that took them north along the border and then back west past Bardia and on to Sidi Rezegh. Meanwhile, British troops near Sollum had lunged west and driven down the coast. On November 26 they caught up with the Afrikakorps and drove it out of Sidi Rezegh. Rommel then opted for a slow and orderly retreat. On December 9, 1941, the Eighth Army lifted the siege of Tobruk. And when Churchill arrived in Washington on the 22nd, Auchinlek was well on his way to occupying Cyrenaica again. Early in January the British took Benghazi for the second time and pushed into the Agheila area, where Rommel had started his first drive the previous spring. Cyrenaica had begun to resemble a football field: so far the British had scored two touchdowns, the Germans one.

Even as Rommel retreated, his supply situation had improved dramatically and he quickly readied another dash downfield. Two factors had helped the surge of the Axis fortune at sea: sustained German bombardment of Malta from Sicily, which greatly reduced RAF ability to use the island as a base for attacks on enemy shipping, and the U-boats, which made their first appearance in the Mediterranean. In rapid succession the subs bagged an aircraft carrier, a battleship and a cruiser. Mines put three more cruisers out of action. On December 18, six Italian frogmen disabled two battleships anchored in Alexandria harbor. This left the British fleet in the area with three cruisers and a few destroyers—just enough to watch Italian ships unload supplies in Tripoli without being able to do anything about it.

Churchill had barely returned from Washington when Rommel began a probing attack across the dunes. The British fell back. The Desert Fox quickly thrust ahead and turned his "reconnaissance in force" into a major assault. His tanks slammed hard through gaps left in the loosely strung British lines. The Afrikakorps raced across 350 miles in 17 days and recaptured Benghazi. On February 7, 1942, it pulled short at Gazala, only 40 miles east of Tobruk.

Until Rommel resumed his dash towards Suez in May, action in the Mediterranean shifted to the battle for Malta, the tiny island 50 miles south of Sicily which was a permanent threat to the safe passage of Axis ships to Africa. The Germans had decided to end that threat by aerial destruction. Week after week the Luftwaffe rained bombs on the British bastion and drove most of the people underground to live in caves, mine shafts and shelters hewn out of rock. But the island's guns kept firing, and fighter planes scrambled into the air day and night to meet the attackers. For Churchill was determined to hold Malta whatever the cost. He sacrificed dozens of ships in efforts to resupply it and kept sending in new fighters to replace those destroyed in combat.

In May a fleet of 60 spitfires took off from carriers and landed safely. Pilots on the ground quickly rearmed and refueled them and took off again to avoid their destruction on the ground. Aloft, the spitfires played havoc with Luftwaffe bombers. In the week that followed their arrival they destroyed 150 enemy planes and lost only three. It was a major turning point of the battle. A second came in June when several ships docked safely and, thanks to good air cover, unloaded supplies. Malta had survived her blitz, and Hitler did not take Raeder's advice to launch a seaborne invasion.

But the Germans used their control of the Africa passage to resupply Rommel in force. Although Churchill poured what men and equipment he could gather into Egypt, Rommel was ready first. He attacked on May 26, 1942, in what would prove his most brilliant and most dangerous campaign: in five weeks he took his Panzers almost within sight of Suez at El Alamein.

He began his drive with a frontal attack on the strong fortifications the British had built from Gazala on the sea to Bir Hakeim, 40 miles to the south. As the moon silvered the desert that night, Rommel climbed into his command tank and led two Panzer divisions on a wide sweep below Bir Hakeim. The next morning his advance armor sent an Indian brigade spinning into flight while motorized infantry overran British positions in the southwest. Meanwhile, Rommel again swung his main force north, behind enemy lines. He planned to push up to the coast and then punch down the high road to Egypt. But on May 28 the Germans suddenly found themselves trapped between positions of the 150th Brigade—a force they hadn't even known was stationed there—and three British armored formations to the east of their own. The Panzers were low on fuel, and the Italians had failed to cut a passage through the mine fields the British had laid to connect their strongpoints—the so-called brigade boxes on which their defense line was based. Had the British counterattacked then in force, they might well have nailed the attackers and caught Rommel in the bargain. But they didn't, and on the 29th Rommel got into a command car to drive off and look for his supply columns. Halfway through the night he found them, hopped into the cab of the front truck and led them back to his scattered tank force.

Then he decided on a bold and unconventional piece of strategy: he would build his own "box" right in the middle of the British positions and use the enemy's mine fields to guard his forces. The Panzers were put inside a ring of anti-tank guns posted behind the mines. To the north, German pressure against the Gazala defenders increased. And German sappers worked feverishly through the night of the 29th to cut at least a small passage through the mine fields from Rommel's position to the Italians on the western side of the British lines. On the morning of the 30th they had done it. Some supplies could trickle into the German box, even though a Free French brigade still held Bir Hakeim and prevented the arrival of reinforcements from the south.

But the precious lifeline was terribly vulnerable. At any moment the 150th brigade could cut it. Accordingly, Rommel determined to destroy the British box, counting on his ring of anti-tank guns to stop any Eighth Army counterattack from the east. He was lucky; none came until June 2. By then the Germans, aided by fierce Stuka attacks, had overrun the 150th brigade positions. German anti-tank guns stopped British counterattacks, and on June 5 Rommel began to attack on his own. In five days he had pushed his way free of the cauldron in which the British had trapped him and sent an armored division south to help the Italians capture Bir Hakeim, which fell on June 10. On the 11th the Germans were in the clear again. Six days later the Panzers entered Acroma and El Adem, and their long guns pointed once again at Tobruk, only 16 miles away. On June 19, Rommel had encircled the port for the second time in the desert war. A violent air and artillery barrage followed which disrupted communications inside the perimeter and destroyed half the mine field outside it. During the night of the 19th the remaining mines were cleared, and at noon on the 20th the Panzers had cracked Tobruk's defenses. The next morning a British garrison larger than Rommel's attacking force surrendered. The German haul was immense and included vast stores of gasoline.

Pausing only to refuel his tanks with British gas, the Desert Fox pushed on immediately, and on June 24 crossed the Egyptian frontier.

The next day Auchinlek once again took personal command of the Eighth Army. Three days later he had taken his dispirited troops all the way back to Fuka and prepared defenses around the El Alamein perimeter, where a major stand was planned to prevent Rommel's breakthrough to Alexandria, only 50 miles away. This was good defensive terrain: a 30-mile-wide gap between the sea and the great salt marshes of the Quattara Depression, which stretched 200 miles south and were impassable even for camels. But Rommel was confident that he could smash the gap's defenses too—so confident, in fact, that on June 29 Mussolini flew to Cyrenaica to await his triumphal entry into Cairo, once more a new Caesar. Hitler sent Rommel a Field Marshal's baton. Suez and the Pyramids glittered on the horizon. The road to the Orient seemed to open wide.

For the next four days the Panzers crunched against British lines, often established only hours before the Germans arrived. But in the fluid battle that raged all across the rocky and ridged desert, the Germans and Italians could not score the kind of massive breakthrough needed to collapse the front. Late on July 3, Rommel had to abandon plans for bypassing the inner El Alamein perimeter. During the following ten days the British beat back German probing attacks, then Auchinlek mounted counterblows of his own. Gradually he pushed the much weakened Germans into the defensive and at the end of the month could have shoved the Afrikakorps out of Egypt had not a belt of German mines stopped him. Rommel had run out of steam at the wrong place. If he could have driven the British out of Alexandria (an excellent port), his supply problems would have been greatly reduced and perhaps the Germans would have carried out the seaborne attack on Malta. As it was, the Afrikakorps' advance had added several hundred miles to Rommel's supply lines; trucks were ferrying in ammunition from Tripoli, a distance of 1400 miles, as well as from the nearer Lybian ports. But even Tobruk was now 370 miles away. And troops destined for the invasion of Malta were sent instead to bolster the Afrikakorps. Meanwhile, planes on the resupplied island made the Africa passage more perilous for Italian ships.

In August, Churchill arrived in Cairo on his way to Moscow. His mood was bitter. He had learned of Tobruk's fall while on a second visit to Washington in June, and it hadn't strengthened his hand in dealing for the North African campaign. The American generals still didn't like the idea even if Roosevelt did. Moreover, on returning home Churchill had nearly lost his job. Criticism of his handling of the war had been on the increase, and the loss of Tobruk brought it to a boil. Churchill survived, but only just. Now he determined to clean house in the Middle East, putting men in command who could finally drive the Germans out. He fired Auchinlek and replaced him with Alexander (his score: retreats in Dunkirk and Burma) as Middle East commander. The Eighth Army went to Bernard L. Montgomery, like Rommel an authentic genius of war but with little of his opponent's charm and wit. Montgomery was cantankerous, overbearing, difficult and insolent, unorthodox in dress and manner, contemptuous of his superiors—and brimful of the confidence of victory. It was a confidence he quickly instilled into the men of the Eighth Army.

First off, "Monty" resorted to elaborate stagecraft to convince Rommel that a British attack was imminent, when in fact all the activity near the salt marshes was fake. The purpose: to trick Rommel into an attack. It worked. Towards the end of August the Desert Fox grew convinced that this was his last chance for Suez and Cairo. His tanks struck south towards the phony British depots, and floundered in the soft sand. The British bashed his flanks. Incessant RAF attacks threatened annihilation. The Germans pulled back, reaching their starting positions on September 3.

Hitler ordered Rommel home for medical treatment. When he returned seven weeks later, it was only to take command of a fleeing army. Montgomery used the time well. Supplies began pouring into Cairo, among them big American Sherman tanks and self-propelled guns. More troops landed almost daily. But this time the gain in Eighth Army muscle was not matched by any increase in enemy strength. The German supply lines had again stretched thin. Convoys just weren't getting through. In October the Africa passage was hopelessly lost. Hitler paid the bitter price for failure to conquer Malta while he had had the chance.

After subjecting enemy defenses to two weeks of aerial pounding, Monty struck on the evening of October 23, 1942. A full moon gleamed down on the desert as a thousand British guns opened up a fearsome barrage. For several hours shells thudded into enemy lines, German soldiers choked in the acrid smell of hot metal and high explosives mixed with the desert dust. At midnight, British sappers began cutting two paths into the enemy's mine fields—the thickest and most dangerous yet laid in the war—and marked them with white tape. Australian and New Zealand infantry marched behind them. Scottish Highlanders advanced to the swirling music of bagpipes. By morning the Eighth Army forces on the northern end of the front had slashed a salient four miles deep. Elements of two armored divisions rolled in after the infantry, but they were not able to break out of the mine fields. The corridor became congested, and the whole offensive seemed in danger of stalling. Monty insisted on pushing ahead nevertheless, and on the morning of October 25 several armored formations were clear of the mines and headed southwest. At midday, Montgomery sent the Ninth Australian Division storming north in an attempt to cut off German formations near the coast. This drive prospered on the 26th, but the rest of the British front failed to generate any real momentum. Accordingly, Montgomery decided to regroup and prepare the more powerful breakout offensive needed now that the Germans had recovered their equilibrium.

By then Rommel was back at the helm, but his command structure was in shambles. General Stumme, his deputy, had dropped dead of a heart attack the day before Rommel's return, and for hours no one had taken command. Once inside the hatch of his command tank, Rommel counterattacked heavily and continued to do so all through the 27th and 28th. But Monty's lines held while the Briton quietly completed the buildup for his next attack. Meanwhile, the Australians continued their advance in the extreme northern sector of the front. On October 31, they cut off the Germans inside a coastal salient.

On November 2, 1942, the Eighth Army launched "Supercharge," the breakout offensive. It went badly at first but then two armored divisions clashed head on. German losses were heavy. When Rommel learned on November 3 that an Indian attack had shattered the southern anchor of his defenses, he disobeyed Hitler's orders to stand fast. That night he began to retreat—a day after he had wanted to, and a day too late. In the next 24 hours he lost 200 tanks and most of his Italian troops. Defeat threatened to turn into rout, and only the heavy rains that fell on November 6 enabled the Desert

Fox to regroup behind Mesa Matruh and begin one of the longest sustained retreats in the history of war: across 1700 miles of Libyan desert into Tunisia. It took three months to complete.

The battle of El Alamein was one of the major turning points of the war. Monty had won it the old-fashioned way—with the sheer weight of artillery and the brute force of infantry. Rommel's sophisticated armor technique could not come into play, and for the Germans the war would never again be the same. Their string of victories had run out.

Rommel must have known it two days after he pulled out of Mesa Matruh and was just across the Libyan border. For on November 8, 1942, General Dwight Eisenhower had led American and British troops ashore in North Africa. Churchill's dream of "Operation Torch" had at last become a reality. Henceforth the Germans would be squeezed inside a giant pincer.

Just after midnight on that November Sunday, an armada of 850 allied ships stood offshore from three North African ports—Casablanca on the Atlantic and Oran and Algiers on the Mediterranean. As U.S. and British soldiers swung over the side and into the landing craft, they still did not know for sure if Vichy forces would fight. But Pétain's rift with the Allies had been too deep. After the French had recovered from their initial surprise, they put up some resistance almost everywhere.

General George S. Patton, who next to Rommel would prove the most flamboyant commander of this war, managed to get his men ashore unopposed on three points along the Moroccan coast outside Casablanca. But as the Americans neared town, the Vichyites fought back furiously. Action around Port Lyautey was especially heavy.

The battle was even hotter at sea. A large Vichy fleet was anchored in Casablanca, and it included the unfinished battleship *Jean Bart,* whose 15-inch guns added power to shore batteries. Then the *USS Massachusetts* steamed within firing range and, after a long-distance cannon duel, left the *Jean Bart* a gutted wreck. Meanwhile, other French ships had sailed out to meet the American fleet. It was no contest. Vichy lost ten ships. On the 11th the French commander surrendered. He didn't have a single ship or plane left.

American troops landed to the east and west of Oran, planning to capture the port in an enveloping operation. French resistance stiffened on the second day when an attempt to capture the port through a direct strike from the ocean failed. But then a British battleship shelled Oran, and on the 10th the French gave up.

Militarily things went much more smoothly at Algiers, where the Allies met little initial French resistance. Before nine A.M. they had captured two key airfields. Later there was some fighting on the approaches to the city, and the French beat off a direct attack by two British destroyers against the harbor. However, the fighting in Algiers played second fiddle to complicated political negotiations completed by dark. At 7 P.M. the city surrendered. Once British and American troops were securely ashore in Algiers, they were quickly grouped into the First British Army under command of General Anderson and sent streaking east to complete the conquest of Algeria. Then they were to sweep through Tunisia and, it was hoped, capture the port of Bizerte and the capital, Tunis. Anderson moved ahead quickly. On November 11 a seaborne force took Bougie. The next day a combined navy-parachute strike seized the port of Bone. On the 16th, British paratroopers occupied the airfield at Souk el Arba, and on the 17th Anderson was fighting in Tunisia itself.

But by then a quick victory in North Africa had already eluded the allies, for German reaction to the invasion had come with lightning speed. On November 11 the Wehrmacht completed the occupation of Vichy France. Two days earlier the first German troops had been airlifted into Tunisia. On the 10th they had established their first defense perimeter around Bizerte and Tunis. Thus, when Anderson entered Tunisia he already found himself opposed by some German units. Still, ten days later the First Army had pushed within a dozen miles of Tunis and stood on a ridge overlooking the capital. It appeared as if the Tunisian campaign might be over in a matter of days.

But by the end of November, General Nehring, who commanded German troops in Tunisia, had become too strong to be pushed easily aside. He had plenty of planes, good airfields and about 100 tanks. Nehring led fierce counterattacks against Allied lines and succeeded in driving green American troops from several key hills. Heavy rains came in December and turned the landscape into a swamp of black mud. Temporary airfields hastily constructed in Algiers became unusable, while the Germans took off easily from bases in Tunisia. Eisenhower, already sporting his famous nickname, "Ike," decided to withdraw to Medjez, 30 miles from Tunis. By Christmas, German strength had swollen to a full Panzer army. The final allied offensive in Tunisia would have to wait.

But military action was only one side of the North African campaign. Perhaps more important were the diplomatic adventures that preceded the landings and the political intrigue that followed. American diplomats had worked for months to persuade French officials in North Africa to support the Allies and allow the landings to proceed unopposed. Veteran trouble shooter Robert Murphy had moved to Algiers from Vichy, for the U.S. maintained diplomatic relations with Pétain right up to the invasion. Murphy was to mastermind the preparations. He quickly won promises of some support from General Juin, the Algiers commander, and several other officials. By October a high-level conference was necessary.

Accordingly, General Mark Clark, Eisenhower's deputy, set out in the submarine *Seraph* for the secret rendezvous, a secluded villa outside Algiers. But the *Seraph* arrived too close to dawn to risk a landing. For the next 24 hours the sub stayed underwater while Clark and his party played bridge. That evening Murphy and the French conspirators drove to the villa in a convoy of cars. One of the Frenchmen spied an Arab guard and quickly gave him 50 francs to keep his mouth shut. The bribe was too large; the guard's suspicion was aroused.

Meanwhile, Clark and his party had climbed into small boats and landed on the beach shortly after midnight. The discussion that followed inside the house examined in detail the military and political problems of the invasion. Several hours later the phone rang: the Arab guard had talked, and Vichy police were on their way. The French officers scattered out of the house. Clark and his group hid in a musty wine cellar. Upstairs, Murphy sat down to play poker with his host, who calmly told the police that the American diplomat had come to buy black-market chickens and had stayed on for a card game. After the Vichyites left, Clark hid out in the woods until dark, when he rowed back to the sub through heavy surf. Just before he reached the *Seraph* a large wave swamped the boat. Clark lost his pants and, with them, an $18,000 bankroll meant for bribes.

Murphy's next recruit was a man his fellow conspirators thought might have the stature and authority to attract the loyalty of Vichy officials. There was one problem: General Henri Giraud lived in unoccupied France. Dutifully, in early November the Allies sent a submarine to pick him up and ferry him to Gibraltar. There Giraud blithely told Clark and Ike that "General Giraud has arrived and is ready to take command." It took two days to convince him that his job was not to lead the invasion but to fly to Algiers after the landing and rally Vichy support. As it turned out, this proved an impossible mission. Several days before the attack, Admiral Jean Darlan, Pétain's heir apparent and second man in the government, arrived in Algiers to visit his sick son. His presence altered the political situation completely, for when Murphy told Juin shortly after midnight on the 8th that a landing was imminent, the general was appalled. With Darlan in Algiers, Juin's authority had melted away. Still, Juin agreed to arrange a meeting with the admiral, and the three men sat down together at two that morning. Darlan was furious, but he agreed to ask Pétain for freedom of action. Several hours later, armed anti-Vichy youths surrounded the villa to make sure Darlan would not escape. But a pro-Vichy police patrol quickly dispersed them and arrested Murphy and Juin. In the morning Darlan took Juin downtown to look over the situation in the harbor. Murphy was left behind to stare pensively at the barrel of a gun pointed at his chest.

By midmorning the admiral realized he could not long hold Algiers and cabled Pétain telling him so. In the evening he sent another cable: he had authorized Juin to negotiate the city's surrender. Several hours later the admiral was in American hands, but far from powerless. He remained the only man whose authority Vichy officials would acknowledge and who could arrange a ceasefire in all of Algeria, a step that would save countless American lives. The tough and dramatic negotiations that followed lasted for two days. Finally Juin asked the Americans for just five minutes alone with Darlan. Clark and Murphy left the room. American guards outside cocked their rifles. When the general and the diplomat returned, the French admiral agreed to order the ceasefire.

But he charged a stiff price. Giraud was frozen out of power. Darlan was left in charge of the French empire in North Africa. The anti-Vichy underground would be crushed, meaning that Murphy's friends would have to go into hiding. Still, the Americans agreed. They felt that the stake in lives was too high not to. On November 13, Ike arrived in Algiers and ratified the pact.

The agreement kicked up a storm in Britain and the United States, where it was denounced as a shabby political deal with a fascist. Roosevelt had to back off and promise that Darlan's government in North Africa was only a temporary expedient, dictated by the needs of war. And FDR and Churchill agreed on the need for pushing all three French leaders—Darlan, Giraud and de Gaulle (who had been excluded from all Torch preparations)—into forming a common regime.

Darlan, however, had other ideas. He moved quickly to keep French fascists in control. As the weeks passed, Vichyite power increased while resentment among anti-Nazi Frenchmen reached the seething point. Things grew worse on December 19 when Gaullist envoys arrived and got nowhere with proposals to merge North African and Free French armed forces.

Then, on Christmas Eve, 1942, events took a sudden and dramatic turn. As Darlan walked to his office, a young man darted from the shadows and shot and killed him. The assassin was arrested and executed two days later on orders from Giraud, who assumed political and military power in North Africa. The allies heaved a collective sigh of relief. The political crisis was over.

FDR now thought the time ripe for a full-dress review of the war and a discussion of future strategy. Churchill and Roosevelt and their staffs met on January 11, 1943, in a hotel outside Casablanca. As usual the two leaders got along famously while their generals disagreed bitterly.

The British came prepared with precise plans for action in 1943. After Tunisia was cleared of Axis forces, the Allies would mount an attack on Sicily or Sardinia and knock Mussolini out of the war before the year was out. At sea the war against the U-boats would have to be intensified; the Germans were sinking a prohibitive half million tons of shipping a month. Finally, the air war was to extend into Germany with the start of strategic bombing. A cross-Channel invasion of France would not be feasible until 1944.

Chief of Staff George Marshall and his aides did not come equipped with such concrete proposals, but British plans left them uneasy. They didn't want to fight a major campaign in the Mediterranean and felt that an attack on Italy would fail to bring about a decision. It would only divert men and equipment better off moved to England for the landings in France, which remained the keystone of U.S. strategy. Moreover, Admiral Ernest King disliked the European war and wanted more ships and supplies sent to Japan. This time Marshall tended to agree. He favored a one-year pause in Europe.

The British were appalled at this prospect, and Churchill managed to win FDR to his viewpoint. The Casablanca compromise, therefore, leaned heavily towards the British view. Sicily was selected as the first European target, with "Operation Husky" to begin on July 9, 1943. In the air the U.S. would fly B-17 daylight raids against Germany; the British would attack at night. The British also agreed on a campaign to retake Burma.

On the political front Churchill and Roosevelt felt that a "shotgun" wedding between de Gaulle and Giraud was a must. It proved a difficult match to arrange. De Gaulle's bitterness against his Anglo-American allies had grown enormously since Syria and his exclusion from Torch. A series of stormy meetings took place after he arrived at Casablanca on January 22. At one point Churchill almost withdrew British support for the Free French, and de Gaulle's relations with FDR were strained at best. Still, after two days of bickering he agreed to join forces with Giraud, as a personal favor to Roosevelt. And on January 24 Giraud and de Gaulle, sweet-sour smiles pasted on their faces, shook hands for the photographers at a final news conference.

There was more momentous news than that to come out of the press briefing, however—Roosevelt's call for unconditional surrender of the Axis. Many historians have claimed since then that this demand prolonged the war unnecessarily, that it stiffened the Axis will to resist and slammed the door on any negotiated settlement of the war. But from the vantage point of 1943, with victory only a glimmer on the horizon, it made good sense both as a morale booster at home and in Russia, and as a warning to the enemy.

Chapter

☆ 8 ☆

When Churchill and Roosevelt parted company a few days after the Casablanca conference, the war in Africa had narrowed to the Tunisian campaign. Rommel had quit Libya and was settling the Afrikakorps into the Mareth Fortifications in southern Tunisia. Montgomery's Eighth Army had crossed the Tunisian frontier early in February but was making slow headway against determined resistance from Afrikakorps rear guards. Further north General Arnim, Nehring's successor, had pushed Anderson's First Army 40 miles from Tunis and seized several key passes through the eastern Dorsal mountain chain. The southern half of Anderson's front was particularly weak, and if the Panzers broke through the Kasserine Pass they could lunge back into Algeria, perhaps even drive as far as Bone and Constantine.

A violent sandstorm swirled through Faid Pass before dawn on February 14 as Arnim's tanks struck west, quickly isolated 2000 Americans and smashed a U.S. tank battalion. Rommel jumped off on the 15th and the next day entered the town of Gafsa, which the Americans had abandoned two days earlier. By the 18th, Rommel was 20 miles from Kasserine and Arnim was 15. Now the Desert Fox decided on a three-pronged attack. One armored column would feint to the west in a direct smash at the Algerian border. The Afrikakorps would pile through the Kasserine Pass and head northwest while the 21st Panzer division plunged through a mountain gap further east. If all went well they would rejoin at Le Kef and drive from there for the Algerian coast.

The screening attack gained 12 miles before the U.S. Second

Corps stopped the German advance. But at Kasserine the sheer weight of tank and artillery fire left the Americans close to rout. On the evening of February 20, Rommel had smashed through the pass and sent his 10th division tanks racing north. All through February 21 heavy fighting raged around the village of Thala, and for many anxious hours it looked as if Rommel would break through. Then, in the nick of time, the U.S. Ninth Artillery Division arrived after a four-day, 735-mile march from Algeria.

On the afternoon of the 22nd the Desert Fox decided he could advance no farther. U.S. reinforcements had arrived, and clearing skies allowed greater use of American airpower. On the 25th, U.S. troops tramped once again through the Kasserine Pass. Soon afterwards they halted their advance and Rommel got the Afrikakorps back into the Mareth line in good order.

For green American troops the battle of the Kasserine pass was the baptism of fire that Guadalcanal had been for the Marines in the Pacific.

The Desert Fox was not content to sit for long behind a Maginot type of defense. (The French had built the Mareth line before the war against possible Italian attack from Libya.) So, on March 6, he sent his tanks against British positions 20 miles away. Montgomery, who had fought Rommel too long not to suspect that an attack was coming, had ringed his bunkers with 500 anti-tank guns. British gunners waited until they could see the hatches of the approaching tanks. Opening up at 400 yards, they devastated the attackers. At nightfall, when Rommel finally retired, he had lost 52 Panzers. Soon after, he returned to Germany and Arnim took command.

Monty's attack against the Mareth line began on March 20 with a head-on smash covered by a fierce artillery barrage. The Eighth Army pierced the defenses but could not break them. But at the same time, Monty had sent a New Zealand corps on a daring 150-mile end run round a forbidding mountain chain to lunge behind enemy defenses.

The Americans had now resumed their offensive from the Kasserine area, and the Germans thus faced entrapment from three sides. Arnim, therefore, pulled out of the Mareth line and retreated north. On April 7, Monty linked up with Anderson's force, and for the next month the Allies ground down the Axis perimeter around Tunis and the port of Bizerte. On May 6, General Alexander, who had taken command in Tunisia, opened a final drive on the capital. British tanks clattered into the city on the 7th while U.S. troops captured Bizerte. It took six days to finish mopping up, but finally, on May 13, 1943, Alexander cabled Churchill: "We are masters of the African shore."

With Africa cleared of the Axis, Sicily and Italy became the next targets. Mussolini's regime had begun to totter. The people and the army had tired of a war they never wanted. A sign of that war weariness came in mid-June when a large Allied fleet approached the tiny island of Pallenteria, 40 miles from the Tunisian coast. Six thousand tons of bombs had been dumped on it in four weeks, and they had been most persuasive. The Italians hoisted a white flag before Allied soldiers had jumped into their landing craft.

Next came Operation Husky, the invasion of Sicily. On July 9, 1943, the biggest armada yet gathered for a seaborne invasion—three thousand ships and landing craft—bobbed in Sicilian waters. Aboard were 160,000 British and American soldiers: Montgomery's Eighth Army and George Patton's Seventh. Bad weather and heavy seas almost led to a postponement of the invasion, but on the morning of the 10th Allied soldiers went ashore and achieved complete tactical surprise. The Italians had taken one look at the high waves lashing the coast the night before and gone to bed convinced the Allies couldn't land. Moreover, they had expected the invaders to hit Sicily's western beaches first because they were closest to Africa. Instead Patton landed in the south, Montgomery in the east.

Initial progress was rapid. Allied paratroopers had seized key airfields before dawn. The Eighth Army captured the ancient Greek port of Syracuse on the 10th; Patton quickly took the towns of Licata and Gela and sent his tanks north and west across the island. Alexander's plans called for Monty to drive up the east coast of Sicily and capture Messina, just five miles from the Italian boot. Patton would act as a shield to ward off an Axis attack against the main thrust. But things didn't work out the way Alexander had planned them. The Germans threw the bulk of their forces on Sicily against Monty's front and stopped his advance on the plains of Catania at the foot of volcanic Mount Aetna. The Eighth Army stayed bogged down there for more than three weeks. Patton, meanwhile, had struck boldly across the island, and on July 22 his tanks rolled into Palermo, near Sicily's northwestern tip. He then swung east down the coast and on July 31 entered San Stefano.

Montgomery, unable to break through on the coast, decided on another swing operation and sent his troops around Mount Aetna, where his artillery literally blasted a road through the mountain. The Eighth Army's progress was slow, painful and costly. Patton, on the other hand, aided by two seaborne landings that outflanked German positions, pushed briskly down the northern coast and on the morning of August 17 entered Messina. The Sicilian campaign was over. Patton won plaudits for his slashing and freewheeling style of armored warfare, Monty the brickbats for relying too much, as he had done in Africa, on crushing artillery barrages.

Nevertheless, Sicily almost cost Patton his command and his career. On a hospital tour the flamboyant general, who usually wore riding boots and strapped two pearl-handled revolvers around his waist, had tongue-lashed several sick GIs and, in a fit of temper, slapped one of them across the face twice with his glove. Finally he stalked out cursing the "cowards" in the sick bay. The incident raised an uproar in the United States. Congress was livid, and demands for Patton's removal were widespread. Ike barely managed to save his top field commander's job. Patton helped his own cause with a public apology.

The Allied victory in Sicily had done more, however, than just conquer the big island. It had toppled Mussolini's already shaky regime. Old, ill and sickened by the loss of Italy's African empire, Il Duce had gradually begun to lose control of events. On July 24, 1943, Mussolini's own henchman called a meeting of the Fascist Grand Council. That rubber-stamp body had not met since 1939, but when it convened it was rubber-stamp no longer. It voted 19 to eight to restore the constitutional monarchy and return Italy to democratic rule. Mussolini still thought he could ignore his opposition, but the next day King Victor Emmanuel III called him to the royal palace and fired him. "My dear Duce," the little king told the man who had made the sovereign into a puppet, "It's no longer any good. . . . You are the most hated man in Italy." Guards quickly hustled the fallen dictator into an ambulance and carted him off to prison.

No one mourned his fall. And after 20 years of his power not a single fascist guard lifted a gun in his defense. For fascism had never bitten deeply into the Italian soul as Nazism had into the German. Italians accepted its petty meanness and the wicked small tyrannies it imposed. They watched the show-off strutting of the fascist leaders with a mixture of amusement and contempt and, in the end, enormous weariness. The nation shrugged off the dictator's ouster as long overdue.

Marshal Badoglio succeeded Il Duce as Prime Minister. Obviously he wanted to take Italy out of the war. Just as obviously he could not admit it while the Germans still fought in Sicily, had some eight divisions scattered in Italy and were pouring in more troops. Allied politicians reacted cautiously to the upheaval—as it later turned out, much too cautiously. Eisenhower had wanted to offer Badoglio immediate and favorable surrender terms. But Washington and London still remembered the disturbance Ike's deal with Admiral Darlan had caused and were not about to give their general that much political freedom again. So Badoglio had to resort to secret diplomacy, a tortuous exchange of messages and protracted negotiations held in hidden houses much on the model of those that preceded the North African landing.

As for the Germans, news of Il Duce's fall hit them hard. Nazi leaders were shocked and confused, afraid the same thing could happen in Germany. Some counseled patience and pointed to Badoglio's pledge that Italy would keep fighting on the side of the Axis. But Hitler knew better. This was one kind of political situation he could gauge in an instant—and his judgment was as true and sure as in the early days of his rise to power. Once again, perhaps for the last time, Hitler proved the cooler and faster poker player.

Nazi troops quickly seized all the Alpine passes that led from France and Germany into Italy. Rommel readied an eight division force able to strike at once if needed. Hitler drew up plans for the Duce's rescue and restoration and for the occupation of all of Italy including the Vatican if necessary. "We can always apologize later," he said. Hitler also planned to disarm the Italian army. He expected a week's grace before putting these plans into action. Instead he got a month and a half.

For Badoglio had turned the negotiations into a Hollywood scenario, complete with disguised envoys and secret meetings in

Madrid, Lisbon and Sicily. He pleaded and cajoled with Ike for better terms than the U.S. general was allowed to offer. The Americans wouldn't budge. Time and again talks threatened to break down as Badoglio, beset by Germans and Americans and his own scheming mind, tried to find a formula that would avoid unconditional surrender. Finally, on September 3, a secret armistice was concluded. Ike agreed not to announce it until September 12 to give the Italians time to make their own military preparations and to launch the Allied invasion in force. (Monty's Eighth Army had landed that day at Reggio on the very bottom of the Italian boot.)

On September 6, 1943, Ike sent General Maxwell Taylor on a secret mission to Rome to reconnoiter prospects for an aerial strike against the capital. Taylor found the airfields already in German hands, the Italian army demoralized. Therefore he vetoed the idea. On the 8th, General Mark Clark's ships carrying troops for Operation Avalanche approached the beaches in the Salerno area below the Bay of Naples. At 6:45 P.M. that evening, Ike, still distrustful of the Badoglio government, broadcast the terms of Italy's unconditional surrender, four days ahead of schedule.

In Rome the king, Badoglio and his government quickly fled to Allied-held territory in the south. The Germans at once put their careful plans into action. The Italian army was disarmed with only scattered fighting. German troops quickly occupied the major Italian cities, including Rome. Wehrmacht units retreating north from Reggio quickly joined other forces to dig in along the ridges above Salerno. On the morning of the 9th, when American and British soldiers hit the beaches, northern and central Italy were already firmly under German control. Four days later Hitler even had a man to put at the head of German-occupied Italy: none other than Benito Mussolini himself.

Il Duce had been moved repeatedly since his arrest, for Badoglio feared that the Germans would make an attempt to rescue him. The fear was well founded, for soon after Mussolini's capture Hitler had charged hawk-faced SS colonel Otto Skorzeny with the rescue of "Italy's greatest son." On August 28 the fallen dictator had been taken from Sardinia to a remote hotel in the mountains near Rome. Skorzeny quickly discovered his whereabouts and on September 12 landed a dozen gliders with 100 men on them on the mountaintop.

Most of Il Duce's guards fled when they saw the black helmets of the SS, and those who stayed refused to fire: Skorzeny had taken an Italian general with him as a persuader. The SS colonel quickly burst into Mussolini's room, stood stiffly at attention and announced: "Duce, the Fuehrer has sent me, you are free." A small spotter plane landed nearby and a short time later flew Mussolini to safety —and to his new role as Hitler's puppet.

Withering German gunfire met the Allied landings at Salerno on September 9, and for the next ten days General Clark's men hid in trenches and caves trying to avoid the bullets and shells poured on their positions from the higher ground that gave the defenders all the advantage. Two days after the landing the Germans were counterattacking in force without much allied air opposition. Fields in Sicily were just too far away to offer fighter protection for very long. Berlin began to boast that the Allies faced another Dunkirk. And indeed, there was a time when General Clark thought seriously about re-embarking his Fifth Army. Slowly, however, the preponderance of Allied firepower and the mass of supplies brought ashore began to tell. Long-range bombers smashed enemy lines. And from the south, Montgomery pushed the Eighth Army up the long Italian toe into the boot proper.

On September 20, Eighth and Fifth Army troops linked up at Auletta, 45 miles south of Salerno. Kesselring realized he could no longer hope to drive the Allies into the sea and began to prepare one defensive line along the Volturno river, 25 miles north of Naples, and other fortifications in the Apennines near Cassino. In the meantime, Clark had begun to push out of his Salerno bridgehead and advance on Naples. Skirting Mount Vesuvius, Clark entered the wrecked shell of that port on October 1, 1943. The Germans had done a thorough job of destruction; they had blown up the water mains, destroyed many historic buildings and left time bombs scattered throughout the city. Disease and hunger were rampant.

With the capture of Naples Allied success in Italy had reached a crest. From then on the Italian war would deteriorate into a bloody slugging match between Allies and German troops that would last until the war was over. Kesselring held the Volturno line until mid-October, then slowly fell back to the north, again and again using the rugged terrain to fight bitter rear-guard actions. The pace of the Allied attack proved agonizingly slow as they flushed the enemy out of every valley and every hillside. On November 20 the Eighth Army was across the Sangro River and closing in on the eastern anchor of the Gustav line, a major fortification Kesselring had readied before the fall of Naples. On the Mediterranean side of the boot the Americans were still trying to pierce the Bernhard line, a secondary fortification.

As Allied forces inched their way towards the Gustav line it became apparent to Alexander that only an amphibious landing closer to Rome offered real hope of breaking the stalemate. Accordingly, plans were made to send an expeditionary force to Anzio, 33 miles south of the Eternal City. On January 22, 1944, 50,000 British and American troops landed almost unopposed at Anzio. For a day the Germans did little to harass the landings, nor did General Lucas, the Allied commander, try to cut swiftly beyond his little beachheads into the Alban hills and crack the German fortifications there. Instead, Lucas fortified and consolidated the positions he had already won, giving Kesselring time to bring up troops from the south. Soon he had three Wehrmacht divisions posted on high ground overlooking the beaches, and he proceeded to repeat his Salerno strategy: bombard Allied soldiers caught in a beachfront trap. For many anxious days it seemed as if this time Kesselring would make good on his repeated boast of Dunkirk II. But as at Salerno, Allied air power and the incredible mass of supplies spilled onto shore saved the day. The Allies hung on but could not break out—and would not be able to until the spring.

In an attempt to take some pressure off the Anzio beachhead, Alexander had made renewed efforts in the south to smash the Gustav line. By the end of January his troops had reached the outskirts of Cassino and could look up at the Abbey of St. Benedict, enthroned on the top of Monte Cassino above town. It would take the combined force of Polish, French, British, New Zealand and American troops almost three and a half months to capture this key anchor of the German defensive system. The battle for Cassino became the fiercest struggle of the Italian campaign, the decision to bomb the monastery one of the most controversial of the entire war.

At the end of January, General Freyberg brought his New Zealand division into the Cassino line and took command of the offensive. Freyberg was a friend of Churchill's; he had defended Crete, fought in the desert and led the sweep around the Mareth line. Certainly his battle credentials were impressive. And in his first attack he took several hilltops and about a third of the town itself. But then Freyberg insisted that the Germans had holed up in the monastery itself and demanded an airstrike against what by any standards was one of the great monuments of western civilization. Clark bitterly opposed the idea. Alexander didn't much like it, but reluctantly gave his approval. On February 15, a fleet of 229 bombers dropped 453 tons of high explosives onto the abbey. An ancient vision of flying stone had been turned into a heap of rubble.

Gratefully the Germans moved troops into the debris, which now offered excellent defensive positions. Kesselring, of course, had not stationed a man in a building that, undamaged, was an obvious death trap. Again and again Freyberg's ground attacks were beaten back. Air attacks just raised clouds of dust above the smashed stones or pockmarked the landscape with bomb craters which quickly filled with water to form natural tank obstacles.

In the spring the Allies finally changed aerial tactics. They settled down to serious strategic bombings, not massive raids, and hit rail lines and yards, roads, staging depots and communications. The Germans had trouble supplying their troops. Gradually the allies rebuilt their strength and in May they were ready. This time they planned to bypass Cassino, rather than risk a straight attack. On May 11, 1944, a massive artillery bombardment erupted along a forty-mile front. At last the allies forded the Garaglione and the Germans were unable to drive them back. On May 16 Kesselring began to pull out of the Gustav line. His winter allies of rain, mud, snow and sleet had given way to sunshine. On the 17th the allies pushed beyond Cassino. The Germans pulled out, the British moved in and a Polish brigade stormed up Monte Cassino to plant their white-and-red banner on top.

The road to Rome lay open. On May 22 the Allies punched through the Adolf Hitler line below the capital. On the 23rd, beefed-up forces at Anzio broke out of their beachhead and linked up with spearheads of the Fifth Army to march down the ancient Appian Way. By the end of May, Kesselring had pulled the bulk of his troops north of Rome to yet another line built across the peninsula.

It was 7:30 P.M. on June 4, 1944, when elements of the 88th U.S. Infantry Division trooped through the gates in the ancient walls that gird the city and stood not far from the cathedral of San Giovanni in Laeterano, the Pope's own church. Then the Americans marched on downtown until they came to the Piazza Venezia. From the palace balcony that overlooked the square Mussolini had often strutted in front of great crowds and delivered his bombastic speeches. That night an American GI of Italian descent climbed on the balcony to give a spoofing imitation of the fallen dictator. A great crowd watched and cheered. Rome was in Allied hands.

Chapter ☆ 9 ☆

While the weary survivors of Field Marshal Paulus' Sixth Army trudged across the frozen waste of Stalingrad towards bitter years in Soviet prison camps, the Red Army swept joyfully through the Don country. The Italian, Hungarian and Rumanian armies Hitler had left to screen the upper Don had been smashed. Grolikov's Voronezh group was within 30 miles of Kursk, Vatutin had reached the Donets and Malinovsky's Stalingrad front threatened Rostov. In the Caucasus, General Kleist saw the specter of a trap: with the Russians on the Don, Rostov was his only overland escape hatch. He began to retreat north and west and managed to get most of his forces through the Rostov gap before the city fell.

By late February, 1943, the Russians had driven far beyond Kursk, captured Kharkov and moved within 20 miles of the Dnieper river. In the south, Voroshilovgrad and Rostov had fallen. Red Army troops had cleared most of the coast of the Azov Sea. To the north of the main front, above Voronezh, only a hundred miles from Moscow, the Wehrmacht had abandoned the iron triangle of Rhzev-Gzhatsk-Viazma, which Soviet troops had failed to take the previous winter. Finally a five-mile-wide railroad corridor had been opened into embattled Leningrad.

Once again a state of exhilaration gripped the Soviet generals. They envisioned the Wehrmacht driven out of the eastern Ukraine and sent their troops plunging recklessly ahead. But the Germans were still much too strong for any such sweeping defeat. By mid-February, Manstein realized that the Red Army was running out of steam and that supply lines were too long and equipment too battle

worn. Quietly he prepared a counteroffensive against the vulnerable
Soviet salient south of Kharkov. On February 20 he unleashed a
blitzkrieg assault that smashed exposed Soviet positions with devastating impact. Stunned, the Russians let go and fell back steadily for
the next two weeks. On March 12, Panzer spearheads entered Kharkov; on the 15th the Germans captured the city for the second time.
Before the spring thaws halted major fighting until July, Manstein
managed to push the Red Army to the east bank of the upper
Donets and dent the Russian lines to the north into a well-defined
salient around Kursk.

Though the battle lines in Russia were relatively quiet that
spring, a political explosion shook the Allies that would have pro-
found impact on the shape of the postwar world: relations between
Moscow and the Polish government-in-exile in London became so
strained that they broke.

They had never been good, for technically the two nations were
still at war, and it had taken a good deal of Allied pressure in 1941
to restore diplomatic ties. This done, the London Poles asked the
Russians for permission to form a new army from among the thousands of Polish prisoners of war still in Russian camps. Reluctantly
Moscow agreed. General Anders quickly raised a 100,000-man force
but, strangely, couldn't find enough officers for it. To make matters
worse, those who did join Anders' army didn't want to fight alongside the Russians; memories of 1939 were too bitter. Churchill solved
the impasse by suggesting that the Poles leave Russia and join the
British Middle East Command, then badly in need of troops to stop
Rommel's drive on El Alamein. Moscow agreed, but the whole episode
left a bad taste.

Stalin now determined to draw up a postwar Polish settlement
on his own terms. Eastern Poland would be incorporated into the
Soviet Union, and Poland compensated with German territories. A
pro-Soviet government would reside in Warsaw. In March, 1943,
Stalin began to plan formation of another Polish army which would
take orders from Polish Communists.

Then, on April 13, Paul Joseph Goebbels dropped a political
bombshell. He announced that the bodies of thousands of Polish officers had been found in Katyn forest near Smolensk. A German-spon-
sored inquiry commission determined that the Russians had shot the

Poles in the back in the summer of 1940 and dumped the corpses into the mass grave at Katyn. For the Poles the German charges at last answered the question of what had happened to the officers who failed to report to Anders' army. The exiles promptly demanded an investigation by the International Red Cross. Moscow refused.

The Polish-Soviet quarrel quickly mushroomed into an explosion: on April 27, 1943, Moscow "suspended" diplomatic relations with the exile government. Soon afterwards Stalin got down in earnest to the business of forming a communist Polish government and army. Later, when the Red Army captured Smolensk, an official Soviet "investigation" was conducted into the incident. The Russians, of course, announced that the Germans had done it. The London Poles did their own investigating and put the blame on the Russians. To this day the issue remains in doubt. Beyond the question of guilt, however, Katyn dramatized the divisive nature of the Polish issue, which was to strain Allied unity during the war and do much to destroy it afterwards.

All during the lull on the Russian front Hitler planned his third summer offensive: the initial attack would continue the drive Manstein had begun the previous February—isolation of the salient around Kursk. One German pincer would punch south from Orel, the other north from Belgorod. Once they met, four Soviet armies would be trapped in the Kursk area. The Germans committed half a million men, several thousand tanks and planes.

The plan was a good one and, had Hitler carried it out as soon as the spring thaws were over, might well have succeeded. But the massive amount of equipment needed wasn't ready then, so the offensive had to wait until early July. The Russians, meanwhile, had easily deduced the enemy's intentions and used the three months' period of grace to turn the salient into an all but impregnable fort. Half a million freight-car loads of arms and ammunition were shipped in, men and hardware skillfully deployed.

Operation Citadel began as dawn broke on July 5, 1943. Model's Ninth Army attacked south along a 25-mile front, and Manstein threw a spearhead of 700 tanks in an assault towards the north. Fierce fighting flamed along both sectors but nowhere did the Germans manage to break through, although they eked out advances of several miles. By July 10, Model had lost two-thirds of his armored formations and went on the defensive. Nowhere had his gains been deeper than ten miles.

In the south, Manstein did a little better. On July 6 his tanks had pierced the first major line of Soviet defense and were hacking into the second. Gradually they ground out small gains. Then, on the 12th, what has been called the greatest tank battle in history erupted in the Prokhorovka area. Two huge tank armadas, 1500 machines in all, collided head on. Great clouds of dust blurred the action. The howl of engines filled the air—soon choked with the black smoke of burning armor and guns. The Germans advanced as much as 20 miles that day, but their losses included 10,000 men and 350 tanks, too prohibitive to continue on the offensive. Moreover, the Red Army had already begun to counterattack massively, and the Germans retreated. Ten days later they had lost all the ground they had won so expensively.

The Red Army now embarked on its first summer offensive of the war. On August 4 the Russians took Orel, north of the salient, and on the 18th they were outside Bryansk. On the southern side of the bulge a massive Soviet drive on Kharkov began to take shape. Hitler issued another of his "fight to the death" orders, which was obeyed for ten days. But on August 23, 1943, the Red Army retook the city.

For the next three months the Russians swept on unchecked. Smolensk fell in September, while further south the Wehrmacht was pushed against the Dnieper. The Nazis hoped to make a firm stand at this natural barrier, but the Wehrmacht had never been very effective at holding river fronts. By early October the Soviets were across the Dnieper north of Kiev. Russian engineers performed incredible feats of bridge-building. They hacked down trees and quickly fashioned them into pontoons, which small boats ferried across the water. Once they were on the other side, German fortifications were quickly reduced. On November 6, 1943, the Red Army entered Kiev, the capital of the Ukraine.

By mid-November, Manstein managed to launch a series of counterattacks, but although he halted the Red Army in many places and pushed it back in a few, his drive never picked up any real momentum and petered out before the month was over. At the end of 1943 the Red Army stood only 60 miles from the pre-war Polish frontier in the center, while in the south Malinovsky and Tolbukhin had swept from the Donets and along the Sea of Azov to the lower Dnieper and the Black Sea. The Crimea was cut off and isolated.

The string of victories continued in the new year. In January, 1944, the two-and-a-half-year siege of Leningrad was lifted. It had taken a year to prepare the breakout offensive, for only brute force —a crushing superiority in men, tanks and guns—could crack the German vise around the city. On January 14 three Russian generals hurled a total force of 375,000 men, 14,000 guns and 1200 tanks against the enemy lines. In two weeks the Soviet armies had advanced 40 miles, and at the end of February their advance units had reached the Estonian border. Further south they had come within 40 miles of Latvia.

The Soviet advance through the Ukraine in early 1944 was highlighted by a major victory at Korsun. On February 3, 1944, the Red Army closed pincers around a German salient on the Dnieper. In a mini-Stalingrad operation, Soviet troops encircled large German forces, defeated a breakout attempt and completed mopping up operations on February 17. The Wehrmacht lost 50,000 men.

In March the Russians began a mammoth offensive to clear the Germans from the western Ukraine and the Crimea, and to drive beyond their own borders into Rumania and Poland. Again a series of sweeping battles was fought over vast tracts of land, through thick swamps and across mighty river barriers. A hundred towns gave their names to major battles, and thousands upon thousands of men died in them. Everything else that winter had been but a preparation for this climax.

The battle line swung in a 600-mile arch from the Pripet marshes in the north to the mouth of the Dnieper river in the south. In mid-April, Zhukov had captured Tarnapol, a hundred miles from the big Polish city of Lwow, crossed the Pruth river at Czernowitz and plunged into Rumania. To his left Marshal Konev had sailed his big T-34 tanks into Umman through a sea of spring mud the Germans had believed impassable. Then he had crossed the Bug and Dniester rivers to reach the Pruth along a 75-mile front. In early April, Konev had forded that river too and pushed his advance to the outskirts of the important Rumanian town of Jassy. In the far south, Malinovsky had advanced somewhat more slowly—rivers are wider at their mouths and harder to cross—to storm into Nikolayev after heavy fighting and enter abandoned Odessa on April 10 almost without firing a shot. A few days later he was at the mouth of the Dniester and had linked up with Konev's forces.

Marshal Tolbukhin launched the final spring campaign: the invasion of the Crimea. He struck on April 11 and needed a month to clear that warm and pleasant land Hitler had once marked out as a vacation paradise of the triumphant Reich. Attacking in overwhelming strength from beachheads established the previous winter, Tolbukhin swept across half the Crimea in two days. By April 18 the Germans had been pushed into a 20-mile perimeter around Sebastapol. Hitler, who had decided to hold the Crimea against all the logic of strategy, when he should have evacuated his army while he had the chance, ordered another "heroic defense" of the port the Russians had held for nine months in the beginning of the war. Tolbukhin needed two weeks to bring up heavy siege equipment. On May 5 he opened a murderous bombardment of the city. It took but five days to smash Hitler's dream of an epic defense.

A month-long lull set in after the conquest of the Crimea. The front had stabilized and now ran from the Gulf of Finland into northern Rumania, close to the pre-war frontiers except for the deep bulge of White Russia (one of the Soviet Republics), where the Germans still clung to positions on the eastern bank of the Dnieper.

Now Moscow prepared for the last summer offensive of the war. First would come a quick strike at Finland to knock that country— which, not surprisingly, had joined the German attack on Russia in 1941—out of the war. Then the Red Army would begin its big summer drive to free White Russia.

On June 10, 1944, General Govorov struck at the Mannerheim line across the Karelian Isthmus. His drive resembled that of the 1939 war, but this time the Finns couldn't stop it. In ten days Govorov had breached enemy defenses, captured the port of Viborg on the Finnish Gulf and reached the 1940 frontier. There the Russians halted in order to give the Finns an incentive for negotiating an armistice—which was concluded on September 19.

Meanwhile, the Soviets put the finishing touches to a huge buildup on the White Russian front, a buildup conducted in utter secrecy. When it was completed, the Red Army had concentrated

166 divisions, 31,000 guns, 5200 tanks and 6000 planes. A fleet of 12,000 trucks was readied to ferry supplies. This was the best-prepared offensive of the war.

The Germans suspected nothing. They were convinced that the Russians would strike next in the south. As for the increased partisan activities in White Russia, they had come at periodic intervals and been ruthlessly suppressed. When the Red Army attacked on June 23, 1944, therefore, it caught the Wehrmacht completely off guard. Within five days rugged German defenses between Vitebsk and Mogilev had been smashed. Two days later the Red Army was across the Berezina river and had begun a pincer assault on the White Russian capital of Minsk. The pincers closed behind the city on July 3; on the same day, Soviet troops entered it. Within four weeks White Russia had been cleared of enemy forces. German losses were heavier than at Stalingrad: 25 divisions destroyed, 350,000 men.

Encouraged by the swift advance in White Russia, the Soviet high command decided to resume the attack in the Baltic and the Ukraine in mid-July. On the 10th, Yeremenko's troops began a drive towards Latvia. In three weeks they had driven west past the Latvian capital to reach the Gulf of Riga and cut the rail communications between Army Group North and the rest of the German land forces in the area. It was one gain the Russians could not hold. Several weeks later General Schoerner massed six Panzer divisions for a counterattack that managed to hack out a 20-mile corridor south of the Gulf of Riga to restore communications with the German rear. Still, the Red Army now occupied more than half the Baltic States.

Konev jumped off in the Ukraine on July 13 to begin a double pincer operation against Lwow. By July 22 he had trapped 22 German divisions, and three days later he encircled Lwow and captured it. By the end of the month he had struck across the San river, reached the Vistula and put a bridgehead across it.

In August, however, the Russian advance slowed. Lines of communications had stretched taut. Troops suffered fatigue, and equipment had become worn out. In the north the Soviets were unable to ford the Niemen and strike across the central Vistula deeper into Poland. Outside Warsaw, Model brought up four armored divisions to counterattack Rokossovsky's troops (whose presence in suburban Praga was to spark the ill-fated Warsaw uprising), and at some points sent them reeling back as much as 60 miles. Towards the end of the month the whole Soviet offensive, from the Baltic to the Vistula 100 miles below Warsaw, came to a halt.

Action shifted to the south as the Russians prepared a knockout blow against the Balkans. Moscow knew that Hitler's satellites had begun to wobble, just as Italy had done a year earlier. One solid punch might well topple the fascist governments there and lead their armies to surrender. It proved a sound guess. Within a month the Red Army had swept through Rumania and Bulgaria, fought inside Hungary and stood on the borders of Yugoslavia.

The Russians attacked on August 20, 1944, along a line that ran from the Carpathian foothills in the west to the Black Sea in the east. Malinovsky slammed his Second Ukrainian Front troops against the combined Rumanian-German force that defended the 340-mile-long front. The Fourth Rumanian Army was brushed aside easily. General Friessner's more seasoned Germans were pulled out of position, and 15 divisions trapped. Once again the Axis had been surprised: Friessner had been sure the Red Army would renew its attack in the center before striking south. The price of this miscalculation was high: 60,000 dead, 100,000 prisoners, two armies all but destroyed. On Malinovsky's left, meanwhile, Tolbukhin struck beyond his Dniester bridgehead to drive across the Danube and down the Rumanian coast to the Bulgarian frontier. Within a week the Red Army had cleared Eastern Rumania; on August 30, Malinovsky entered the Rumanian capital of Bucharest.

When he did, Rumania had changed sides. On August 23 young King Michael staged a coup against the fascist dictator Ion Antonescu and put all the German generals in Bucharest under arrest. Hitler was confident he could crush the uprising quickly, restoring Antonescu or some other fascist general. But suddenly he couldn't find one willing to act as his front man, and the Germans didn't have forces strong enough to launch a major drive on Bucharest. As a result, the Nazis did little more than shell and bomb the capital, not enough to make a real difference.

A coalition government of all pre-war parties, including the Communists (who did not then play a dominant role) was formed, and early in September the new regime signed an armistice with Moscow.

As the Red Army drove into Rumania, neighboring Bulgaria grew increasingly jittery. Sofia was a member of the Axis but had declared war only on the western powers. A Bulgarian ambassador still resided in Moscow. On August 26 the Bulgarians reaffirmed their "neutrality" and promised to intern any Germans in their country. But this was no longer good enough for Moscow, which was well aware of strong pro-Soviet sympathy among the Bulgarian people. On September 5, 1944, Russia declared war, one of the shortest on record. It lasted two days, without a shot being fired. The Bulgarians welcomed the Red Army as liberators, formed a coalition government and declared war on Germany. In October the Germans decided to pull out of Greece, paving the way for bitter political turmoil there later that year.

By the end of September the Russians had cleared most of Rumania and were battling the Germans in Hungary. Bulgarian and Red Army troops had entered Yugoslavia, where they quickly linked up with Marshal Tito's partisan army. On October 4, Partisans and Russians threatened Belgrade; by the middle of the month the Yugoslav capital had been liberated. Delirious thousands lined the roads to cheer their own soldiers and those of the Red Army.

Further north the Russians had struck through the Banat into Hungary, and soon half the country was in their hands. But the Wehrmacht dug in and held fast. The Red Army was on the high road to Vienna and the rich industrial basin of Central Europe. That prize would be defended bitterly. For the next several months progress in the southeast would be painfully slow.

Nor had the Russians made much headway in the center of their vast front. In October they were still stalled outside Warsaw and had not been able to strike beyond the Vistula. For Warsaw lay on the road to Berlin, and this route, too, the Germans would defend with utmost ferocity. What enthralled the world that summer, therefore, was not the Red Army, but the struggle waged by the Polish Home Army for their capital, a struggle that ended about the time that Belgrade was surrounded.

The Polish insurrection in Warsaw was one of the tragic epics of the war. It created much bitterness and mistrust between Moscow and the West. For when General Bor-Komarowski gave his underground army the signal to strike at 5 P.M. on August 1, 1944, Rokossovsky's patrols were fighting in Praga, on the other side of the Vistula from Warsaw. The Poles were sure it could only be a matter of days before the Red Army arrived. When it didn't, many in Poland and the West were convinced that failure to ford the Vistula had more political than military motives, for Bor-Komarowski was loyal to the London exiles, and only ten days earlier Polish Communists had set up a "Governmental Committee" in Lublin. Moreover, Stalin gave only surly and evasive replies to Churchill and Roosevelt's urging that he help the Poles.

For all the distrust and suspicion that has lingered through the years, however, there is good evidence to back the Russian claim that they simply were not strong enough on August 1 to crack determined German resistance. When Rokossovsky's armored patrols reached Praga, they had been advancing continuously for 40 days. Fuel and ammunition were low, tanks in bad repair and losses very heavy. Finally, the appearance of Model's four armored divisions put the Russians on the defensive: they did not stop retreating until August 26, and they moved forward again only very slowly.

As for the uprising itself, it began in a great burst of hope. The underground army had been built up to a strength of 300,000 men. As German civilians evacuated town and dogfights popped across the sky, Bor-Komarowski was sure his rebellion would succeed. Certainly he felt that Soviet radio broadcasts had given him every encouragement. And the response of local Poles was all that he could have wished. Men, women and even children flocked to the colors. People poured out of their houses to build barricades and nail Hitler pictures on them so the Germans would have to shoot at their beloved Fuehrer. Polish flags, lovingly sewn from bedsheets and slipcovers flamed from house fronts and windows. German street signs were torn down. Within 24 hours the Poles had occupied the gas works, the electric power plant and four city districts. Two days later they held the downtown area and the post office; a week after the uprising had begun, the rebels controlled 40 per cent of the capital. But still no help came from the Russians.

Hitler began to throw heavy reinforcements into Warsaw. The Nazis used tanks and flamethrowers against the Home Army. The long muzzles of anti-aircraft guns ringing the city were lowered to fire on the rebels. German gunboats raced down the Vistula to pound

Polish bunkers on shore. Day by day the plight of the Home Army grew more desperate. They ran low on ammunition and other equipment. Early in September they broadcast an urgent appeal for help: "We have not eaten bread for ten days." Finally Russian and Allied planes dropped some supplies by parachute, but the Poles managed to get only a few of them. It was not enough. Slowly Warsaw began to die again. People lived without gas, electricity or water mains. There were only scraps of food. Methodically the Germans shot Warsaw into rubble. On September 27 the rebel radio broadcast this forlorn message: "We have a desperate feeling of loneliness and frustration. . . . Perhaps you do not realize under what conditions we live and fight." On October 2, 1944, the Poles could fight no longer. "Warsaw is no more," the radio said. "There are only ruins left." At 8 P.M. the Home Army stopped shooting.

The uprising cost 300,000 lives. When it was over, a vengeful Hitler ordered the city's complete destruction.

The Red Army continued to sit opposite Warsaw for another three months. Not until January 17, 1945, did the Russians enter it and begin their final drive into Germany itself.

Elsewhere on the northern front Soviet troops scored substantial gains only in the Baltic. Govorov attacked from Narva on September 15 and quickly drove across northern Estonia. On the 22nd he was in Tallin, the capital. On October 3, the Russians grabbed three large islands that dominated the entrance to the Gulf of Riga. Farther south, Yeremenko finally smashed German defenses around Riga and entered the Latvian capital on October 15. On his left the armies of the First Baltic Front crashed through to the Baltic coast, trapped 30 divisions in Latvia's Courland peninsula and laid siege to the town of Memel. Finally, heavy artillery barrages succeeded in pushing the Germans back to the very frontiers of East Prussia. Only desperate Wehrmacht counterattacks succeeded in stabilizing the front at the end of October.

As winter approached, the Red Army was poised for the strike into the German heartland itself; great armored spears were pointed at Berlin and Vienna.

Chapter
☆ 10 ☆

German tanks were at the outskirts of Smolensk as Josef Stalin sat down in his Kremlin study on July 18, 1941, to write a letter to his new ally, Winston Churchill. "It seems to me," Stalin wrote, "that the military situation would be considerably improved if there could be established a front against Hitler in the west—in northern France."

It was the first of many Russian requests for the opening of a second front to relieve the hard-pressed Soviet armies. For the next three years Moscow pleaded, cajoled, blustered, threatened and insisted that the Allies launch a cross-Channel invasion of France. And just as stubbornly Churchill refused to move until he was sure such an invasion could succeed. It wasn't easy. At their first face-to-face meeting in Moscow in August, 1942, Stalin grew downright insulting: "Are you so afraid of the Germans you dare not attack?" he asked the man who had defied Hitler's hordes when Britain stood alone. Churchill sat tight on his famous temper. He knew the meaning of failure: Hitler might well nurse the war into stalemate, perhaps even win it. And four days after he left Moscow the disastrous attack on Dieppe gave the world a tragic and bloody example of such defeat. Six thousand Canadian troops tried to land on the beaches of the seaside resort. Few even made the seawall at the head of the beaches. The Germans raked the attackers with gunfire from the bluffs above. The whole raid lasted less than six hours. Canadian casualties— killed, wounded or missing—approached 4000, and all the equipment landed was lost.

No, an assault on Hitler's "Fortress Europe" was out of the question until U.S. factories had produced the needed equipment,

American yards had built the armada of ships needed to carry it to England and Allied navies had secured the Atlantic sea lanes.

American factories quickly poured out a torrent of hardware—300,000 planes, 85,000 tanks, 315,000 field guns, two million trucks and 17 million rifles before the war was out. U.S. yards built 28 million tons of shipping. Liberty ships splashed into the water on an assembly-line basis. But the challenge of the German U-boats was harder to meet. It took until May, 1943, to defeat Admiral Doenitz' submarines, and before that time he came close to cutting the lifeline for good.

For all their initial successes in the war, the U-boats did not truly come into their own until the defeat of the German surface fleet—specifically, after the sinking of the *Bismarck* in the spring of 1941. The big battlewagon had sailed out to raid the North Atlantic convoy lanes. Challenged by two British battleships, *Bismarck* sank the *Hood*, damaged the *Prince of Wales* and fled. A British torpedo bomber found the monster before it reached port, slammed a torpedo amidships and crippled its steering. Two British battleships finished her off a day later. The remaining big German ships, *Tirpitz*, *Scharnhorst* and *Gneisenau*, threatened arctic convoys to Russia from bases in Norway, but when *Scharnhorst* actually sailed out to intercept one, it was sunk. *Tirpitz* then played hide and seek in Norwegian fiords with RAF bombers until the British finally nailed it in October, 1944.

The story of the U-boats was far different: by mid-1942 they sank ships faster than U.S. yards could build them. In July the subs had sunk 69 ships, in August 108. Between August and the following May the U-boats—now hunting in wolf packs—destroyed 3,700,000 tons of shipping. At the turn of 1942–43, Allied admirals were close to admitting defeat. Then advanced technology began to pay off: improved radar, more sophisticated depth charges, better air cover. Gradually the U-boats lost ground. They still sank a prohibitive half a million tons of shipping a month, but the price was rising. In March and April, Admiral Doenitz lost 27 U-boats. A climax was near.

Early in May a wolf pack of 17 submarines attacked an Allied convoy, but the accompanying air and sea escorts quickly struck back and sank seven and damaged four of the underwater prowlers. The rest slunk back to port. The battle was a harbinger of disaster.

By the 24th, Doenitz had lost 31 submarines in May alone, and he called the wolf packs home for good. The U-boats continued to harass the shipping lanes, but did not threaten to cut them. The Atlantic was secure.

Supplies for the invasion of France could now flow more freely than ever before into British ports. In August, Roosevelt and Churchill met again, this time in Quebec, to finalize plans for Overlord, the second front. They set May 1, 1944, as the date of the invasion, agreed that an American would have to command it (Chief of Staff George Marshall was the favorite candidate), selected the Normandy beaches as target and approved the technical equipment for the attack, including landing craft and floating harbors, the so-called mulberries, which ships could tow across the Channel. Finally, they decided to ask Stalin to attend a big-three conference to review the war effort.

Stalin was agreeable but insisted that the foreign ministers meet first to do the spadework. On October 12, 1943, talks began in Moscow. They dealt with the Balkans, Italy, Austria, the future of Germany, Nazi atrocities and Overlord, the one overriding issue for the Russians. The Moscow Pact that emerged from the meeting was important. The Allies pledged to destroy German militarism, restore democracy in Italy and re-create a free and independent Austria. And they tried to slow down the size and pace of Nazi slaughter with a special declaration on atrocities: "Let those who have not imbued their hands with innocent blood beware lest they join the ranks of the guilty, for [we] will pursue them to the uttermost ends of the earth. . . ." The declaration was a vain hope. The Germans refused to listen.

On November 27, 1943, Roosevelt and Churchill arrived in Teheran for their meeting with Josef Stalin. The Briton viewed the entire matter with foreboding. Security was virtually nonexistent. Persian horsemen, stationed 50 yards apart, lined the route from the airport. Great crowds mobbed Churchill's limousine. Once it even stalled for three or four minutes in the crush. Never had the Prime Minister been more easy to assassinate. Small wonder he urged FDR to stay at the Soviet embassy near the British compound and thus avoid the long daily trip to the U.S. villa.

The big three agreed quickly on the Overlord concept and on

Anvil, the strike into southern France from the Mediterranean that was to accompany it. But Churchill's plans for an invasion of the Balkans won little support from either Stalin or FDR. Roosevelt, however, did win Russian support for his United Nations Organization, which would succeed the old League after the war. Indeed much of the U.N.'s shape and structure was settled at Teheran, which helps explain the conference's crucial place in the political history of World War II.

After a series of lavish banquets that featured fervent toasts of friendship and understanding, the Allies issued a communiqué that looked "with confidence to the day when all the peoples of the world may live free, untouched by tyranny."

Early in December, FDR decided to name Eisenhower, not Marshall, as commander of Overlord, and on Christmas Day 1943, Ike, Montgomery and General Omar Bradley moved to London to prepare the invasion.

England quickly turned into one huge arsenal, bursting with tanks, guns, trucks, bulldozers and jeeps. Planes stood wing to wing at dozens of fields—10,000 in all. An armada of 5000 ships jammed British ports. And still it was not enough. D day was postponed a month to add the extra output of U.S. shipyards, and Anvil was delayed even longer to provide more landing craft. On land a million soldiers trained for the invasion. In the air, Ike changed the thrust of attack away from massive bombings of the cities towards strategic targets: transportation and fuel supplies. In May alone, Allied flyers destroyed 900 locomotives and 16,000 freight cars, and wrecked 18 of 24 bridges across the Seine.

As D day neared, invasion plans were finalized: massive naval and aerial bombardment would soften up the coast; then an initial force of 150,000 men would land on five gently sloped, hard-surfaced beaches between Caen and Cherbourg on the Normandy coast. Weather would determine the precise date of the attack.

Now the meteorologists took over. Each day they pored over maps and charts to study the tides, the winds, the chance for rain, the cloud cover. For most of May the outlook stayed promising: spring weather, flat seas, not much wind. June 5, 1944, was tentatively selected as D day. Then, on June 3, the forecast turned bad. A typical December depression had begun to move across the North Atlantic.

That meant high winds, low clouds, rains and rough seas. The next morning heavy rain fell, and Ike decided to postpone D day by 24 hours to June 6. Soggy clouds still darkened the sky that night when Eisenhower drove to the mansion where his twice-daily weather briefings were held. Miraculously the outlook had improved. A high-pressure area stalled off Spain had begun to move north; chances were good that it would interrupt the bad weather for at least a day. Time ran short. If Ike stayed with the 6th he had just half an hour to send out preliminary instructions to the fleet to assemble. "The question is," the supreme commander said more to himself than to the others, "how long can you hang this operation on the end of a limb and let it hang there?" Not a minute longer, Ike decided, and the go signal went out to the ships.

A bright moon peeked through scattered clouds on the night of June 5 and silvered the decks of ships maneuvering into the five assault groups that would plow through carefully mine-swept channels to the French coast. The U.S. First Army was to land at two beaches —the VII Corps on "Utah," on Cotentin Peninsula south of Cherbourg, the V Corps at "Omaha," 15 miles away on the other side of the Vire river. The British Second Army would attack three target areas between Caen and Bayeux. Three airborne divisions were loaded into planes to land further inland and pull enemy attention away from the shore. The U.S. 82nd Airborne was to attack around St. Mère Église, the 101st north of Carentan and the British Sixth Airborne near the eastern fringe of the assault zone.

At 20 minutes after midnight on June 6, 1944, the first British gliders touched down on French soil, about nine miles inland near Caen. Within 15 minutes the soldiers had gained control of two bridges across the Caen canal and the Orne river. In the air Allied planes bombed the coast and dropped dummy parachutists, fireworks and strips of metallized paper that glowed fiercely. The Germans must have thought all Normandy was under aerial attack.

Out at sea, warships began hurling shells at the French coast, still clothed in pre-dawn darkness. Behind them, landing craft splashed into the water and soldiers climbed down the gunwales of bucking ships. As the sky streaked gray, shelling increased. Soon acrid smoke hung like a curtain over the shore. On the dot of H hour, 6:30 A.M., the first 20 landing craft beached on the yellow sand of Utah beach. As the GIs went ashore, not an enemy gun opened up from the bluffs above. The Americans had landed a mile below their intended target, and luckily the Germans had not stationed any artillery there. By nightfall, Utah was secured—a perimeter of 36 square miles occupied at the cost of 197 casualties. Much of the credit for Utah's success went to the two U.S. airborne divisions, which, though dispersed, had drawn most of the German troops in the area away from the beaches.

Omaha was a much more tragic story. Ideal for defense, the beach sloped up gently from the ocean for 300 yards to a natural shingle sea wall, reinforced on top with concrete pillboxes and other fortifications. Moderately high bluffs further inland proved too steep for tracked vehicles to climb. The four ravines that led out of the beachhead "trap" had been heavily mined. Moreover, Allied shelling hadn't been heavy enough to silence German guns, which spat fire from all sides as the Americans went ashore. Many died wading through the last few feet to dry land; some of the wounded fell into the water and drowned. Tanks were immobilized before they could struggle ashore. The men and machines who made it spent most of D day morning huddled in the sand amid growing chaos and confusion that was fed by steady enemy gunfire. At one point Omar Bradley even considered pulling his Omaha troops back and sending them to Utah.

But then raw courage turned the tide. A brigadier pulled out his pistol, hollered at his men to "get off this beach" and charged up the hill. A sergeant took his squad through a mine field on a suicidal run, made it, poked his bazooka against a pillbox and knocked it out. By late afternoon, infantrymen had clawed their way up the bluffs; tanks struggled up the ravines. That night the Americans had pushed a mile and a half inland and overrun the enemy coast defenses. Omaha would hold.

On the British beaches—Gold, Juno and Sword—the going was easier. The British had landed an hour later than the Americans, and the Royal Navy had laid down a heavier artillery barrage. Armor moved into action more quickly. Heavy rocket fire covered the advance. By evening, Gold and Juno had joined into a single front, while the Sword force had pushed inland far enough to make contact with the airborne troops.

The epic day was over: 155,000 soldiers had gone ashore and captured 80 square miles of land. A sigh of relief—and gratitude— went round the Allied world.

As for the Germans, they had been caught unprepared. The "impregnable" Atlantic wall Goebbels had boasted so much about had not been finished. Defense strategy was muddled at best. And Hitler had appointed Rundstedt and Rommel as commanders, although the two men differed on how best to halt the invasion: the Desert Fox had wanted to concentrate his armor right on the beaches and stop an Allied landing; Rundstedt favored letting the enemy ashore, then counterattacking to drive him into the sea. Hitler's compromise was irrational. He kept infantry on the beaches, the armor in back. As a result, the Wehrmacht could bring up very few tanks to support the infantry when the invasion began.

Moreover, the Germans were plagued by bad luck. Rommel was in Germany visiting his wife and did not reach the front until the evening of D day. Six key generals were off holding war games, and two armored divisions Rundstedt might have thrown into battle couldn't move: they took orders from Hitler personally, and on D day the Fuehrer slept until two P.M.

Five days after the landing the Allies held an 80-mile strip of Normandy coast and in places had pushed twenty miles inland. About 16 divisions were ashore. Two of the mulberries—the floating ports Churchill and Roosevelt had discussed at Quebec—were installed offshore and allowed a steady flow of supplies to stream onto the beaches. Overhead the Allies had quickly established complete air superiority. There had been one major failure, however: Monty had not captured Caen, a key target ten miles inland. As a result, the massive Allied sweep through Normandy was delayed.

The Americans advanced in two directions: the Omaha force moved towards St. Lô, the Utah troops cut across Cotentin peninsula towards the Gulf of St. Malo. But progress was agonizingly slow. The GI's fought across terrain made to order for defense and hard on armor—mostly small fields surrounded by hedgerows: 15-foot-high fences, half earth and half hedge, designed to protect cattle and crops from Atlantic storms and as tough to smash as concrete. It took four U.S. divisions eight days to cover 17 miles. And not until June 18 had they hacked out a narrow corridor to the sea.

Still, Bradley was now in a position to mount twin drives against the port of Cherbourg, on the tip of the peninsula, and Normandy to the south. A day later, however, the worst storm in 70 years battered the coast and wrecked the mulberry off Omaha (the British one survived). With the flow of his supplies thus drastically reduced, Bradley had to settle for a more modest target, the capture of Cherbourg. By June 29 the last enemy resistance in the harbor forts was subdued.

Allied engineers managed to rig up a pier in the wrecked port within 48 hours, so that a ship could dock. But the facilities would take much longer to repair, so Cherbourg could not yet serve as an alternate supply funnel to U.S. troops. Operation Cobra, the attempt to break out into Normandy, would have to be postponed until mid-July. In the second half of the month, however, bad weather repeatedly delayed the operation. And the Germans made the Allies pay dearly for the meager few miles that they managed to capture in local attacks.

But while the campaign in Normandy stalled, a political explosion ripped the Reich that almost, but not quite, did away with Adolf Hitler. It had been a long time in the making, for opposition to Hitler and his cutthroats dated back to the thirties, and plots against him were hatched throughout the phony war. Then victory in the west silenced the Fuehrer's enemies. Not until Germany's defeats in Russia did opposition to the Nazi regime revive and spread rapidly. By the end of 1942, plotters were active in the Wehrmacht intelligence (the Abwehr), the army, the diplomatic corps, the churches and the aristocracy. Slowly a shadow cabinet emerged ready to take power once Hitler left the political stage. Now all that remained was to push him off it. There was only one way: assassination.

The first attempt came on March 13, 1943, when two officers smuggled a bomb aboard Hitler's plane just before it left Smolensk for East Prussia. It failed to go off. There were other attempts later that year, but they all failed. The Fuehrer moved around too much and was hard to nail. Gradually the plotters faltered. The SS pushed the Abwehr aside and took over intelligence activities. But just as the resistance seemed about to collapse, it won a vital new recruit: Klaus Philip Schenk, Count von Stauffenberg, a brilliant staff officer who became disillusioned with the Nazis in Russia. He lost an eye and a hand in Tunisia but continued to work in the Home Army, whose leader, General Olbricht, had joined the plotters and supplied the soldiers needed to carry out a coup. In 1944 Stauffenberg, now a colonel, became the Home Army's chief of staff and conferred often with Hitler. He was the logical candidate to kill him. Early in July he walked into two meetings with the Fuehrer, a bomb in his briefcase. The first time Hitler was alone, and Stauffenberg wanted to bag more Nazis. On the second occasion Stauffenberg slipped out to telephone the plotters to go ahead; when he returned to place the bomb, Hitler was gone.

Now time ran short. The SS was on the trail of the plotters. Orders had gone out to arrest one of the leaders. Stauffenberg's third chance would have to be his last. It came on July 20, when he was called to attend a briefing at the Fuehrer's headquarters in Rastenburg, East Prussia. He entered the conference room, where Hitler and his generals stood around a big oaken table covered with maps at 12:37 P.M. The bomb in his satchel was timed to go off in less than ten minutes. Unobtrusively he placed the briefcase next to the Fuehrer, listened to a general report on the worsening Russian situation, then muttered an excuse and went out. A minute or two later the bomb went off. It was a minute or two too late.

For someone, somehow, had pushed the briefcase just far enough away so that the table's heavy wooden legs and top protected Hitler from the full impact of the blast. The explosion smashed windows and walls and blew a hole in the roof. Debris choked the room. The Fuehrer's trouser leg was torn off. A beam bounced off his back. An arm hung paralyzed from his shoulder. Both eardrums were damaged. But as Field Marshal Keitel led him out of the gutted room, Hitler was not only alive but in full control of his faculties; so much so that in the afternoon he could tell the visiting Mussolini that his salvation was a sign from the gods: he was destined to win the war.

But Stauffenberg was convinced Hitler had died. He told an accomplice to phone the news to Berlin while he raced to the airport to board a waiting plane for the flight to the Reich's capital. Unfortunately the telephone connection to the plotters was bad. The man at the other end wasn't sure he had heard correctly, wasn't sure if Hitler was indeed dead. The tragic misunderstanding led the conspirators to sit on their hands and wait for confirmation. When the young count arrived at their headquarters on Bendelstrasse, nothing had been done. Stauffenberg started firing orders at once. But still the machinery of revolt moved slowly. Olbricht hesitated. Former Army Chief of Staff von Beck arrived as if he were coming to tea. Rebellious officers in Vienna, Prague and Paris began to move— but as slowly as if they had all the time in the world. They had only minutes.

By late afternoon telephone and cable lines, which Stauffenberg's friend at Rastenburg had managed to disrupt, were restored. By early evening the radio, which, incredibly, the rebels hadn't seized, broadcast bulletins that Hitler was alive. The officer sent to arrest Goebbels wasn't in on the plot, and the wily propaganda minister quickly persuaded him to help crush it. The SS rallied. By nightfall it became obvious that the rebels had failed. Loyal troops arrived at Bendelstrasse. Stauffenberg and Olbricht were taken into the courtyard and shot. Von Beck was allowed to shoot himself, but the old man botched it; a sergeant finally put a bullet through his brain.

At one the next morning, Hitler went on the air. He was indeed alive, and he'd heap bitter vengeance on the plotters. In the next few months the SS arrested 8000 suspects. Kangaroo courts sentenced five thousand to death. Perhaps the most prominent victim was Field Marshal Erwin Rommel. Although he sympathized with the plotters, Rommel lay in a hospital the day the bomb went off. On July 17 Allied fliers had shot up his car and wounded him badly. A stroke of fate implicated his name. One of the conspirators had tried to kill himself. When he emerged from surgery he cried out one name: "Rommel." Later another plotter admitted under dreadful torture that Rommel had once said: "Tell the people in Berlin they can count on me." For Hitler it was enough. On October 1, 1944, he sent two Generals to Rommel's home: the Desert Fox could swallow poison or face the disgrace of a People's Court. If he committed suicide he would be given a state funeral and his family would be unharmed. Rommel chose poison. Hitler kept his word: the Desert Fox was buried with all the pomp the fast-fading Third Reich could muster.

In Normandy, Operation Cobra finally began five days after the bomb went off at Rastenburg. Strategically, the operation was to resemble a door being swept open. The British would provide the hinge at Caen, where they tied down a large German force; Bradley's Americans would be the door itself. In five days the GIs had pushed the door down to Avranches, at the bottom of Cotentin peninsula. By that time George S. Patton's Third Army had been carved out of the unwieldy mass of the First Army and carefully tailored to his measure as a general. It was a fast, mobile, tactical striking force. Patton quickly put it to good use. After his tanks had crashed through Avranches, they raced 40 miles southwest to Rennes and prepared to swing into Brittany.

But Bradley again changed plans, for he sensed the opportunity for a dramatic sweep east across Normandy to the Seine, a sweep that might trap a large German force. Instead of invading Brittany, therefore, Patton moved to cut it off. He sent one corps racing south towards Nantes at the mouth of the Loire river. A second corps thundered east towards Le Mans, 50 miles away.

Hitler ordered a counterattack towards Avranches to cut Patton's lines of supply and communications. The Germans still occupied positions above the chain of armor the Third Army was dragging across Norman fields. Kluge, who had replaced Rundstedt, obeyed reluctantly. He would have preferred to keep his northern escape routes open. The German attack began on August 7 and made some headway. But clearing skies brought rocket-firing Allied fighters to the scene. They littered the battlefield with wrecked Panzer tanks, their heavy armor plate rent open like sardine cans. By nightfall the attack had failed. The next morning tanks of the Fifteenth U.S. Corps were inside Le Mans. The outline of the trap Bradley hoped to fashion emerged more clearly. If Patton could race north for 60 miles and grab Argentan while the British attacked in the south towards Falaise, two German armies would be caught in a pocket between Falaise and Argentan.

However, when the Fifteenth Corps reached Argentan it met unexpectedly stiff resistance, and it was not until August 19 that the Falaise gap was closed. Field Marshal Model, who had just replaced Kluge—Hitler had begun changing Generals as fast as a losing football coach switches quarterbacks—managed to get about

40,000 men through an escape hatch at the village of St. Lambert. Still, German losses in the battle of the Falaise gap were heavy: 10,000 dead, 30,000 men and almost all their heavy equipment captured.

Meanwhile, Patton had opened a three-pronged attack on the Seine. While fighting still raged at Falaise, Third Army troops captured Orleans, Chartres and Dreux. By August 20, they were at Troyes and Fontainebleau, east of Paris, while Haislip had put two regiments across the Seine at Mantes-Gassicourt, west of the capital. Coming out of the Falaise gap, Montgomery had sent four corps in pursuit of Model in the hope of trapping the Germans inside two bends of the Seine southeast of Rouen. But the enemy held only a short front there and was able to prevent any more crossings of the river. The Allies could not attack his rear. By August 24, Model had got the bulk of his troops on the other side of the river. Meanwhile, the British quickly closed on the southern bank of the Seine to the sea.

But what about Paris? The city was cut off, and Model was in no position to reinforce it. General von Choltitz had a garrison of only 20,000 men inside. Still Ike made no move to capture it. In fact he was determined to avoid a battle. He remembered too well the horrors of the frontal assaults on big cities such as Stalingrad and Warsaw. And he wondered how he would feed a starving city of four million.

But Charles de Gaulle had no such compunctions. He wanted Paris captured quickly and captured by Free French troops. There were two reasons: de Gaulle wanted to establish his own authority before the faction-ridden underground, with its strong communist element, took over, and he feared a bloodbath, for by August 20 Paris was in full revolt. City Hall and police headquarters were already occupied by the FFI, the underground army. Barricades went up in the streets, and Choltitz was under orders to burn the city to the ground.

De Gaulle, therefore, told Ike that he'd move a French division against the capital—with Ike's consent if possible, without it if not. Reluctantly Eisenhower agreed. On the evening of August 24, 1944, General LeClerc had fought his way to the suburbs that ring Paris. Inside the city, fighting spread. French flags blossomed from windows and balconies. That night LeClerc sent a lone tank clattering into Paris to show his own banner. When Captain Dronne flung open the hatch outside City Hall, the men on the steps began to sing the *Marseillaise*. It was the first of the moments of glory. Choltitz did not interfere. He knew the Germans in Paris were defeated. Later, when the bells of Paris churches rang in the coming victory, Choltitz called Model's headquarters and let the Nazi generals listen.

As the sun splintered against the rooftops the next morning, the first French soldiers marched through the ancient gates into the city and headed for the Place de la Concorde. A sudden burst of heavy fighting erupted before they reached it. But somehow it no longer mattered, perhaps not even to those who died in that last hour. For that morning was unreal, touched by a strange splendor. With each passing hour the face of Paris changed. At 12:30 the tricolor fluttered from the Eiffel Tower; at two it hung from the Arc de Triomphe. The rule of jackboot and swastika was all but over.

De Gaulle arrived in the afternoon and quickly took charge. Henceforth, he told the underground, he, not they, would give the orders. The next day de Gaulle lit the eternal flame above the unknown soldier's grave and, together with major resistance leaders, marched from the Arc de Triomphe to the cathedral of Notre Dame as two million Parisians watched and cheered. A sudden fusillade greeted him outside the church, a last good-bye from bitter traitors who had collaborated with the Germans. Coolly the general looked up at the rooftops and strode into the cathedral. "The Magnificat rose around us," he wrote later. "Was it ever sung more ardently?"

Yet, for all its drama, the liberation of Paris was only a footnote in the amazingly rapid conquest of France. On August 15 the Allies landed on the French Mediterranean coast to carry out the delayed Anvil operation. A week later they had captured Toulon and Marseille and were streaking up the Rhone valley. On September 3 they were outside Lyon and had pushed through the mountains of the Haute Savoie. By mid-September they had captured Dijon, cleared most of Burgundy and linked up with Patton's forces at Epinal near the Swiss and German frontiers. The speed of their advance had been matched by that of the armies storming out of Normandy and across the Seine. Monty and Patton had practiced a type of blitzkrieg that

Guderian and Rommel might have envied. Towns and river barriers fell like ninepins. On September 8 the British were in the Belgian seaside resort of Ostende. To their right, the U.S. First Army had captured Brussels and Antwerp. And Patton had hacked his way through the Argonne forest to reach Verdun and occupy the banks of the Moselle from Nancy to Metz.

What next? Allied supply lines were stretched too taut. They reached from Belgium all the way back into Normandy. Key channel ports were either still in German hands or lay in rubble. Fuel was desperately short. Clearly Ike could no longer support the lavish drive that had taken his armies across France in six weeks. He would have to make a choice between two conflicting plans of battle, Montgomery's and Bradley's. There were only enough supplies to support one of them fully.

Monty favored a northern strategy: a drive from his advance positions in Belgium through Holland into the north German plain, and from there a double strike against Berlin and the industrial Ruhr. The plan had an extra dividend, as it would overrun V-1 and V-2 bases.

These were Hitler's secret weapons. The V-1s were pilotless jet planes with a ton of TNT in the nose cone. They had subjected London to a second blitz all summer and now, with the French Channel coast launching pads gone, bombarded Brussels. The V-2s were the first true rockets, the grandaddies of today's sophisticated space hardware. They had a longer range and, unlike the noisy V-1s, flew in utter silence.

Bradley disagreed with what Monty called "a powerful, full-blooded thrust into the heart of Germany." He saw an attack into Holland as "a 60-mile salient driven up a side alley to the Reich." Moreover, he knew that if Monty's scheme were adopted, his own Twelfth Army Group would play only a defensive role. Finally he had a plan of his own: an attack through Metz and the Saar into central Germany that would enable him to wheel east from Frankfurt and cut Germany in two.

Ike compromised. He ordered a general drive towards the Rhine by all the Allied armies that would nevertheless allow Monty to make an airborne assault against Arnhem on the lower Rhine in Holland. Operation Market Garden began on September 17. Three airborne

divisions were dropped between Eindhoven and Arnhem, with orders
to grab the bridges across the many canals and rivers in that area.
Once they had done that, the British Second Army was to cut a
narrow corridor from the Dutch border to the Rhine. The two U.S.
divisions in the operation had little trouble. The men of General
Maxwell Taylor's 101st Airborne quickly seized the bridges across
the Zuid Willemsvaart Canal in the north of their landing area. In
the south they found the Wilhelmina Canal bridges wrecked, but
they managed to scramble to the other side anyway. The next morning they were in Eindhoven, and a few hours later linked up with
the British. Further north, General James Gavin's 82nd Airborne
landed men virtually on top of the Maas river bridge at Grave,
moved rapidly across the Maas-Waal canal and did not encounter
stiff enemy resistance until Nijmegen.

But the British First Airborne was in trouble from the moment
the "red devils" jumped. Field Marshal Model was sipping a glass
of wine on a hotel terrace when he saw the first parachute open. An
SS division raced quickly to the landing scene; a second rushed
across the bridge at Arnhem and dug in on the southern bank of the
Rhine. The British paratroopers managed to assemble their forces
on the north side of the river and even pushed a batallion to the
bridge. But they could not hold it, and the Allies were unable to
move up fast enough from Nijmegen to bring relief. It took Gavin
three days to clear the town, and the Germans fought bitterly for
every mile they gave up on the road to Arnhem. All a Polish parachute brigade could do was help evacuate 8000 trapped British soldiers. By September 25 the last red devil was back on the other side
of the river. For all the British heroism in the week-long battle,
Arnhem was a major defeat. About the only consolation was that it
had given Monty what a German general called "an excellent springboard from which to launch the final attack on Germany."

But the British would not be able to use that springboard until
the turn of the year. For the next ten weeks the Allies did little more
than close on the frontiers of the Reich and, in a few places, breach
them. Aachen was captured on October 13. Patton smashed into the
Saar and attacked the Siegfried line. The French reached the Rhine
and took Strasbourg. But these were isolated instances. On the whole,
the Germans had stabilized the western front and gained time to

mount a counteroffensive of their own, which would become known as the Battle of the Bulge.

They had begun preparing for it in August. "November, when the enemy cannot operate in the air," a German general wrote, would be a good time. Plans were ready in October. Once again the Wehrmacht would hunt for victory in the Ardennes, where they had so often won in the past. And once again the Allies ignored history and stuck to the myth that the forests were impassable, as they had done in 1940. Only weak forces manned the 80 miles of woods and ravines.

Hitler made a massive commitment of troops and supplies. He grouped 28 divisions, ten of them armored, into three Panzer armies; readied 2000 fighters—including 80 revolutionary jets—to protect 400 bombers; and pulled together 30,000 tons of ammunition and six million tons of fuel. And from his stable of generals he trotted out a veteran battlehorse for one last race, Field Marshal Karl Gerd von Rundstedt.

On December 15, 1944, Rundstedt issued an order to his troops: "Soldiers of the west front, your great hour has struck. Everything is at stake." At dawn on the 16th the Germans opened up one of the greatest artillery barrages of the war. They even brought up 14-inch guns on flatbed railroad cars. One result of the hour-long pounding: telephone communications were destroyed from one end of the front to the other. An ominous pause followed. Then the great hulk of Tiger tanks crunched through the fog and behind them, eerie in the milky white mist, row upon row of white-clad Wehrmacht soldiers.

That night the Panzers swept towards the Meuse as if it were that balmy May of victory of 1940, not the winter of defeat of 1944. The surprised Americans—mostly overtired veterans and raw recruits —could offer only scattered and ineffective resistance. On the 17th the northern flank had carved out a salient 12 miles deep and six miles wide. The next day German armor crossed the Ambleve river. In the evening of December 19 Rundstedt's tanks stood 15 miles from Liège. Nothing, it seemed, could stop their crossing the Meuse. For this was a tough and ruthless campaign where all the rules of proper conduct went out the window. At noon on the 17th, for example, SS tanks bumped into a U.S. convoy of trucks and jeeps some two miles from Malmedy. An SS lieutenant made the 125 Americans get out with their hands up and herded them into a field. Then came the chatter of machine guns. Only a few survived to tell of the massacre.

Operation Greif was even more chilling. Squads of specially trained German soldiers were dressed in U.S. uniforms and sent behind the Allied lines. Able to imitate Americans almost to perfection (down to striking matches inward, not outward), they were to disrupt communications and traffic and spread what other mischief they could. They did some damage: the worst, paradoxically, when a jeepload of them was captured, and confessed the mission. Fear and panic spread quickly. Ike was put under extra heavy guard. And a sentry almost refused to let Bradley pass because the general didn't know the name of pinup star Betty Grable's latest husband, bandleader Harry James.

Not until December 19 did the Allies realize that this was no spoiling attack but a major offensive which local action could not contain. Confusion was rampant. Patton wouldn't be able to counterattack until the 22nd. Bradley could no longer survey the situation. Quick and drastic action was needed. Ike now put Monty in charge of two U.S. armies. The Briton quickly reinforced the Meuse Bridges, built a mobile striking reserve and managed to hold the northern shoulder of the German advance.

But in the center the Panzers flowed on. On the 20th they were outside the strategic roadhub of Bastogne. Fortunately General Anthony McAuliffe commanded a strong force of 18,000 men there. For the next 36 hours McAuliffe's Shermans battled the big Tigers to a standoff. Then Rundstedt decided to bypass the town and put it under siege. On the morning of the 22nd, with Bastogne surrounded, two German officers drove into town under a flag of truce. The Americans could not possibly escape—would they surrender? McAuliffe's reply has become a legend. He spat out just one word: "Nuts." Bewildered, the Germans asked the U.S. colonel who had delivered the message what it meant. "In plain English," the colonel said, "it means go to hell."

As he spoke, help was already on the way. Patton had begun his counterattack, striking heavily at the enemy's southern flank. On December 23, skies cleared for the first time since the Battle of the Bulge had begun. Allied planes entered the fray with devastating effect. By nightfall the Second Panzer Division pulled short only four miles from Dinant and the Meuse. At Bastogne, McAuliffe's field guns beat back repeated German attacks, the last one on Christmas morning. On the 26th, Patton's tanks lifted the grim siege. All along the front that day the German tide had halted and even begun to recede. Hitler's last big gamble had failed.

On January 3, 1945, the Allies counterattacked along roads clogged in deep snowdrifts and thick with ice. Bad weather hampered air support. But slowly the First Army hammered the Bulge from the north and the Third from the south. On January 8 the German armies had been driven from the neck of the Bulge. On the 16th the two American armies joined forces, and at the end of January the Wehrmacht was back where it started.

Thus, at the beginning of 1945, Adolf Hitler's thousand-year Reich of the Germans burned dangerously at every corner. The Allies prepared to storm into the Reich from the west. In Italy, Alexander readied a final drive through northern Italy from positions beyond Rimini and Pisa, two-thirds of the way up the boot. The Russians had taken the Balkans and were perched on the borders of the industrial heartland of Central Europe and on those of East Prussia. Germany itself had begun to resemble one giant heap of slag and rubble as city after city came under the hail of Allied bombs. Dresden was wiped out in one furious night of fire, the greatest man-made inferno in all history. The dead of Rotterdam and Coventry, Belgrade and London were finding their vindication.

In Berlin, Hitler and Goering, both half mad, sustained and ravaged by drugs, dreamed of yet another miracle weapon to turn the tide, or of some last desperate trick to split the alliance and save their rule. It was a vain hope. The next four months would wreak such havoc on the Reich as to make the death of the Nordic Gods, the Ragnarok of Norse mythology, seem a harmless little joke.

Chapter
☆ *11* ☆

As Allied armies converged on the borders of the old Reich and the day of victory in Europe approached, the strains tugging at the Anglo-American alliance with Russia began to show. Major areas of disagreement included Germany, the United Nations, Yugoslavia, Greece and Poland. By early January these differences had reached the point where both Roosevelt and Churchill thought another big-three meeting necessary. Stalin agreed, and the Crimean resort of Yalta was selected as the site.

What had happened in the areas of conflict was briefly this:

The United Nations. Two months of talks at Dumbarton Oaks in Washington had failed to produce agreement on the future structure of the world body. Negotiators hadn't even come up with an acceptable voting formula. Russia wanted 16 seats in the General Assembly, one for each Soviet Republic. But the West was unwilling to concede Moscow that many votes.

Germany. At the second Quebec conference in September 1944, Secretary of the Treasury Henry Morgenthau, Jr., had proposed to Roosevelt and Churchill a plan to strip Germany of her ability to make war by dismantling her industry and turning the militant Germans into peaceful farmers. Churchill was dubious about a scheme that would condemn future generations to poverty but agreed to it because he needed Morgenthau's support for big postwar U.S. loans to Britain. However, other members of FDR's administration were more outspoken. They argued that the Morgenthau plan would hurt Europe as much as Germany by depriving other nations of this important industrial base. Moreover, it would fuel German resentment and renew its will to fight on another day. The plan was shelved, but not before becoming an issue in the 1944 elections and providing Goebbels with a field day. Still, what would the Allies do about a defeated Germany?

Yugoslavia. By the time Yalta rolled around, the problem had become largely academic. Tito's Communist partisans had defeated the royalist Chetnik guerrillas and, because Tito never stopped fighting the Germans while Chetnik leader Mihailovic collaborated with them, won strong British support as well. As a result, Churchill, who had met and liked Tito, agreed to leave the future of the monarchy to a postwar plebiscite. But since the partisans had liberated most of the country by themselves, Tito was not about to give up power voluntarily. A convinced communist, he was sure to lead Yugoslavia into the Russian camp.

Greece. Initially the situation there had resembled that in Yugoslavia. Communist and non-communist guerrillas had sprung up almost simultaneously and begun at once to fight each other, the royalist government-in-exile in Cairo and, sporadically, the Germans. Chaos ruled the underground, and in the summer of 1944, when it became clear that the Wehrmacht would soon withdraw to avoid entrapment by Russian armies advancing through the Balkans, Churchill decided to intervene to avoid a communist takeover. A British force under General Scobie occupied Athens on October 12 but was not strong enough to pursue the retreating Germans. As a result, communist partisans quickly entrenched themselves in the countryside. In December they moved on Athens. Inside the city the Communists called a general strike. The civil war was on. The red guerrillas would have won it quickly had not the British opposed them with force. After a month of bitter fighting, Scobie drove the Communists back into the mountains, where they awaited a more propitious time to resume the civil war.

Poland. This would prove the most difficult problem of all, for Stalin was bound and determined to incorporate eastern Poland into the Soviet Union in exchange for large chunks of German territory. The London Poles, however, refused the trade. The most they would accept—and that only under heavy pressure—was a "line of demarcation" drawn roughly along the 1940 border. Predictably, Stalin demanded that the "line" become the final frontier. At a meeting in Moscow with Churchill in October, 1944, the Soviet dictator even trotted out his Lublin puppets, who dutifully told the British leader they'd redraw Poland's borders to conform with the Kremlin's wishes. At the turn of the year Stalin moved to sharpen the Polish division: he recognized the Lublin "committee" as Poland's provisional government.

For Churchill the lesson of political conflict with Russia was clear; henceforth the Allies would have to let political goals dictate military strategy. He realized that Stalin would push as far west as his arms would carry him and that Moscow would insist on a ring of friendly states around the Soviet Union. He was willing to go halfway in meeting Russian security needs, but he also wanted to keep as much as possible of eastern and central Europe cleared of Russian troops. This was the reason for his intervention in Greece and his proposals for carving up the Balkans between East and West.

But as sensible and practical as Churchill's policies were, they smacked too much of the old power politics for the Americans. FDR had already quarreled with Churchill's Balkan plans, and he pressured the British into political talks that resulted in a regency in Greece. (Yet after the war was over and the Communists started to fight their civil war in earnest, the United States reversed itself and, under the Truman Doctrine, helped democracy survive.) The United States took a similar attitude on other outstanding issues. In short, it all boiled down to American insistence that the war be won first, political problems solved afterwards. The result of this U.S. policy was disastrous: it allowed the Soviet Union to penetrate much further into Central Europe than it otherwise could have. For example, Ike worried so much in the final weeks of the war about the Germans holding out in a nonexistent Alpine redoubt that he halted the swift advance of his armies towards Berlin and into Eastern Europe. The lines of the cold war that followed so quickly on the end of the "hot" one were, therefore, drawn much more in Russia's favor.

By early February the stage was set for the Yalta encounter. Churchill met Roosevelt at Malta. He was shocked at FDR's frail appearance; clearly the President had become a desperately sick man since winning reelection to a fourth term. Together they flew to the Crimea to tackle a thick and thorny agenda.

Few fundamental decisions were made about Germany; the big

three simply decided to postpone them. About the only concrete agreement to emerge concerned the immediate division of Germany into four zones of occupation, with the French zone carved out of the British and American areas.

The Russians made some concessions on the U.N., settling for three General Assembly votes instead of 16. They quickly accepted proposals for a big-power veto in the Security Council designed to protect the interests of the major nations—the United States, Britain, the Soviet Union, France and China—and to avoid any breakdown in peacekeeping machinery. And Stalin agreed to hold the U.N.'s founding meeting on April 25, 1945, in San Francisco.

Poland came next. There was no longer any debate on Soviet incorporation of eastern Poland in exchange for German territory— Stalin had carried the day there—although Churchill warned against stuffing "the Polish goose so full of German food it died of indigestion." The new borders would run roughly along the Oder and Neisse rivers and include within them half of east Prussia and the old free city of Danzig. Poland's future government, however, was not as easily settled. Stalin flatly refused to replace Lublin with another, more broadly based regime. At most he was willing to enlarge or modify it, providing he had a veto on the London Poles nominated to take part. Argument was long, bitter and inconclusive despite the tenuous agreement finally hammered together. It called for inclusion of "democratic leaders in Poland and from Poles abroad" in a "Provisional Government of National Unity" which would pledge to hold free elections as soon as possible. But the pact lacked teeth to back the fine words of its text. And the promises it contained were easy to break.

As for the Far East, Stalin had no wish to take his war-weary people into yet another battle, but he'd go for the spoils provided the price were right. His demands included cession of naval bases and several island chains in the Pacific, as well as autonomy for Outer Mongolia.

Despite the fragile nature of the Yalta agreements, the big three sat down for a final banquet with great good cheer. Wine and vodka flowed freely. Toasts were the friendliest ever. As Churchill put it somewhat too hopefully, "The fire of war has burned up the misunderstanding of the past."

Scant attention was paid during the meeting to the battlefields of Europe. There was really no need. Only good news flowed from the front. German positions were crumbling everywhere. In Poland the Red Army began its final offensive in mid-January. By the end of the month, Soviet tanks had reached the Oder river and stood less than 50 miles from Berlin itself. On January 12, Marshal Konev's First Ukrainians struck beyond the Vistula from their Sandomierz bridgeheads. In two days they had torn a 40-mile gash in German lines and advanced 25 miles. On the 14th, Zhukov's First White Russian Armies attacked north and south of Warsaw while Rokossovsky sent his Second White Russian front charging towards East Prussia. When the Red Armies entered the shattered Polish capital on January 17, a 180-mile-long and 80-mile-wide breach had been torn into German lines. On the 19th, Konev was in Cracow, Zhukov in Lodz, 70 miles west of Warsaw and Rokossovsky near the borders of East Prussia.

The momentum of the more than two million soldiers gathered into the three Russian fronts proved unstoppable. On the 20th, Konev stormed across the German frontier about a hundred miles southeast of Breslau and raced for the Oder, which he reached on the 23rd. In the north, Rokossovsky punched to within a few miles of the Bay of Danzig by January 26, almost cutting East Prussia in two. In the center, Zhukov had bypassed Poznan to breach the frontier, and he reached the Oder on the 31st. Early in February, Konev had hacked out a bridgehead across the Oder south of Breslau while Zhukov had put one across north of the city.

But by the middle of the month the Soviet offensive began to sputter. In the southeast the Carpathian mountains slowed the Russian advance. Fierce German resistance in Silesia proved too strong to break yet, while enemy forces in Pommerania to Zhukov's north had been reinforced by troops evacuated from East Prussia. As a result, the Soviet advance was funneled into a relatively narrow salient, blunted by the 50-odd-mile front held along the Oder. Before resuming their forward momentum the Russians would have to deal with enemy troops in Silesia and Pomerania and clear out garrisons left behind in Poznan, Breslau, Koenigsberg, Danzig and other cities. Nor did the Red Army make much progress in the southeast. Budapest fell after a two-month siege on February 13, but a week later

General Friessner managed to counterattack with some success and thus prevented the Russians from exploiting their Budapest victory.

By the end of February, therefore, the whole gigantic eastern front took a deep breath while the Red Army gathered strength for the final push on Vienna and Berlin. As it did, the attack in the West gathered new momentum.

It had been slow going. For after the Germans had been driven out of the Bulge, Allied strategic differences remained unsettled. Ike still favored Bradley's plan for an attack on Frankfurt; Monty clung to his northern strategy. Again Eisenhower compromised, as he had in September; the Allies would drive on the Rhine together and then decide what to do next. At this the British exploded. They were convinced Montgomery's plan would get them to Berlin before the Russians, and for the British, at least, political considerations loomed very large. The vehemence of his ally's opposition forced Ike to compromise for a second time. Monty could attack in the north before the other armies reached the Rhine, but he'd have to do it without the support needed for success. The concession only made the British angrier, for they saw it as another example of U.S. inability to weigh the importance of political and military goals. The patchwork plan that was finally adopted called for Montgomery's 21st Army group to attack first and secure the Rhine between Duesseldorf and the sea. Next, Bradley's Twelfth Army group was to drive the enemy out of the Saar and close on the Rhine between Mainz and Duesseldorf. Finally the 6th Army group, the U.S. Seventh and the French 1st Armies, was ordered to clear the Germans out of a pocket around Colmar and occupy the Rhine between Mainz and the Swiss frontier.

Montgomery jumped off first, attacking on February 8 along a front between the Maas and the Rhine. The Germans were ready for him. They had blown up dams and opened dikes so that thousands of acres between the two rivers were hip-deep in water. And on patches of dry land the Wehrmacht fought stubbornly to delay the advance of the First Canadian Army. Not until February 21 had Monty's men sloshed through the flooded landscape to reach the Rhine and push the Germans onto the other side. Before they retreated, the Wehrmacht blew up all the bridges on this sector of the front.

Artificial floods stopped the Ninth U.S. Army's advance too. The Americans were supposed to attack towards Duesseldorf on February 10; but before they could move, the Germans blew up the one dam across the Roer river they still held and the masses of water that spurted through the countryside paralyzed the U.S. assault. The Ninth Army wasn't able to get an amphibian vessel into the Roer until February 23, but three days later the Americans had secured the eastern banks of that river and reached the Rhine above Duesseldorf, where they swung north to link up with the British. Then Monty opted for caution and waited another two weeks before he attempted a crossing and an attack into the Ruhr, Germany's industrial heart which Hitler was desperate to defend.

Early in March the Twelfth Army group's offensive had got a full head of steam too. Hodges' First Army struck for Cologne and Bonn, and Patton's Third attacked northward parallel to the Moselle river towards Coblentz. On the left of Bradley's front General Collins' Seventh corps barged across the Erft river and headed for Cologne. The Germans tried hard to defend the city, even lowering anti-aircraft guns to blast advancing tanks. But they didn't have the manpower or the equipment to do it. On March 3, Collins had tanks on the Rhine above the city, and on the 5th U.S. armor clattered past the magnificent gothic cathedral—which, incredibly, was still almost intact amid the surrounding rubble of Cologne.

On Collins' right the U.S. Third Corps advanced towards the Ahr river, a Rhine tributary. General Milliken was under orders to cross the river and join forces with Patton. But he still saw a chance to reach the Rhine first. On March 7 a U.S. platoon, part of a Ninth Armored Division tank-infantry strike force, came to the bluffs overlooking the Rhine at Remagen. As the platoon commander looked down, he could hardly believe his eyes: the Ludendorff railroad bridge was still intact. The Americans raced to the river. An explosion shook the bridge and timber and metal whirled in midair, but the span held. Minutes later the GIs raced down the footpaths on either side of the railroad track. The Germans on the other side laid down a curtain of hot metal, but the Americans won their race with death to the eastern bank. "We took cover in some bomb craters," one of the men reported later. "Then we just sat and waited for the others to come." They weren't far behind. Engineers snipped every wire they saw that might lead to other demolition charges. They shot heavy cables apart with carbines. Within 20 minutes a hundred Americans had crossed the bridge; 24 hours later Ike had pushed 8000 across. And before the bridge finally collapsed ten days later, five divisions had marched over it and secured the bridgehead against enemy attack.

Spurred on by the unbelievable stroke of good luck at Remagen, Allied armies closed fast on the Rhine. By the 10th, Patton was in Coblentz. Three days later he wheeled sharply to the right and stormed across the Moselle towards Mainz, Worms and Mannheim. At the same time, Patch's Seventh and de Tassigny's First French armies attacked north along a line from Strasbourg to Saarbruecken. Ten days later Patton stood south of Mainz, and on the night of the 22nd he sneaked a division across the Rhine to establish a second bridgehead. Allied armies now held the river's western bank from the Swiss frontier to the sea. The storied stream of German legend could not offer the Reich's heartland protection for much longer.

On March 23, Montgomery struck massively across the Rhine to threaten the Ruhr and northern Germany. Once again the hero of El Alamein began the attack with his personal trademark: a devastating artillery barrage aimed at the seven crack divisions of the First German Parachute Army dug in on the other side. Two thousand guns pounded the enemy for more than an hour. Then advance guards of four divisions jumped into assault boats and crossed the wide river. Light enemy resistance enabled them to establish and hold a long, if shallow, bridgehead. The next morning two thousand planes flew across the river and parachuted 14,000 men, guns and equipment into the Wesel area. The drop was one of the most successful of the war, enabling Monty to deepen and widen his bridgehead quickly.

Now there was no holding the Allied armies. The Rhine front was quickly turned into shambles. Patton took Mannheim on March 25. Four days later his tanks reached Frankfurt. Darmstadt, Limburg and Kassel fell soon thereafter. In the north, Monty's successful strike across the Rhine paved the way for a giant pincer operation against German forces in the Ruhr. The

U.S. Ninth Army had struck out of the Wesel bridgehead to drive east as far as Hamm, then wheeled south behind the Ruhr pocket, in which Model commanded a force of 325,000 men. On March 26, Hodges broke out of the Remagen bridgehead in stunning force and headed north. The two pincers closed near Lippstadt on April 1. Model fought on for another 18 days before his troops surrendered, and the despondent Field Marshal went off into the woods to shoot himself.

Thus, at the end of March, the heart of Germany lay exposed. The Ruhr was surrounded. The British Second Army had struck 25 miles beyond the Rhine on a 20-mile front. The Canadians were busy cleaning the Germans out of northern Holland. To the south the First and Third armies had left the Rhine far behind them. And at the bottom of the front, U.S. and French troops poured through the state of Wuertemberg.

In contrast to the western front, March proved relatively quiet in the east. Fierce German resistance prevented a breakthrough at the Oder, so Zhukov and Rokossovsky concentrated on reducing the forts in their rear. Danzig fell on March 30, Koenigsberg on April 9.

Most of the action took place in the southeast, in Hungary, where Friessner's counterattacks in February had stabilized the front. Encouraged by this local success, Hitler shifted the Sixth Panzer Army, barely recovered from the ordeal in the Ardennes battles, to Hungary. There they participated in a miniature Battle of the Bulge. Friessner attacked southwest of Budapest on March 3 and drove towards the Danube, but his tanks ran out of fuel before he reached the river. By March 15 the Russians had pushed the Wehrmacht back to its starting position, and for the next two weeks Malinovsky and Tolbukhin ground on relentlessly. On March 29, Tolbukhin crossed the Austrian frontier, and soon his armored spearheads were astride the road that led from the south through Wiener Neustadt to Vienna. Malinovsky pushed along the Budapest-Vienna highway and captured Bratislava on April 3. Four days later he was in Vienna's eastern suburbs, and on April 11 the Russians had pushed the Wehrmacht across the Danube. On the 12th the Austrian capital was liberated. As a farewell present, the Nazis, entrenched on the northern bank of the Danube, shot gothic St. Stephen's cathedral into flames so that only the charred ribs of that lovely church remained standing.

The gaudy military gains made in the two months following the Yalta conference stood in sad contrast to a rapidly deteriorating political situation. The shadow of the cold war now brooded ominously over Europe. The spirit of Yalta had been quite eclipsed by it, for Stalin had begun to break the promises he had made in the Crimea as soon as the ink was dry on the final communique.

Free elections in Poland were quickly a dead letter, especially after Stalin noted the sullen hostility that the Poles displayed towards the Red Army. Nor would the Russians agree to enlarging the Lublin government. Molotov simply turned down every London Pole the British suggested. In Rumania, Moscow had forced young King Michael to fire General Radescu, his democratic premier, and replace him with a veteran Communist, Petru Groza. The Russians refused to let U.S. planes land in Budapest during shuttle bombing runs. Allied officials were denied entry to Soviet prisoner-of-war camps. Moscow stalled on any agreement for the occupation of Austria.

As Churchill watched Moscow's post-Yalta policy unfold, he became more determined than ever to get to Berlin first. But he had not counted on Ike's fixation on the Nazi Alpine fortress—a nonexistent figment of Goebbel's propaganda. The mountain fastness would have to be conquered before the Germans had a chance to settle in, the Supreme Commander was sure, and so he halted the drive on Berlin and slowed the advance towards Eastern Europe. What's more, he wrote Stalin a note on March 28 telling him what he planned to do, and didn't clear it with London or Washington.

Churchill was furious. He felt that Ike had no business dealing directly with Moscow, and thought his description of Berlin as "nothing but a geographic location" ludicrous. But there was little he could do about it. A delighted Stalin had sent Eisenhower a gushing letter: yes, Berlin was just a spot on the map, the Russians weren't sending first-line troops against it (a lie). In Washington, Marshall stood solidly behind his field commander. So did FDR, for by early April the failing President was desperate to stay on good terms with Stalin. He was convinced that big-three understanding and harmony were the key to world peace, and he was willing to take a lot more Soviet provocation to gain his end. By the second week in April, Churchill's quarrel with Ike had been smoothed over.

Roosevelt was then in Warm Springs, Georgia, for years his favorite vacation home, which he had turned into a center for the treatment of his own disease, infantile paralysis. In the past he had always returned refreshed and strengthened from these trips, but this time his recuperative powers seemed to have left him. He was having his portrait painted on April 12. It was about 1:15 when he put his hand to his temple and said, "I have a terrible headache." Then he slumped forward, unconscious. Two hours and twenty minutes later he was dead without having recovered consciousness. He was 63 and had served as President for 12 years, longer than any man in U.S. history.

In Washington Vice-President Harry Truman was called to the White House without knowing why. He arrived at 5:25 P.M. and was taken to see Mrs. Roosevelt. "Harry," she said, "the President is dead." Stunned, Truman could not find his voice. Finally he said, "Is there anything I can do for you?" Eleanor Roosevelt's reply has become a classic: "Is there anything WE can do for YOU? For you are the one in trouble now." Two hours later Truman put his hand on a Bible and swore to preserve and defend the constitution of the United States. "I dropped my hand," he wrote later. "The clock beneath Woodrow Wilson's portrait marked the time at 7:09."

As men and women wept unashamed across the nation, the world mourned with the United States for its fallen leader. Black flags blossomed in London, Paris and Moscow. The House of Commons took the unprecedented act of adjourning in FDR's honor. Russian newspapers appeared bordered in black. Even the Japanese paid tribute to their dead enemy. Only in Berlin did Hitler and his hyenas cackle with joy. Goebbels heard the news first. "Bring out the best champagne," he cried, "and get me the Fuehrer on the telephone." Moments later he said dramatically, "My Fuehrer, I congratulate you. Roosevelt is dead. It is written in the stars that the second half of April will be the turning point."

Some turning point! The day FDR died the Ninth Army had crossed the Elbe below Magdeburg and stood only 60 miles from

Berlin. In the east the Russians were only 35 miles away. And in the days that followed, the Allied sweep turned into a chase. Patton crossed the Czech frontier on April 18; Monty raced north towards Denmark. German cities fell like ninepins—Jena, Chemnitz, Brunswick, Nuernberg, Karlsruhe. Allied divisions covered as much as a hundred miles a day. But Ike still did not believe that victory was only days away. Stubbornly he refused to take the political spoils, his for the plucking. He abandoned the advance on Berlin and halted Patton's drive on Prague, although the Third Army could have captured it with ease long before the Russians got there in May.

The Red Army began its final drive on Berlin before dawn on April 17. Tensely, Zhukov sat in his command bunker at the Oder and looked at his watch as the seconds ticked away. "Now comrades, now," he shouted as the hand swept up to 4 A.M. Almost 150 searchlights flamed across the dark sky. The lights burned in dead silence for several seconds. Then three green flares vaulted into the air, and fire and lead burst from the muzzles of 20,000 guns. Shock waves made the earth tremble. A hot wind whipped through trees and villages. The blanket of shells obliterated everything: men, houses, machines, trees. General Chuikov's Eighth Guards moved forward.

To the south, Konev attacked through a thick smokescreen that his fighters had laid across the Neisse river. Assault boats splashed through the ice-choked river under a heavy artillery barrage. Engineers followed behind pulling pontoon bridges after them. Twenty minutes later Konev held his first bridgehead.

Five days later the two marshals had men on the Autobahn ring around Berlin. On April 25 their armies linked up; Berlin was surrounded. Further south, at Torgau, Russians and Americans shook hands at the Elbe. Germany was cut in two. Only days were left.

Hitler spent them in the great underground bunker he had built near the Berlin chancellory. On April 20 he celebrated his 56th birthday with a party. That night Himmler, Goering and Ribbentrop said good-bye. They were leaving Berlin. The next day Hitler ordered a massive counterattack, but there were no longer any troops to carry it out. On the 22nd the Fuehrer learned that the Russians were outside Berlin, and he threw the greatest temper tantrum of his life. Everyone had betrayed him, he shrieked, and nothing but treason, corruption and cowardice were left.

The week of sheer insanity that followed teemed with plots and counterplots and hysterical outbursts. The bunker resembled a madhouse. On the 23rd, Goering sent a cable from Berchtesgaden: shouldn't he take power now that the Fuehrer had decided to die in Berlin? Hitler ordered Goering's arrest, and the SS in Bavaria obeyed. On the 24th the fat marshal sat in jail. In Luebeck, Himmler negotiated with the Swedes about an armistice. And all the while, the Russians pushed closer to the bunker. On the 28th they were only blocks away. Now Hitler prepared to die. Vials of poison were handed those who wished to die with him. Later that day the Fuehrer heard of Himmler's talks with the Swedes. "He raged like a madman," an eyewitness reported. "His color rose to a heated red, and his face was virtually unrecognizable."

At 3 A.M. on April 29, Hitler married his constant but secret companion of the last 12 years, Eva Braun. After a champagne toast Hitler dictated his last will and testament, in which he appointed Grand Admiral Doenitz as his successor and new Fuehrer and expelled Goering and Himmler from the Party. At dawn he went to bed. On April 30 he held his usual noon military briefing: the great German empire had shriveled to a single city block. At 3:30 P.M., according to some accounts, Hitler and Eva Braun went to their bedroom. There was a revolver shot, then silence. When the surviving Nazis went inside, they found the Fuehrer sprawled on his bed, his face smeared with blood. He had shot himself through the mouth. Eva Braun had swallowed poison. Their bodies were carried into the bunker garden; gasoline was poured over them, and they were set on fire. The next day, May 1, Goebbels had a doctor kill his six children, then ordered an SS man to shoot him and his wife. Deputy Fuehrer Martin Bormann tried to escape. There's evidence that an artillery shell killed him outside the bunker, but since his body was never found rumors that he is still alive persist.

It was all over in Berlin. The red banner had fluttered over the Reichstag hours before Hitler died. And on May 2 what was left of German forces in Berlin surrendered.

Slowly the fighting in Europe was coming to an end. In Italy,

Alexander had begun his final drive on April 9. Two weeks later the Allies were across the Po river and sweeping through the north Italian plain and into the Alps. On the 25th the Italian underground rose and liberated a string of northern Italian cities from Venice to Milan. On April 29 the Germans accepted terms of unconditional surrender, and the day the Wehrmacht quit in Berlin, May 2, a million soldiers put down their arms in Italy. When they did, Mussolini had been dead for three days.

In fact he had died only hours before Hitler. Il Duce had tried to negotiate with the partisans through the Archbishop of Milan. The effort got nowhere, so Mussolini and his mistress, Clara Petacci, tried to escape into Switzerland. A band of guerrillas, who stopped the German column with which Il Duce was traveling, recognized him. They dragged the hated dictator and his mistress out of the car and shot them both. The two bodies were taken to Milan and hung head down on meathooks in a public square.

In Germany, Doenitz assumed his new role as Fuehrer and proceeded to do the only thing he could—arrange the surrender. On May 4 the Wehrmacht surrendered Holland, northern Germany and Denmark to Montgomery. Two days later Jodl arrived at a red-brick schoolhouse in Rheims, Ike's headquarters. Hours passed as the Germans negotiated the last details of defeat. Finally, at 2:25 A.M., May 7, 1945, Jodl signed the instruments of unconditional surrender. On the 8th the ceremonies were repeated in Berlin, with Keitel signing for Germany and Zhukov for Russia.

The war in Europe was over. It had lasted five years, eight months and seven days, left the continent strewn with ruin and rubble and cost 20 million lives. Six million alone had perished in the death camps.

But at least and at last it was finished. And the surge of joy and relief that flooded the world on VE Day could not be contained by the prospect of a war yet to be won in the Pacific and by a future that held in it the cold war. In every capital the streets and squares were black with people. Churchill, a smile of triumph lighting his cherubic face, stood on the balcony of Buckingham Palace next to King George VI to acknowledge the delirious cheers of the multitude. Two million people thronged Red Square in

Moscow to dance and sing in the streets. New York's Times Square exploded with a joy never seen on any New Year's Eve.

The mad monster of Braunau was dead, his Thousand Year Reich a heap of rubble and his henchmen—Goering, Ribbentrop, Seyss-Inquart and the others—in jail. Only Himmler had elected to die by poison. The bestial nightmare in Europe was over. For those who had survived it, the light at the end of the tunnel shone with the brightness of a thousand suns.

part II
THE PACIFIC

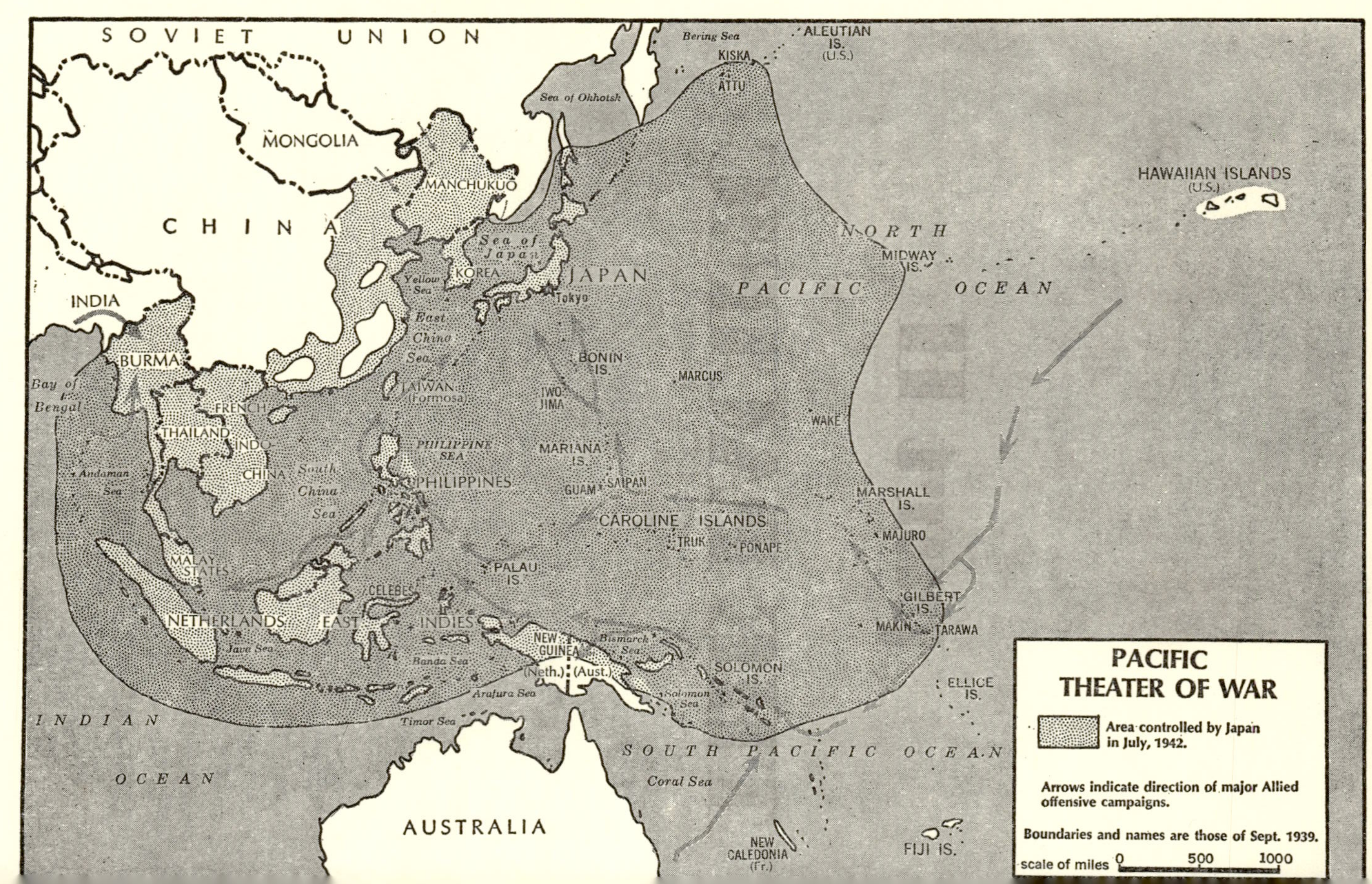

PACIFIC
THEATER OF WAR
Area controlled by Japan in July, 1942.
Arrows indicate direction of major Allied offensive campaigns.
Boundaries and names are those of Sept. 1939.
scale of miles
0
500
1000
SOVIET UNION
MONGOLIA
CHINA
MANCHUKUO
Sea of Okhotsk
Bering Sea
KISKA
ATTU
ALEUTIAN IS. (U.S.)
HAWAIIAN ISLANDS (U.S.)
NORTH
PACIFIC
OCEAN
MIDWAY IS.
Sea of Japan
KOREA
Yellow Sea
JAPAN
Tokyo
East China Sea
INDIA
BURMA
Bay of Bengal
FRENCH INDO-CHINA
THAILAND
Andaman Sea
MALAY STATES
South China Sea
TAIWAN (Formosa)
BONIN IS.
IWO JIMA
MARCUS
WAKE
PHILIPPINE SEA
MARIANA IS.
GUAM
SAIPAN
PHILIPPINES
CAROLINE ISLANDS
TRUK
PONAPE
MARSHALL IS.
MAJURO
GILBERT IS.
MAKIN
TARAWA
CELEBES
PALAU IS.
NETHERLANDS EAST INDIES
Java Sea
Banda Sea
NEW GUINEA (Neth.) (Aust.)
Bismarck Sea
SOLOMON IS.
Solomon Sea
Arafura Sea
Timor Sea
ELLICE IS.
INDIAN OCEAN
SOUTH PACIFIC OCEAN
Coral Sea
AUSTRALIA
NEW CALEDONIA (Fr.)
FIJI IS.

Chapter ☆ 12 ☆

On a Sunday morning in December at U.S. Pacific Fleet headquarters in Pearl Harbor, next door to Honolulu, scattered clouds drifted across the blue sky arching over Hawaii. The flower-scented air held out promise of another warm and pleasant day. Admiral Husband Kimmel, the fleet's commander, was up with the sun to prepare for an early golf date with General Walter Short, the army commander. At a nearby mobile radar station two army privates watched the screen. It was just 7 A.M., Sunday, December 7, 1941. Suddenly there was a wild blip. It looked like a swarm of aircraft approaching the islands from a distance of 137 miles. Quickly the privates telephoned their superior officer, a young second lieutenant. But Kermit Tyler was unimpressed. "Forget it," he told the privates. The planes either belonged to a U.S. aerial task force now at sea or were a flight of B-17 bombers expected from the mainland. The blip grew larger. The planes were 92 miles away. A second phone call to Tyler. The answer: "Don't worry about it." At 7:39 A.M. the blip went off the radar screen. The planes were 22 miles from Pearl Harbor.

The port's docks were full of ships—86 of them, including eight battleships berthed neatly, two by two, in battleship row. Crew members on the ships were still asleep; others had gone off for weekend shore leave. It was now a few minutes before eight. A roar of engines filled the sky—seconds later the crump, crump of high explosives. Kimmel rushed out of his house, still knotting his tie. Wave after wave of planes flew overhead, already at rooftop level, their wings emblazoned with red insignias—the rising sun of Japan. They headed straight for battleship row, torpedoes already loose and ready for firing.

A total of 189 Japanese planes flew in that first attack, and they caught the sleepy-eyed Americans completely by surprise. Torpedoes and bombs thudded into the massed ships with sickening impact. Planes lined up at nearby Wheeler Field were raked with bombs and machine gun fire. A bomb fell down the funnel of the battleship *Arizona*, breaking the ship in two. Torpedoes bit into the side of the *West Virginia*, and soon her whole superstructure was a mass of flames. The *Oklahoma* had her sides split open like a sardine can and flipped over so that her bottom showed through the water after she sank. Bombs tore gaping holes into the *Pennsylvania* and the *Maryland*. A bomb slammed the *Tennessee* into dockside.

Groundfire against that initial strike was scattered and ineffective, and a second wave of enemy planes did not encounter much heavier resistance. Finally a few U.S. planes managed to struggle into the air, and quite heavy anti-aircraft fire greeted the third and final wave of attackers. But by 9:45 it was all over. The eight U.S. battleships were either sunk or damaged, a host of other ships destroyed. The Japs had knocked out 188 U.S. planes and damaged 159 more. Almost 2400 Americans lay dead, another 2000 wounded. Japanese aircraft carriers, standing several hundred miles off the Hawaiian Islands, had sent 363 planes against Pearl Harbor. All but 29 came back safely.

News of the attack hit Washington at 2:22 P.M. local time. Secretary of State Cordell Hull was just preparing to receive two Japanese "peace" envoys when he was handed the Pearl Harbor flash. The diplomats entered his office and proceded to read him a long list of rambling accusations in the best Ribbentrop style. Hull let his visitors finish, then lit into them with the roughest tongue-lashing in modern diplomatic history ("I have never seen a document more crowded with infamous falsehoods").

The next morning, President Franklin D. Roosevelt went before a joint session of Congress to tell the lawmakers of the attack. "Yesterday, December 7, 1941, a date which will live in infamy," he described it, and he asked for a declaration of war. Congress promptly voted one.

For all the suddenness of the sneak attack on Pearl Harbor, war with Japan had not come all that unexpectedly. Relations with the Mikado's empire had been deteriorating for many months; in fact, they had been strained ever since the Japanese invasion of China in 1937. That act of aggression—a logical continuation of the Nipponese conquest of Manchuria in 1931—had put Japan on a collision course with the United States. For American commercial interests in China were widespread and U.S. historical ties to the mainland long and deep. Gradually U.S. support for the Nanking government deepened to the point where Washington paid most of Chiang Kai-shek's war bills. Later the U.S. put economic pressure on Japan by cutting off shipment of strategic materials, such as scrap iron.

But the Japanese appetite for expansion was not checked. Their warlords claimed they needed *Lebensraum* too. And after the fall of France and Holland the war party in Tokyo cast covetous eyes at French Indochina (today's Vietnam, Laos and Cambodia) and the Dutch East Indies (Indonesia). In the summer of 1941, Tokyo snagged one of the prizes. Vichy authorities agreed to Japanese occupation of Indochina. On July 21, Japanese troops marched into Saigon.

That was too much for the United States. President Roosevelt demanded prompt Japanese withdrawal and proposed neutralization of the country under international controls. Then, without waiting for a reply, he slapped stiff economic sanctions on Japan, including an oil embargo. The Japanese had oil stockpiles for 18 months, but that wasn't enough to continue fighting in China. By early August, therefore, Japan had determined to go to war if the sanctions weren't lifted. On the 6th, Tokyo rejected FDR's proposals for neutralization of Indochina, refused to withdraw from the country and demanded an end to the oil embargo. The United States, of course, found this position unacceptable. Yet for the next four months it formed the basis of negotiations between the two countries.

Inside Japan, moderate Premier Prince Konoye gradually lost control of the government to the war party headed by General Tojo, the defense minister. In October, Konoye urged concessions towards the United States. A cabinet crisis followed, and Tojo emerged as new premier. War was now only a matter of timing, diplomatic talks a camouflage.

Tojo's war plans called for the swift conquest of Southeast Asia:

Japanese troops would sweep through the Philippines, the Dutch East Indies, Hong Kong, Singapore, Malaya and Burma. Later they would mount an attack on Australia. The strike against Pearl Harbor would keep the United States off balance while Japan completed occupation of an empire whose resources would make her a self-sufficient industrial state.

Meanwhile, the diplomatic wheels spun as uselessly in Washington as they had two and a half years earlier in Berlin. On November 14, 1941, two new ambassadors arrived in the United States with orders "to make a touchdown." But they barely carried the ball across the ten-yard line. For now both sides had begun handing each other perfectly unacceptable ultimatums whose conditions had lost all touch with reality. What's more, Washington and Tokyo knew it.

The United States also knew that war was imminent. Warnings were flashed to major U.S. bases in the Pacific to prepare for an attack. Japanese ships and troop movements had increased across the Pacific. But heavy fog protected one large task force that left port on November 26 and steamed through the North Pacific towards Hawaii. Not until the pre-dawn hours of the 7th, when a U.S. destroyer sank a Japanese midget sub, was its presence suspected in the Hawaii area. By the time a report of the action reached Admiral Kimmel, the first enemy planes had long since taxied down the carrier deck some 275 miles from Pearl Harbor. As they approached Hawaii, a boy rode a bicycle furiously down a road towards U.S. headquarters. When the first bombs fell, he dived into a ditch. Clutched in his hand was a message from Washington warning of an imminent attack on Pearl Harbor. A breakdown in communications had forced routing it through commercial channels, and it had arrived too late.

After Pearl Harbor the Japanese wasted little time putting their plan of conquest into effect. On December 8 they plastered Malay beaches near Kota Bharu and Singora with shells and bombs before the vanguard of a 200,000-man army, stationed in Indochina and Thailand, sailed across the Gulf of Siam to land almost unopposed. To the west, Japanese planes began to pound Luzon, the largest island of the Philippine chain, and two days later, on the 10th, the first troops swarmed ashore under cover of a heavy air and sea barrage. Other enemy task forces attacked the three U.S. islands in the mid-Pacific. Guam fell easily. On Wake a handful of U.S. Marines fired their five-inch guns so effectively that they held off the Japanese for two weeks before surrendering. An attack on Midway was beaten off. Finally, a battle in the South China Sea gave Tokyo's warlords unchallenged mastery of the Pacific east of Hawaii —and proved once again that in this war ships were no match for air power.

On December 8 the battleships *Repulse* and *Prince of Wales* led a strong British squadron from Singapore out to sea: the British feared Japanese air attack and did not want to be caught in port the way the Americans had been. But the Japanese had readied 300 planes in Saigon to hunt them. For two days they searched in vain. Then, on December 10, the Mikado's pilots found their target. Banking out of the clouds, the planes swooped low to attack the ships with high explosives, torpedoes and armor-smashing bombs. The *Repulse* took five torpedo hits and sank. A half hour later the *Prince of Wales* went down. The Japanese lost three planes in the two-hour battle.

For the Allies it was unmitigated disaster: not a single capital ship fit for action was afloat between the Indian Ocean and Hawaii. As for the Japanese, within two days of Pearl Harbor they had succeeded in igniting all of Southeast Asia. By Christmas they had taken Hong Kong and pushed deeply into the Philippines and Malaya.

Once ashore in Malaya, the Japanese moved briskly down the cigar-shaped peninsula. The British had thought the jungles impassable (just what the Allies had believed about the Ardennes) and left them only weakly defended. The Japanese easily disposed of what opposition they found, for they quickly proved themselves much superior jungle fighters. British soldiers were weighted down with all the paraphenalia of modern war: steel helmets, canteens, gas masks and heavy packs. Moreover, they depended on mechanized transport for supplies. The Nipponese needed none of these things. Like the Vietcong of our own day, they were lightly armed, lived off the land and wore simple cotton dress. A two-wheeled ox cart served them better than tanks did the British. By the end of December the invaders had knifed halfway down the peninsula towards the prize that hung like a ripe pear at its end—the island port of Singapore.

The British had spent $200 million to make it an impregnable fort—against a seaborne attack. Every gun on Singapore pointed towards the ocean. But no one had bothered to protect the island's landward side, with its water reservoirs and airfield, from an attack across the narrow strip of water that separated the port from Malaya. By mid-January the Japanese had reached the causeway. The British blew up the bridge across it and dug in for what they confidently expected would be a long siege. But Singapore's administration had grown complacent. There was labor trouble, and the long retreat had demoralized the army. On February 14, General Yamashita smashed across the causeway and grabbed the water reservoirs. The garrison surrendered.

The Japanese did not wait to complete the conquest of Malaya before striking against their next target to the west—Burma. This Texas-size nation, straddled between India on the one side and China, Laos and Thailand on the other, was of vital strategic importance: across its hills and through its jungles wound the 800-mile-long Burma road, the major supply artery to China. If the Japanese could cut it, they would choke off the flow of war material to Chiang Kai-shek's hardpressed armies.

Once again the Mikado's soldiers encountered little British opposition. Jagged mountains and dense rain forests did much more to slow their advance. The Japanese opened the campaign in mid-January with a march through the Kawkareik Pass. Quickly defeating an Indian division there, they struck next for the port of Moulmein, which fell on January 25. Early in February they crossed the Salween river and pushed for the Bilin river, where some of the heaviest fighting of the campaign took place. In early March the Japanese reached the Sittang river, the last natural barrier to Rangoon. And on March 7, Sir Harold Alexander, the last British commander at Dunkirk, took his troops out of the burning and heavily bombed Burmese capital. (It would be Alexander's last retreat. Five months later he succeeded Auchinlek as commander in the Middle East and, together with Montgomery, began to fashion Rommel's defeat in the desert.) Retreating up the Sittang and Irrawaddy rivers, the British set the oil wells at Yenangyaung on fire and finally reached Mandalay in mid-April. Meanwhile, the Japanese struck for the terminal of the Burma road at Lashio, pushing tanks into the city on April 30. The next day the British decided to abandon Mandalay and flee across the Ava River. For the next month British forces and a Chinese army under the command of an American general, "Vinegar" Joe Stillwell, engaged in a desperate race with their Japanese pursuers to reach the Indian frontier. At the end of May, after a journey of incredible hardship and heroism, they made it. The monsoon rains then put an end to the Japanese advance and gave the British time to fortify the border. With the Burma road gone, supplies were now flown to China across the "hump" of the towering Himalayas by a daring band of American freebooters: Claire Chennault's Flying Tigers.

While still engaged in Malaya, the Philippines and Burma, the Japanese opened yet another drive of conquest, this one into the Dutch East Indies, an area rich in oil, rubber, tin, manganese and other resources. The islands were garrisoned by weak Dutch forces, and the Japanese had little trouble landing troops on them. Borneo, the Celebes, Bali and Timor were among the first attacked. On January 23 a pickup Allied fleet waylaid a Japanese convoy in the Makassar Straits between Borneo and the Celebes and sank several ships. But the action did little to stop Japanese momentum. On February 14 the invasion of Sumatra, the largest Indonesian island, began. Two weeks later another Allied fleet, under command of a Dutch admiral, engaged superior Japanese naval forces in the Java Sea. The battle lasted for three days, and at first the Allies held their own. Then enemy superiority in the air and the prevalence of Japanese submarines began to tell; the Allied squadron was annihilated, and the last barrier to an attack on Java, the most populous island in the East Indies, was removed. Within ten days the conquest of Java was completed, and on March 9 the last Dutch forces there surrendered.

During the first few months of 1942 the Japanese also extended their conquests into the south Pacific. Landings were made in the Solomons, New Britain and the Bismarck Archipelago. On March 7, Japanese troops swarmed ashore in New Guinea: the dagger of Nippon was now pointed straight at Australia.

By this time, the battle for the Philippines, too, had been all but lost. General Douglas MacArthur had obeyed an order from President Roosevelt and flown to Australia to take up command of the defenses of the "down under" continent. After Pearl Harbor, MacArthur did not have the manpower to oppose the many Japanese landings on Luzon. His forces consisted of 19,000 American soldiers and 12,000 Filipino scouts (as well as the 100,000 half-trained men in the Philippine army). He had little air support, and there were no U.S. ships in the area to intercept the invaders. Instead of meeting the enemy everywhere, therefore, he let the Japanese advance through Luzon almost unopposed while he marched his troops into Bataan Peninsula, across the bay from Manila. The capital was declared an open city on December 26. The next day, the Japanese demonstrated their contempt for such civilized rules of war with a heavy bombardment that destroyed the port. On January 2, General Homma marched his victorious army into Manila. The battle of Bataan now began in earnest.

MacArthur hoped to fight a holding action there until the United States could bring in enough men and supplies to permit a counterattack. But American ships were unable to run the Japanese blockade of Philippine waters. Food ran short; soldiers were put on half-rations. Many of the Filipinos fighting with MacArthur gave up and went home. Malaria sapped the strength of those who remained to fight. In February, Homma called on the Americans to surrender, a demand MacArthur scornfully rejected.

But Washington saw the situation in a more sober light. The best the Americans could hope for was to fight a delaying action. For that MacArthur was too valuable a general; his talents were needed in Australia. The task of holding Bataan was now entrusted to General Jonathan Wainright. He continued to resist for three weeks after MacArthur left the islands. But then the Japanese brought in a new army, fresh from its triumph in Malaya. On April 1, 1942, General Yamashita began a two-pronged drive against Bataan: he landed troops behind the U.S. lines and pounded the front itself with murderous artillery fire. The Japanese didn't need much time. On April 9, Wainright took what forces he could extricate from the Bataan debacle to the island fortress of Corregidor in the middle of Manila Bay.

The men who fell into Japanese captivity were made victims of a callous brutality that matched Nazi excesses. American and Philippine prisoners were lined up in rows of four and taken on an 80-mile death march through dense jungles. Guards beat many of the prisoners to death, often on the slimmest pretext. Water was so short that some of the marchers were driven half mad. Malaria, dysentery and other diseases were rampant. Those too weak to keep up with the rest were murdered by guards. The march's survivors were herded into boxcars and taken to a prison camp. The train ride in the airless cars proved almost as bad as the march itself.

Wainright kept Corregidor's guns firing until early in May. Then the Japanese forced a landing on the island, and on May 6 the Americans surrendered. Thus, within five months of Pearl Harbor, Japan had gobbled up an empire half the size of the United States, which had a profusion of every raw material a modern war machine needs. Moreover, the Japanese were in a position to strike not only at Australia but also at the U.S. lifeline across the southern Pacific.

In this orgy of Nipponese victories there had been only one American offensive, and that was more warning than threat. On April 18, 1942, Colonel Jimmy Doolittle had flown a group of B-25 bombers from the decks of an aircraft carrier task force through to Tokyo, where they dumped their bombs. The physical damage was slight, the psychological shock much greater. After Doolittle's raid, the Japanese never felt wholly safe again.

In early May, Tokyo's warlords made a first attempt to cut the Pacific supply route to Down Under: U.S. planes spotted a strong force of ships sailing through the Coral Sea (between Australia and the Solomon Islands) in the direction of Port Moresby, on the southern tip of New Guinea facing Australia. A task force built around the U.S. aircraft carriers *Lexington* and *Yorktown* moved to intercept the enemy. The battle of the Coral Sea that followed proved a "first" in naval warfare: ships did not exchange a single shot in three days of fighting. Fleets of planes took off from carrier decks to bomb enemy vessels, often flying past each other through thick cloud cover. Both sides lost heavily. The *Lexington* was sunk. But although the battle was a standoff, Admiral Yamamoto gave up his advance on Port Moresby and Australia. He regrouped his forces for another attack on the U.S.-held island of Midway, at the extreme end of the Hawaiian chain. Presumably, he would move from there to Hawaii proper.

By all odds Yamamoto should have won the battle for the mid-Pacific base without much trouble. He had assembled a fleet of 200 ships, including 11 battleships (some sporting 18-inch guns) and eight carriers. But the Americans had luck, daring and good leadership on their side, and these would prove more important.

The Japanese admiral planned first a feint against the Aleutian Islands—tossed far out into the Pacific from Alaska like so many stepping stones—designed to trap Admiral Chester Nimitz into sending the bulk of his fleet north, leaving Midway undefended and ripe for quick occupation. But Nimitz refused the bait. He kept his carriers close to Midway (the United States still didn't have a battleship nearer than San Francisco) and stationed so many planes on its airfield that they crowded the runway. Again air power decided the outcome.

Before dawn on June 4, 1942, U.S. planes spotted a large enemy task force, grouped around four carriers, steaming towards Midway. The island base was promptly alerted, and an hour later the Americans were able to beat off the Japanese air assault, shooting down about a third of the attacking planes. The enemy did some damage to the airfield but left it in still usable condition. Yamamoto, therefore, determined on a second strike. The decks of his carriers were littered with refueling planes when the brash Americans arrived overhead for a counterstrike. It was unsuccessful. Enemy gunners knocked down all but six of the 41 attacking torpedo bombers. But before that battle was over, U.S. dive bombers from the *Hornet* and *Enterprise* arrived to lay down a carpet of bombs on the Japanese ships. Three of their carriers were set on fire and sunk. Later in the day, U.S. planes hunted down the fourth carrier and sank it. The U.S. lost 60 planes and the *Yorktown*, but the victory was cheap at the price. For on the next evening Yamamoto decided to break off the action and called back a naval strike force headed by two cruisers already on the way to Midway to deliver a seaborne attack. The Japense ships started a general retreat towards the north. They did capture a consolation prize, however—two barren but strategic islands in the Aleutian chain.

Midway was the most crucial battle of the Pacific war, for it stopped the flood of Japanese expansion in the Pacific and began the long and bloody process of reversing the tide of her empire.

And the United States had done it with a crippled fleet. After Midway the Americans had only three aircraft carriers left compared with Japan's five, but U.S. shipyards had already laid the keels for 13 big flattops and 15 smaller ones. In a matter of months this huge fleet would begin ferrying thousands of U.S. planes closer to enemy possessions. It was an outpouring that Japanese shipyards could not hope to match. In fact, they could not even make up the losses suffered at Midway. More immediately, the battle secured the vital supply lanes to Australia and assured the United States of a mighty base from which it could launch a counterattack.

Chapter ☆ 13 ☆

At the battle of Midway in June, 1942, Japan had reached floodtide. Her empire stretched from the Indian border to the Aleutians, from the East Indies almost to the edge of the Hawaiian islands. And although the Japanese held more water than land, anyone could draw on a map the frontline Tokyo had to defend—or expand. It ran from the northernmost of the Japanese home islands east across the bottom of the Sea of Okhotsk, below the tip of the Kamchatka Peninsula and on to Kiska in the Aleutian chain. From Kiska the line turned southeast for many thousands of miles, past Marcus and Wake Island, the Marshalls and the Gilberts, to the Ellice Island group. There it swung sharply west to run below the Solomon Islands and New Britain, cut across the northern half of New Guinea, skirted around the East Indies and finally reached the coast of Burma.

The lines from Kiska and the Indies that converged near the Ellice chain formed the head of a triangle or salient that bit deeply into the Pacific. It delineated Japan's outer defenses. The base of the triangle curved from Tokyo past the Bonin islands and Marianas, along the head of New Guinea (the big island is shaped like a bird) down to the island of Timor in the Indian Ocean. This was Japan's inner defense line that protected the rich East Indies, the Philippines and the Japanese home islands themselves.

In the weeks that followed Midway, both American and Japanese planners pored over maps to figure out what to do next. Obviously Tokyo wanted to expand the perimeter; just as obviously the United States wished to crack it. Since the Japanese still held the initiative, even after Midway, they made the first move—in two directions:

towards Port Moresby on the Coral Sea side of the Papuan Peninsula in New Guinea, and towards the New Hebrides, New Caledonia
and Samoa. The first drive threatened Australia, the second the vital
shipping lanes from the United States to "down under." The United
States moved fast to contain both threats, but even as it did, it had
already worked out an elaborate and long-range program of crushing
the Empire of the Rising Sun.

The attack against Port Moresby began on July 22, 1942, when
Japanese troops went ashore at Gona and Buna on the Papuan
coast. They began to drive straight across the peninsula towards the
Coral Sea and met only light Australian resistance. By early August
they were already pushing into the Owen Stanley range, whose
peaks soar up to 14,000 feet, and had captured the Aussie base at
Kokoda. But the Kokoda track led through increasingly tough and
more hazardous terrain. It slowed the invaders down to a crawl, and
General MacArthur was handed a few precious weeks in which to
prepare his defenses.

The threat to the shipping lanes, the New Hebrides and New
Caledonia, however, was more immediate. In late July, U.S. intelligence learned that the Japanese had almost completed an airfield on
the island of Guadalcanal, on the southern edge of the Solomon
chain. It was within easy bomber range of all three targets. The base
had to be captured before it became operational.

Then it was August, 1942, one of the more crucial months of
the war. In Africa the British were regrouping after their retreat
deep into Egypt. In Russia, General Paulus drove his Sixth Army
pell mell through the Don Bend towards Stalingrad.

On August 7 three U.S. flattops escorted a 19-ship convoy and a
strong naval striking force to Guadalcanal. After navy guns had laid
down a withering barrage, U.S. marines swarmed ashore and met
almost no resistance. They moved quickly across the relatively open
country at the northern end of the island and took the half-finished
airfield without a fight. The Japanese had fled in confusion and left
huge stores of supplies behind, even half-eaten meals. Slowly the
marines advanced into the jungles beyond the base, with scattered
sniper fire the only resistance.

Rain fell the second night the Americans were ashore and
turned their camp into a soggy misery. Few slept that night, espe-

cially when the dull thud of gunfire offshore rent the night and flashes of fire traced the picture of a major naval battle against the dripping black sky. A strong enemy squadron had sneaked into the channel between neighboring Tulagi and Guadalcanal and blasted U.S. ships out of the water. When the battle was over, the Japanese had sunk four U.S. cruisers, damaged several destroyers and given the waters around Savo Island a new name—Iron Bottom Bay.

Fortunately the Japanese commander, Admiral Mikawa, retired up the slot—as the Americans called the channel through the Solomons—before dawn, and never knew the extent of his victory. It saved the Americans from a much more crushing defeat. U.S. commanders, however, were fearful of a repetition of the disaster and decided to withdraw their warships from Guadalcanal waters. Without naval protection few convoys got through. Soon the marines ran short of supplies; a week after the landing they were down to two small meals daily. And, to make matters worse, the enemy came down from the hills to harass the Americans in earnest for the first time.

For two weeks the marines fought back without air cover while the Seabees, the navy's lightning-quick corps of engineers, completed the airstrip that the Japanese had started. Finally, on August 20, the first Grumman Hellcat touched down on Henderson Field. Slowly the marines enlarged their perimeter, but until November it was never more than seven miles long and four miles wide.

Tokyo, meanwhile, began a massive and sustained effort to land reinforcements on Guadalcanal, no matter how badly its supply fleets were mauled at sea. The first attempt came on August 23, when a large convoy of troopships protected by aircraft carriers, battleships and cruisers sailed down the slot. American planes from *Henderson* and the carriers *Enterprise* and *Saratoga* scrambled fast to meet the enemy fleet. Japanese losses in the two-day battle were heavy: a carrier sunk, another flattop, a battleship and half a dozen cruisers damaged, a hundred planes shot down, several troopships sunk. Yet, despite the high cost, the enemy had managed to land additional troops. A fast force of destroyers had escaped U.S. detection and unloaded soldiers on Cape Esperance at the northern tip of the island. It was the first "Tokyo Express"—squads of fast destroyers that dashed down the slot at night to bombard U.S. positions inland while soldiers climbed over the sides and waded or swam ashore.

Gradually Japanese strength on the island increased. And in the second week of September, evidence mounted that a major attack was in the offing. It came on September 12. In the afternoon enemy bombers knocked out a radio station at Henderson and destroyed three planes on the ground. That night Japanese ships opened a heavy naval barrage. Small boats brought troops ashore. Marines who held a ridge covering the approach to Henderson were pushed back, but their front was not broken and at dawn the Japanese retreated into the jungles. When darkness came, the attack resumed. Two thousand men slammed at a ridge manned by only 300 Marines. Again fighting lasted until dawn. Guns painted bright fireworks into the sky. The Japanese slapped their rifle butts and howled, "U.S. marines be dead tomorrow." The chatter of small "Nambos" machine guns added to the din. Marines dragged heavy machine guns, able to slice attackers in half, to the hilltop. They bit pins out of hand grenades and rolled them down to halt wave after wave of enemy soldiers. But the Japanese kept coming with that utter contempt of death the Americans would encounter again and again in this war. By midnight the marines had even got 75-mm howitzers and 105 cannon atop the hill. The attack had to be halted and the hill held; otherwise the enemy could deliver a quick and destructive blow to the airbase. At 2:30 A.M. the Japanese stopped shooting for 90 minutes and the Americans could let their gun barrels cool. When fighting resumed at four, the sting had gone from the attackers. Small arms fire petered out by dawn. The hill had held, the threat to Henderson been met.

During the next month the marines managed to expand their own perimeter a little and drive the enemy from his more exposed bridgeheads. But the wearying jungle patrols did not bring about a decision. On October 11 the Japanese made another effort to land massive reinforcements and turn the balance of battle in their favor. Luckily a U.S. scout plane spotted the convoy and its large escort far up the slot. American ships hastily put out to sea and that night surprised the enemy fleet off Cape Esperance. The battle ended in a clear-cut U.S. victory. The Japanese lost eight ships, including four cruisers. Only one U.S. destroyer was sunk. The next day a large American convoy landed with the first U.S. army replacements for the battle-weary marines. But in this seesaw battle the advantage didn't stay long with the Americans. Three days later the enemy sent in another convoy, and it managed to land a great number of troops.

The Japanese commander on Guadalcanal decided on another offensive to drive the Americans off the island. The attack began on October 24 with a massive artillery barrage which forced the marines to fall back. Then the Americans managed to get big guns of their own into the line and marines beat back repeated banzai charges. After two days of incessant attack the Japanese withdrew. That day, October 26, another crucial naval battle, the fourth of the Solomon campaign, began to shape up off nearby Santa Cruz island. The Japanese had gathered a strong air-sea squadron in a bid to harass shipping in the lifeline to Australia. But although a kamikaze—a suicide plane—sank the carrier *Hornet,* Japanese losses were much heavier. A major offensive thrust against the vital lane had been blunted.

About two weeks later U.S. scout planes spotted yet another huge Japanese fleet northwest of Guadalcanal. A force of cruisers and destroyers quickly sailed out to meet the much stronger enemy— U.S. battleships were too far away to join the action. On the night of November 13, Admiral Cunningham steamed brazenly into a semi-circle of Japanese ships arrayed offshore to cover a troop landing. His fast ships zipped past the cumbersome enemy battlewagons to bombard them at close range and dash away before the huge gun turrets could crank down to their level. The Japanese were soon shooting at each other, not the Americans. But then they found the range: a big shell smashed the bridge of the *USS San Francisco* and killed Cunningham. Soon the Americans had only three destroyers left undamaged, and they decided to retire. But the enemy was already beaten. The next morning, planes from the *Enterprise* spotted three more columns of enemy ships and drove them to cover. When U.S. battleships finally arrived on the scene, the Japanese turned tail and ran. Their losses had been almost as large as the fleet they brought: 28 ships sunk, including two battleships and eight cruisers, eight other ships damaged and five thousand soldiers drowned. The Americans lost two cruisers and seven destroyers. It was the biggest of the battles fought in Guadalcanal waters. The fifth and last naval engagement was fought on November 30, 1942, and again the Japanese won; but they failed to realize the extent of their victory and therefore didn't exploit it.

For the next two months the GIs mopped up enemy resistance in the jungles. American planes bombed Japanese bases nearby so hard that they became all but useless. And the Tokyo Express began running in the opposite direction—taking soldiers off the island. The Japanese had started losing badly in New Guinea early in 1943, and all reinforcements were sent there. On February 8, 1943, the last Japanese soldier slipped quietly out of Guadalcanal. The campaign had cost the Mikado 40,000 dead. The Americans had lost 1600 dead, but the Marines and soldiers who survived were battle-hardened veterans. For the American fighting man in the Pacific, Guadalcanal was the baptism of fire. Like El Alamein and Stalingrad (which had surrendered only five days before) it was one of the turning points of the war.

On Papua, meanwhile, General MacArthur had made good use of the time granted him by the slow pace of the Japanese advance across the Owen Stanley chain. An airfield was completed near Port Moresby before the end of August, and when the enemy landed at Milne Bay on the southern tip of Papua on August 26, General Kenney, the U.S. Air Force commander, had planes overhead to meet them. Bombed mercilessly for three days and unable to crack Australian defenses, the Japanese soon evacuated the bridgehead, their hopes of building a pincer operation against Port Moresby (the thrust through the mountains along the Kokoda track was to be the other arm) dashed.

Still, the Japanese advance through the mountains had made good progress. By mid-September they were 20 miles from the airbase. But there the Australians held and on September 23 began pushing the exhausted Japanese back up the Kokoda track. By October 16 the Aussies had reached Templeton's Crossing, just beyond the highest crest of the Owen Stanley range.

Some of the worst battle conditions of the war dominated fighting along the Kokoda track. Jungle paths were steep and muddy, the sheer activity of crawling along them exhausting and draining. Tropical disease was rampant. Most of the retreating Japanese were sick, and all were hungry. Supply problems across this mountain fastness were virtually insoluble. The Australians even found evidence of Japanese cannibalism.

Meanwhile, MacArthur made a seaborne landing some miles south of Buna and Gona, where the Japanese had landed the previous July. By mid-December, Australian and U.S. troops had taken both towns after bitter fighting in which the Aussies used tanks for the first time in the campaign. The Allies had also supplied Australian troops on the Kokoda track from the air and landed troops in back of the Japanese. As the Japanese situation worsened in Papua, the Tokyo high command decided to give up its position and concentrate on holding the Huon Peninsula and the ports that guarded its approaches. On January 13, 1943, the Japanese began to evacuate troops from Sanananda, the only terminal of the Kokoda trail still in their hands. The town fell on January 22.

Thus, by early February, both Japanese efforts to expand their southern flank had been defeated: the enemy had been cleared from southern Papua and Guadalcanal. The Allies could now put into action the long-range battle plans that had begun to take shape after Midway.

The Pacific had been divided into three fronts. In the central Pacific, Admiral Chester Nimitz' ships would strike against the Marshalls and the Gilbert island chains before attacking the key enemy base at Truk in the Caroline group. At the same time, General MacArthur and Admiral Halsey would begin a pincer attack on Rabaul, a key base on New Britain and the spider that directed the Japanese net. MacArthur would smash up the New Guinea coast and then invade New Britain. Halsey would climb up the "ladder" of the Solomon islands, conquer New Ireland and converge on Rabaul. The plan looked good on paper; but the actual campaign took 16 months to complete, and at times progress was agonizingly slow. Huon peninsula, for example, was not cleared until the end of December, 1943.

The drive on Salamaua, the first gateway to Huon, really began at Wau, 30 miles to the southeast at the head of Bulldog Track (another road inland). The Australians airlifted a brigade into Wau. At the end of January the brigade repulsed a Japanese attack, then went over on the offensive. It took them four weeks to advance 15 miles to the outskirts of Mubo, and they then spent the next few months bogged down outside the village in patrolling and holding actions. Their attack towards the coast did not resume until May. This kind of fighting was typical for much of the New Guinea campaign.

The Japanese, meanwhile, decided to send massive reinforcements to Lae from Rabaul in order to mount a second attack on Wau. On March 1, 1943, an American plane spotted the large convoy sailing north of New Britain through the Bismarck Sea. The next day B-17s flew through hazy clouds to skip bombs over the enemy ships. Three of them went down in this raid. On March 3 the convoy had sailed close enough to the new Allied air base near Gona to permit a major strike by B-25 medium bombers and P-38 fighters. For two days bombs rained down on the ships while the P-38s shot Japanese fighter escorts from the sky. When it was all over, the Mikado had lost 61 planes, 22 ships and about 15,000 men. Allied losses: one bomber, three fighters, 13 men dead.

The Battle of the Bismarck Sea was a crucial engagement, for it clearly spelled out the limits of Japanese power. Henceforth, they would not be able to supply stranded or isolated garrisons or move reinforcements to threatened areas at will. In fact, it marked the end of Japanese initiative in the Pacific, which now began to pass to the Allies. From this battle on, the Empire of the Rising Sun would fight a defensive war.

For most of the spring of 1943, however, there was little evidence of this change as something of a lull gripped the whole Pacific theater. The Allies used the time for a bombing campaign against the Solomons and to build up land and naval forces in the southwest Pacific. Soon 150,000 U.S. soldiers were stationed in MacArthur's theater.

Major fighting resumed in May when the Americans landed on Attu, one of two islands in the Aleutian chain still in Japanese hands. (The Japanese had landed on Attu, Kiska and Amchitka after the battle of Midway, but withdrew from Amchitka in January, 1943.) Fighting on Attu was heavy with enemy resistance, which was as fierce as any in the war. GIs had to push Nipponese soldiers through ankle-deep mud and crawl up jagged cliffs after them. Finally, on June 2, after three weeks of battle, the Japanese tried one last suicide charge. More than 2000 men stormed down a cliff overlooking Attu harbor, allegedly shouting, "Japanese drink blood like wine." Nobody did any drinking that day, and the banzai chargers were mowed down almost to the last man. That ended fighting on Attu. The Americans reoccupied Kiska on August 2 after the Japanese had abandoned it. At the same time, Patton and Montgomery were just completing their 39-day conquest of Sicily. In Russia, Soviet tanks smashed at the outskirts of Orel.

The Australian campaign in New Guinea came to life again in May, and for most of the summer the Allies waged a bitter fight to capture both Salmaua and Lae. Early in September, MacArthur decided on a double strike. First, Australian troops landed east of Lae. The next day a U.S. regiment parachuted into an airbase 19 miles west of town and quickly captured it. Then the Americans began to advance down the Markham river towards Lae, now threatened by a pincer attack. The Japanese fought fanatically to hold every plantation and every palm grove; but on September 15, U.S. and Aussie patrols met in the center of town. Salamau was occupied on September 11 after efforts to seal escape routes and trap the enemy garrison failed.

A week after the capture of Lae, MacArthur jumped into Huon proper with a seaborne landing north of Finschhafen. The town was occupied on October 2, 1943, and for the next three months the Allies slowly pushed up the Huon coast towards Sio. Once the Huon coast was secure, the Allies would control the sea approaches to New Britain, the major target of MacArthur and Halsey's campaigns. Halsey's attacks in the Solomons turned into a preview of the U.S. island-hopping drive towards the Japanese homeland: it concentrated on capture of key bases, and left less important ones to wither on the vine.

Halsey struck first against the Russell Islands. Marines from Guadalcanal landed there unopposed on February 21, 1943. In June, Halsey's ships attacked the New Georgia group. Rendova was overrun in a week, and U.S. guns emplaced on the island began shelling Munda airfield on New Georgia. On July 5 two U.S. regiments scrambled ashore near Munda to fight a wearying repetition of the Guadalcanal battle: they gained little ground, were hemmed in on all sides by jungles and enemy soldiers and withstood a shattering series of counterattacks. Finally massive reinforcements arrived, upping

U.S. strength to two divisions. On August 1 the Americans broke through to the edge of Munda field and, after several days of heavy fighting, captured it. The New Georgia campaign, however, continued for several more weeks as the Japanese resisted in the south of the island just as tenaciously as in the north.

Choiseul and Bougainville were the next targets. On October 27, marines struck at Choiseul in a diversionary maneuver designed to confuse the enemy, and pulled out five days later. On November 1 the Americans stormed ashore at Empress Augusta Bay on Bougainville, the largest and northernmost of the Solomon islands. The story of the Bougainville campaign is already familiar: fast and sustained Japanese air strikes that were repeatedly beaten off, a major naval battle near Empress Augusta Bay, the slogging jungle fighting to expand the small initial perimeters and attempts to reinforce the defenders by sea. Land needed for construction of airfields was seized within a month, but Bougainville itself was not finally conquered until mid-January, 1944.

With the Huon and Solomon campaigns ended, the Allies struck next at New Britain. The capture of Rabaul itself no longer figured in Allied planning. The base, MacArthur was sure, could be neutralized from the air and the two prongs of the Allied attack pushed forward across New Guinea and into the Admiralty islands. Rabaul itself had already been subject to constant aerial bombardment. On Christmas day a large Allied convoy sailed through the Vitiaz and Dampier Straits, between Huon and New Britain, to land elements of two marine divisions on Cape Gloucester, while army troops went ashore on Cape Arawe on the southern coast of the island. Heavy surf made the initial landings difficult, and once the Marines were ashore the terrain again provided most of the opposition. The Marines sank up to their hips in mud and water or became entangled in the network of roots under their feet. The first American fatality occurred when a tree fell on a Marine's head. Once past what the mapmakers had somewhat optimistically described as the "damp belt," fighting grew heavier. But on January 1 the American commander could cable MacArthur: "I have the honor to present you Cape Gloucester as a New Year's present." For the next two months the Americans slogged grimly through the jungles to clear about a third of the island.

In January, 1944, the air assault on Rabaul was stepped up greatly: 100 planes attacked daily. By January 29, Tokyo itself conceded that the situation had reached "a serious stage." In February the U.S. captured tiny Green Island, a hundred odd miles from Rabaul, and quickly built an airstrip there. A month later they took Talasea and its airstrip, only 160 miles from Rabaul. The base was as good as neutralized; indeed, the Americans had already leaped far beyond it.

On February 29, 1944, MacArthur opened a campaign to capture the Admiralty islands, some 300 miles north of New Britain, with an attack on Los Negros. Elements of the First U.S. Cavalry went ashore from fast destroyers, deployed on the model of the Tokyo Express. Within a week the Americans had cleared most of the island, again only after savage fighting. On the 12th they landed on Hauwei, and on the 15th they began the attack on Manus, the largest island of the group. Most of the enemy resistance was broken by March 25, although fighting on the Admiralty islands continued into May.

On March 20 the Americans had also made an unopposed landing on Emirau, 650 miles from Truk. This stroke not only completed the isolation of Rabaul, but also outflanked the second major enemy strong point at Kavieng on New Ireland. Tokyo, therefore, decided at the end of March to move its southwest Pacific headquarters to Hollandia, 600 miles west of Salamau on the New Guinea coast. But MacArthur was able to think and act faster than the Japanese. He had already struck far beyond Huon when he jumped to Saidor, 100 miles north of Finschhafen. He determined on an even bigger leap—right into Hollandia before the Japanese got their headquarters fully established there. If the attack succeeded, large Japanese armies would be left stranded along the coast and the Americans put in a position to mount a final drive for the conquest of New Guinea and to the Philippines beyond it. A huge force of carriers and cruisers was gathered to protect the invasion fleet, which arrived off Hollandia in April. Again the attack featured naval bombardment of shore positions. Dive bombers flew close air support. Rocket-firing assault boats covered the actual landings, which were spearheaded by amphibious tanks. Within five days MacArthur had grabbed his most important targets, the airfields, and early in May the Allies were securely established in the Hollandia area. But MacArthur continued to leap-frog up the coast. On May 17 he landed a hundred miles further up at Arare. Two days later he seized the small offshore island of Wadke. Seabees began repairing the airstrip, while enemy gunners still shelled the hangers.

Next, MacArthur jumped 200 miles to Biak island in Geelvink Bay. The 8000 defenders fought desperately for three weeks to hold it, but on June 22 the Allies had captured Biak's three airfields and the battle was over. On June 30, MacArthur moved to end the New Guinea campaign: he attacked Sansapor, a town that sat like a beady eye in what the Dutch had called the Vogelkop (the bird's head) Peninsula. Caught off guard, the Japanese offered only scattered resistance.

In the year since the Allied attack on Salmaua, the Allies had covered more than 1200 miles and left 135,000 enemy soldiers stranded along the coast or on islands. Moreover, Sansapor was only 600 miles from the Philippines. As he looked out across the ocean after his tremendous victory, MacArthur knew he was closer then ever before to redeeming the pledge he had made when he had left those islands 28 months earlier: "I shall return."

Indeed, it had been a tremendous year for the Allied cause: Africa had been cleared, Sicily and Italy invaded, Rome captured, the beaches of Normandy secured and the Wehrmacht driven out of Russia proper, while Soviet tanks stabbed into Poland and the Balkans.

In the central Pacific, Admiral Chester Nimitz had started his own drive a few months after MacArthur and Halsey had begun their 1943 campaigns against Huon and the Solomons. His problems were complicated by the much larger area in which he had to fight and his lack of land bases. There was nothing beyond Hawaii, and consequently Nimitz needed more ships and planes. He began to get them in quantity only in mid-1943. Then hundreds of ships and thousands of planes joined his command. Floating factories equipped to handle underwater welding on the spot sailed behind the fighting ships. An armada of supply and repair ships was kept close to the fluid battle lines. Nimitz' fleet could roam the Pacific at will and strike at half a dozen enemy targets at once. The Japanese never knew where an attack might come and therefore had to spread available forces much too thinly. Their situation resembled that of Poland in 1939: Nimitz could smash a huge phalanx of ships against one weakly guarded position.

Nimitz opened his campaign with air raids against Wake Island in July and August. On August 31 his planes smashed Marcus Island, a mid-Pacific dot due north of the Carolines and the Marianas. September and October saw bombardment of the Marshalls and the Gilberts. In November, Nimitz determined to land on Makin and Tarawa in the Gilberts. Carrier-based planes bombed both islands to prepare for the invasion. On November 20, 1943, U.S. ships bobbed off Makin. Fortunately, the Japanese did not contest the landing, for about half the assault force had to wade ashore across a pot-holed and boulder-clogged reef. After a few days of sometimes bitter fighting that included a banzai charge by drunken enemy soldiers, Makin was in U.S. hands. The Americans were confident Tarawa would fall as easily. They were wrong.

Tarawa is a typical Pacific atoll—a string of tiny islands, perhaps a dozen in all, linked by coral reef and grouped around a shallow lagoon. Most of the Japanese garrison was concentrated on Betio, a strip of land that hunched out of the water for three miles and was only a mile wide. Some 3000 Imperial Marines manned a heavy net of concrete and steel-covered pillboxes. U.S. ships steamed up to the atoll on November 21 to launch a fierce aerial and naval barrage. U.S. marines came ashore confident that nothing and nobody could have survived such a bombardment. A fleet of landing craft and amphibious tanks chugged towards shore and entered the clear blue waters of the lagoon. The white sands of the beach gleamed ahead of them. The landing, however, was anything but placid. Deep water reached to within 15 feet of shore, and an intricate system of underwater barbed wire defenses made the scramble ashore an obstacle race. Once on the beach the Marines were subjected to withering gun fire. Amazingly, the Japanese had withstood the bombardment well and soon threw tanks against the invaders. Marines wading ashore behind the initial wave of attackers were caught on the reefs in an inferno of crossfire. At one point in those first few hours Colonel David Schoup radioed the battleship *Maryland:* "Issue in doubt." Later the marines stabilized their positions and proceeded to dynamite defenders out of pillboxes or burn them out with flamethrowers. U.S. casualties were enormous. Hundreds died on the first day alone. Finally, after four days of the bitterest fighting anywhere in the Pacific campaign, the Japanese made their last, ritual banzai charge and the battle was over. The Marines had lost nearly 1000 dead and 2000 wounded.

Nimitz now moved against the Marshalls, another collection of atolls, and selected the largest of them, Kwajalein, for attack. The island was 66 miles long and 18 miles wide, and the Japanese had built several excellent airfields there, making it a valuable prize. This time, though, Nimitz moved carefully. He bombarded the Marshalls for two months before sending out his carriers to protect the huge task force he had gathered for the invasion. On January 29, 1944, Admiral Marc Mitscher sliced his flattops past the outlying atolls and that night began a sustained three-day barrage that dumped a total of 15,000 tons of high explosives on the island. Kwajalein turned into a mass of scars. Every tree had splintered or been turned into a charred stump. Three-quarters of the garrison were killed or wounded before the first U.S. troops stormed ashore. A heap of rubble littered the island. Yet despite death and destruction, the fanatic Japanese put up fierce resistance. Once again the Americans had to inch their way across the island, pillbox by pillbox, and watch in horror the senseless Japanese suicides. One enemy soldier ran up to a U.S. tank, held out a hand grenade and waited until it went off. It blew him to bits and left the tank unharmed. Kwajalein fell in the first week of February.

On February 17 the carrier *Saratoga* led a task force against Eniwetok, 350 miles to the northeast. Again the pattern was familiar: the heavy naval barrage to cover the invasion, the hand-to-hand fighting, the banzai charges, the last suicide attack. The atoll fell on February 22, 1944.

Conquest of the Marshalls put the American flag 2700 miles west of Pearl Harbor and less than a thousand miles from Truk, the key base in the Caroline chain. Since the Japanese had fortified it, no outsider had seen it. Early in February two Liberator bombers flew a reconaissance mission over Truk and came back with pictures that showed the harbor crammed with 25 ships. The American admirals decided on a major gamble: they would strip newly conquered Kwajalein and send Mitscher's carriers and a strong squadron of warships on a raiding mission against the big base. On February 16, with Truk only 45 flying minutes away, Mitscher sent his planes screaming down the carrier decks. Dogfights quickly popped across the sky over the enemy stronghold. Hours later the Japanese had lost 127 planes in aerial combat; another 87 were destroyed on the ground. Meanwhile, the U.S. surface fleet had spotted an enemy flotilla steaming into open water 60 miles away. The ships were quickly engaged, and many were sunk on the spot. The Americans then sailed their vessels around the allegedly "invincible fortress" in a display of mockery and disdain. Japanese losses in the raid totaled 23 ships sunk, seven damaged.

Next came the U.S. attack against the Marianas. Admiral Raymond Spruance's Fifth Fleet was swollen into the largest invasion force yet seen in the Pacific. Again a key island in the group was selected as the major target, the one with the best airfields. The others would be bypassed as so many had been in the Gilberts and Marshalls. This time the brunt would fall on Saipan. Marc Mitscher's carriers were in position off the Marianas on June 11, 1944. For four days planes blasted Saipan, Guam, Tinian, Rota and Pagan. They did good work. When Spruance's armada came into view of Saipan on June 14, every coastal gun had been knocked out and not a single enemy plane flew out to meet the invaders. Still, the Americans laid down another shattering barrage that turned the coastline into a mass of bruises. Under this canopy of shells three American divisions went ashore. The well-entrenched Japanese offered fanatic resistance right at the beach. The landings were a nightmare of hand-to-hand combat, of saber against bayonet. But after two days of savage slogging the Americans had established a beachhead several miles deep and prepared to lunge for a nearby airfield.

But Tokyo was determined to hold Saipan no matter what the cost, for once the big B-29 bombers were established there they could threaten the home islands themselves. Accordingly, Admiral Ozawa assembled a huge fleet that included nine carriers, five battleships and seven heavy cruisers. He planned to send out his bombers while the two fleets were still so far apart that U.S. planes could not make the round trip without refueling. The Japanese aircraft wouldn't have to fly that far: after dropping their bombs they could refuel at Guam, one of Tokyo's island "aircraft carriers."

Spruance guessed Japanese intentions, though, and had placed his ships—among them 13 carriers and seven battleships—a hundred miles from Guam to wait for the enemy. The Battle of the Philippine Sea that followed on June 19, 1944, was the last great carrier engagement of the war and ended in an American victory as decisive as Midway, though achieved much more easily. In fact, some who took part were later to call it the Great Marianas Turkey Shoot. After eight hours of aerial combat the Japanese lost more than 300 planes. At one time 15 enemy fighters were on fire simultaneously and dropped into the sea like burning torches. The next afternoon the Mikado's fleet began a retreat towards the northwest. But Mitscher sent his planes after the fleeing enemy. The result: one carrier sunk, two others disabled. Total losses in this disastrous expedition totaled 50 ships.

On Saipan the defeat at sea had little effect on the defenders' determination to die to the last man and to fight with the bitter ferocity that had begun to mark their despair. It took the Americans 25 days to reduce the small island. They fought through dense and stinking jungles and sent patrols up the cave-marked cliffs on Mount Tapotchau. By the end of June, Saipan had been cut in two and another airfield won. Yet the attrition on both sides continued to mount rapidly. Marines kept firing until they had no bullets left. The Japanese staged one banzai charge after the other. Gradually the Americans advanced up the island and pushed into the western coastal plain.

As the campaign entered its fourth week the enemy held only the northern pocket of the island. On July 6 came the last suicide charge. General Saito ordered 3000 of his soldiers to hurl themselves against U.S. lines and kill ten Americans each before they themselves died. As wild shouts of "banzai" tore through the jungle the human wall exploded against units of the 27th U.S. infantry division. The sheer physical weight of the attackers dislodged the Americans but did not break their lines. More than 2000 Japanese died and were buried in a mass grave later. General Saito opted for ritual suicide: he cut open his wrists, nodded to an aide to shoot and slumped forward. On July 9 it was all over. Saipan had been conquered. The Japanese had lost 24,000 dead. American casualties were the heaviest of any island campaign: 3500 dead, 13,000 wounded.

Loss of Saipan and Guam, which was overrun on July 22, 1944, meant that the U.S. troops had breached the inner line of Japanese defenses. The salient that only two years earlier had bitten so deeply into the Pacific had been eliminated. The way was now cleared for an attack on the Philippines that fall.

After Saipan, by all logic of battle, Japan had lost the war and should have sued for peace. General Tojo did draw the consequences of the Marianas defeat and resigned as Premier. But General Koiso, his successor, did not. He continued to fight.

Chapter

☆ 14 ☆

In mid-September, 1944, Admiral Halsey sent planes from his 3rd fleet carriers roaming across the Philippine Islands in a series of concerted attacks. They met little opposition and reported that the islands' defenses appeared weak. The opportunity was clear: a much faster and more daring strike against the Islands than had been planned, in order to prevent the enemy from beefing up his defenses. Strategy was swiftly changed. The Americans would attempt a direct landing on Leyte in the Philippine chain on October 20, two months earlier than planned. It would be a bold stroke—the first seaborne invasion protected entirely by carrier-based aircraft.

The fleet that bobbed in the waters off Leyte at sunrise on the 20th was the largest ever assembled in the Pacific: 700 troop, supply and combat ships, four mighty task forces of carriers, battleships, cruisers and destroyers. Scores of planes buzzed constantly overhead. Other forces committed to the invasion were: General Krueger's 200,000-man Sixth Army, General Kenney's 2500-plane Far East Air Force, Halsey's Third Fleet and Kinkaid's Seventh Fleet.

Ten days before the landing, the Americans had delivered a crushing blow to the Japanese air force. Halsey had sent 1000 aircraft to blast enemy bases from Okinawa to Taiwan, and the Japanese lost 600 planes in a week. It was a bitter defeat, for it severely crippled a grand design of Tokyo's warlords: an ambitious naval and air attack to forestall any American landing in the Philippines and crush the U.S. fleets in the bargain. Dubbed Sho-1 and Sho-2 (Victory-1 and -2), the plan involved most of the Imperial Navy, but now it would have to be carried out almost without air cover.

By October 18 the Japanese realized that a major attack was on the way. Two days later two powerful squadrons commanded by Admirals Kurita and Nishimura reached Brunei Bay on Borneo. Operation Sho was under way. Kurita planned to sail his flotilla, including two 64,000-ton battlewagons, through the San Bernardino Straits and attack the Americans in Leyte Gulf. Nishimura would take his ships through Surigao Strait below Leyte and join Kurita's attack from the south. A third force under Admiral Shima would steam down from Formosa and follow Nishimura's wake to provide extra punch. Meanwhile, Admiral Ozawa took Japan's four remaining carriers, two battleships, several cruisers and destroyers down from the inland sea to the Philippines. His was a desperate and tragic mission. On the face of it he commanded the most powerful of the Japanese forces. But his carriers had only 100 planes and few pilots who could fly them. He was paying the price of defeat in the air a week before. Instead of leading a proud and strong task force, Ozawa would be the decoy, sent out to tempt Halsey's fleet away from Leyte Gulf while Kurita and Nishimura pounded Kinkaid and the American transports offshore from Leyte.

Kurita and Nishimura left Brunei on October 22, 1944, but two American subs soon spotted Kurita's ships off the outer Philippine Island of Palawan, and alerted the U.S. Third Fleet. On the 24th the Japanese admiral entered the Sibuyan Sea and was in range of Halsey's planes. Beginning at 9 that morning the Americans flew 250 sorties against Kurita's force. The enemy slunk to cover but two hours later, with the U.S. planes gone, headed once again for the San Bernardino Straits and Leyte.

It was late afternoon. Bull Halsey studied Intelligence reports from his pilots, which told of Ozawa's big carrier force to the north. This was the main enemy strike, Halsey was sure. If Ozawa's carriers got close enough, his planes could fly shuttle bombing runs to Leyte and back. At eight that night Halsey set off in pursuit, and didn't leave even one destroyer guarding the entrance to San Bernardino Strait. He was sure Kinkaid would keep the Straits under aerial observation and could stop any attempt by Kurita to break through. Ozawa had played his role well.

Nishimura, meanwhile, had sailed into the Surigao Straits that separate Leyte from the island of Dinagat. He was weaker than he had hoped to be: Shima's ships lagged far behind. Even worse, Kurita's hesitation to the north left Kinkaid free to concentrate on Nishimura. The American posted eight cruisers and six battleships at the mouth of the Surigao Straits, and sent destroyers and PT boats to harass the enemy inside it. The strategy worked like a charm. Destroyers fired torpedoes up close, sank one battleship and damaged another. The big guns at the straits' entry finished the job. Only two vessels escaped. Nishimura went down in his flagship. Hours later—it was now before dawn on October 25—Shima arrived, surveyed the situation and, concluding that his small force faced annihilation if he accepted a fight, turned tail and ran.

Kurita received word of Nishimura's defeat about 5:30 that morning. His ships had already passed through San Bernardino, and he decided to continue south towards Leyte Bay anyway. At first luck was with him, for Kinkaid and Halsey had had a misunderstanding: each thought the other would protect San Bernardino's mouth, but neither did.

Shortly after dawn the Japanese squadron encountered a puny American force of destroyers and small aircraft carriers with but a handful of planes on their decks, under command of Rear Admiral Sprague. The Americans were no match for the much more powerful enemy force. But Kurita became confused and, believing he faced a U.S. squadron at least as strong as his own, hesitated. Sprague, however, had no illusions about his own desperate position. He quickly sent out planes to harass the enemy, laid down smoke, hid in rain squalls and again and again struck daringly against the enemy. But gradually Japanese superiority began to tell. Sprague held out little hope for his own survival. Then, suddenly, Kurita broke off the engagement. He had never corrected his initial mistake and remained convinced that he faced a big task force instead of a few scattered ships. Sure that he had dealt his enemy a punishing blow, Kurita began to retreat back up the San Bernardino Strait. He did not want to risk his "victory" for the few empty remaining ships still off Leyte. But Sprague was not yet out of danger. Japanese Kamikaze or suicide planes rode out of the sky, pilots aiming their snouts at U.S. ships. Several were damaged and the carrier *St. Lo* sunk.

That same morning, October 25, Halsey and his carrier commander, Marc Mitscher, had finally caught up with Ozawa's carriers off Luzon's Cape Engano. U.S. planes screamed down the carrier decks at daylight and pounded the defenseless Ozawa until midafternoon. By that time he had lost all four carriers, a cruiser and two destroyers. But his losses would have been much heavier had Halsey not taken the bulk of his fleet south in midmorning to rush to Sprague's help. For three hours Halsey had ignored a flood of messages; then with heavy heart, he left Mitscher's carrier strike force to finish the job and sailed away. "At that moment," Halsey later wrote, "Ozawa was exactly 42 miles from the muzzles of my 16-inch guns. . . . I turned my back on the opportunity I had dreamed of since my days as a cadet."

There was a double irony here: not only had Halsey lost his chance to sink Ozawa's fleet, but he arrived too late to catch Kurita. He sank a single enemy destroyer.

The three-day battle of Leyte Gulf was the largest in the Pacific and the last of the big naval engagements. The crushing Japanese defeat ended any threat the Imperial Fleet could pose to the Leyte landings.

The Americans had swarmed up the island's beaches on October 21, 1944. Among those who waded through the choppy water to shore was the tall, imposing figure of Douglas MacArthur. A promise had been redeemed. "People of the Philippines," the always dramatic American commander intoned, "I have returned. By the grace of Almighty God our forces stand again on Philippine soil. . . . Rally to me."

It took more than two months of bitter fighting to subdue stubborn Japanese resistance on Leyte. The campaign was similar to that fought on other islands except, perhaps, for the added frustration of bad weather that turned much of Leyte into a soggy swamp and prevented establishment of U.S. air superiority until the battle was almost over. But by Christmas day (when in Europe the Battle of the Bulge was nearing a climax) the Japanese commander was ordered to evacuate his 15,000 remaining troops. He had begun the island's defense with a garrison of 65,000 men. U.S. losses too were high: 5000 dead, 14,000 wounded. Despite the collapse of organized resistance, isolated units fought on there until March, 1945.

The invasion of the main Philippine island of Luzon on January 9, 1945, was next. It would prove the biggest of the Pacific land campaigns, the only one to compare to the large-scale battles fought in Europe. Again Krueger's Sixth Army spearheaded the invasion; Kinkaid's Seventh Fleet—by now dubbed "MacArthur's navy"—protected the landings in Lingayen Gulf, on the other side of Manila Bay. There were overtones of D day: massive aerial bombardment, dummy parachute drops, guerrilla actions to confuse the enemy, a naval pounding and finally the landings themselves. At the end of the day 68,000 troops were ashore and had secured a beachhead 15 miles long and three miles deep. As he had at Leyte, MacArthur again splashed ashore that first day to repeat his "I have returned" theme.

Initially, opposition was light. Flooded rice fields, marshes and streams proved bigger obstacles than the enemy. General Griswold's Fourteenth Corps drove briskly through the valley that lies between Lingayen and Manila. Not until the 23rd did the Americans encounter real opposition, near the town of Bamban that guarded Clark Field, a major enemy base. After two days of heavy fighting the Americans captured it. On the left flank General Swift's I Corps had swung into the mountains of northern Luzon; they met fierce resistance and once again had to blast the Japanese out of their network of caves and other fortifications man by man.

On January 29, 1945, the Eleventh corps landed north of Subic Bay and quickly sealed off Bataan Peninsula. MacArthur did not want any Japanese repetition of his own retreat into that pocket of land three years earlier. Next the Americans made an airborne landing at Nasugbu, on the southern tip of Manila Bay. The way was cleared for a pincer attack on Manila itself. The Japanese battled fiercely for another month to hold the capital. Fighting raged inside the city for two weeks, with the attackers forced to flush the enemy out of one fortification after another. It took two days, for example, to reduce the mighty 16th-century citadel of Intramuros, whose stone walls measured 40 feet across at the base. Few Japanese soldiers were left alive when the city finally fell.

In mid-February the Americans attacked the island fortress of Corregidor that sits astride the entrance to Manila Bay, where General Wainright had held out heroically for many weeks in 1942. U.S. paratroopers landed on the island on February 16 following many weeks of sustained bombardment. But shells and bombs had not broken Japanese resistance, and it took two more weeks of heavy fighting to clear Corregidor.

With Manila Bay secure, supplies could flow more freely to Allied forces, and the final assault into the northern mountains of Luzon began. The battle was long, fierce and costly. General Yamashita's large force fought with what had become routine suicidal bravery. The Americans brought up bulldozers and tanks to reduce fortifications, lowered demolition charges through gun slits and poured burning oil on the defenders. There was just no other way to get them out. Resistance on Luzon continued into June, and there was fighting on the island till the war ended. Elsewhere in the Philippines the Americans invaded one island after another and did not formally end the campaign until July.

While MacArthur struck through the Philippines, Admiral Nimitz prepared the next stage of his own island-hopping campaign. He had taken Saipan and Guam in the Marianas in the summer of 1944. That fall he prepared to attack his next target, Iwo Jima in the Bonin Group. Eight square miles of volcanic ash, pockmarked with caves, strewn with harsh, ugly rocks, hostile, bleak and ugly, the pear-shaped island with volcanic Mount Suribachi rising like a stalk from the southern end was a key to Pacific strategy. It lay only 750 miles from Tokyo, and the Japanese had made it into a major airbase. They had also constructed a jungle of underground fortifications on the island that 72 days of sustained aerial bombardment and three days of close-range naval pounding did not reduce.

But the Americans were sure no one and nothing could have survived such a bombardment. It was the costly mistake of Tarawa all over again—and again the Marines would have to pay for it in blood.

An armada of 450 ships stood off Iwo Jima at dawn on February 19, 1945. More than 480 landing craft loaded to the gunwales with troops splashed through the water around and between the big vessels grouped in semicircle formation near the landing beaches. Bombarding warships moved to within a thousand yards of shore and plastered it with shells. Overhead, planes laid down a carpet of bombs. Then the first wave of 68 LVTs crunched into the volcanic sand. It was 9:02 A.M. At first the Marines reported only light resistance. But 20 minutes later the earth itself erupted in gunfire. Bullets whistled out of slits in the ground, and shells burst out of rocks and cracks in the stone. The Marines, no more than 300 yards inland, suddenly found themselves pinned down.

Nevertheless, by 10:30 elements of all eight attacking Marine battalions were established ashore and, more importantly, had brought their equipment safely with them. Tanks, bulldozers, other heavy equipment followed. At nightfall 30,000 Americans crowded the beaches. The next morning the island's southern stalk was in American hands. That night Marines fought on the foot of Mount Suribachi. Their casualties so far: 3650 killed and wounded.

Three days of fierce, bloody, hand-to-hand combat followed. Inch by inch the Americans clawed their way up the mountain. On February 23 a 40-man patrol made it to the top. An American flag was hauled up and a handful of Marines stuck it triumphantly in to the ground. AP photographer Joe Rosenthal had made the climb with them and at the climactic moment the shutter of his camera clicked. The photograph became the most famous of the war and won Rosenthal a Pulitzer prize. Today the scene stands embodied in bronze across the Potomac from the Lincoln Memorial in Washington.

But, for all its pictorial drama, the capture of Mount Suribachi was only the beginning. As the Marines turned north, hopefully to sweep across the island, they ran into one defensive line after the other, each seemingly stronger than the previous one. Artillery counted for little. Tanks couldn't operate on the terrain. And the enemy's mania for suicide was stronger than ever: the Japanese cared nothing for their own lives as long as they killed Americans. All in all it took 34 days before the final, useless, hopeless, death-defying banzai charge by 300 of the enemy.

The toll of battle was dizzyingly high: out of a Japanese garrison of 23,000 only 1083 were taken prisoner and the Americans lost 6821 dead. But in strategic terms the prize was worth the cost. On April 7, 107 P-51 fighters took off from the island for the first time to escort flying fortresses on a daylight raid against Tokyo.

Nevertheless, Iwo Jima left U.S. commanders with one nagging doubt. If it took this kind of maximum effort to reduce a speck of dust in the ocean, what would be the cost of an invasion of Japan itself? It was the kind of doubt that helped set off a mushroom cloud over Hiroshima on August 6 and burst the light of a thousand suns into the sky.

Now it was Okinawa's turn. The largest and most important of the Ryuku group, it lay only 325 miles from Japan. Its capture was a necessary prelude for the invasion of the home islands themselves. The customary naval and aerial bombardment began on March 22, 1945. Soon a fantastic fleet of nearly 1500 ships that had sailed from a dozen ports neared Okinawa. More than 180,000 soldiers and marines were aboard the 430 assault troopships. A thousand planes littered the decks of the huge carrier force.

As awesome as this force was, however, it was a sitting duck for Japan's last, desperate weapon—the kamikazes, an elite corps of pilots determined to die for just one chance to hit an enemy ship. And as the fleet maneuvered off Okinawa, the kamikazes buzzed out of the sky like hordes of angry wasps, each pilot waiting for the opening that would allow him to plunge his plane into a flaming dive of death and destruction. Their toll at Okinawa was heavy but not decisive: they damaged two carriers, a battleship, a cruiser, four destroyers and six other ships. Hundreds were shot from the sky without ever reaching their target. The Kamikazes remained a threat all through the 82-day Okinawa campaign. But in the end they had little impact on the course of the war.

The invasion itself followed on April 1, 1945. The Japanese let the Americans land almost unopposed. At the end of the first day 50,000 men were ashore. A day later they had pushed three miles inland on an eight-mile front. A week after the invasion the Americans had cut the island in two and held a third of it. And on top of that, U.S. planes had sunk the pride of Japan's dwindling fleet, the 64,000 ton super-dreadnought *Yamato*, which had sailed south to annihilate the invaders. The ship got to within 270 miles of its target before being sunk.

But then resistance stiffened, and by mid-April the Americans were again fighting bitterly for every yard of ground in the sickeningly familiar pattern of fanatic resistance. Not until early June did the invaders capture the capital of Naha. But the 15,000 enemy soldiers continued to fight. Then, on June 22, 1945, with the Americans only a hundred yards away, the two Japanese commanders committed ritual suicide.

With the fall of Okinawa and the clearing of the Philippines the last phase of the war in the Pacific had begun. The Americans had all but completed planning for the invasion of the home islands in November. And the Japanese position in the "forgotten war" of Asia in the China-Burma-India theater was also deteriorating rapidly.

After the British lost Burma in May, 1942, there had followed a year of total inaction. The airlift across the mountains assured that at least a trickle of supplies got to Chiang Kai-shek's forces, but that was all. Then, in 1943, the Allies began planning an offensive strike into Burma. Guerrilla raids by Orde Wingate's swashbuckling Chindit brigades deep into the Burmese jungles had proved the Japanese vulnerable—if enough troops and supplies could be committed to the attack. But that was a matter of time and priorities. Burma ranked low in both, and it was not until January, 1944, that the British began probing operations near the frontier. Unfortunately, the Japanese had noticed the enemy buildup and determined to strike first, launching a full-blooded offensive through the state of Assam and into the Indian plains beyond it.

They came close to success. Three divisions attacked across the Chindwin river and the Burmese border into the Assam mountains. Their targets were the key British bases at Kohima and Imphal. Operation U-Go started on March 7. For several weeks Japanese columns pushed on steadily, forcing British and Indian units to evacuate their strong points. On March 29, 1944, as the Russians were just preparing to drive into Rumania, the Fifteenth Japanese Division cut the road between Imphal and Kohima, while elements of the Thirty-third Division moved up from the south. By early April the enemy had bottled the British Fourteenth Corps into a perimeter around Imphal. But the surrounded force was a strong one: 155,000 men, 11,000 animals and food and supplies for five weeks. To the north, elements of General Sato's Thirty-first Division reached Kohima on April 5 and besieged the town for two weeks.

The British, meanwhile, airlifted an Indian division from the south and concentrated other forces at Dimapur. These then drove to the relief of beleaguered Kohima, raising the siege on April 19. After that the steam went out of the Japanese attack. They still occupied strong positions, and many weeks of heavy fighting followed. But the danger to India and to rebuilding land communications to China was over. Moreover, the Japanese slowly began to starve to death while the British troops at Imphal received a steady flow of supplies via air—everything from construction equipment, tanks and guns to pigs. The Japanese were reduced to a diet of grass and water; few supplies could get through to them on overgrown jungle paths, and when the monsoon rains came they lived in a sea of mud. In June, 1944, Japanese resistance broke. The attackers had lost half their strength and would have been annihilated had they not retreated.

Far to the north a Chinese-American army under command of General Stillwell fought slowly through the jungles. Right behind them, engineers continued construction of a new supply artery to China, the Ledo road. Stilwell's target was Myitkyina. He took an airfield right outside town on May 17, but could not capture the town itself until August 3. He found 187 Japanese left alive in it.

Two weeks after Myitkyina's capture the British Fourteenth Army swept the last Japanese soldiers back across the Burmese border in the Kohima-Imphal region.

Admiral Lord Louis Mountbatten, the Supreme Allied Commander in the C-I-B theater, prepared a sweeping offensive designed to clear the enemy out of all Burma. It could not start in full force until the rains ended in November and dry weather set in. By early December the Fourteenth Army had taken Naba, not far from the Irrawady river. To the north, Chinese armies drove for Wanting, where the Ledo road would be able to link up with the old Burma road. They crossed the Salween river in January, 1945, and reopened the overland route to China on January 27.

For the next four months the Allied armies slogged determinedly forward amid some of the most appalling difficulties faced by any army in this war. Burma is a country of few roads and dense jungles. It is veined by swiftly flowing streams and rivers, some as wide as the Mississippi. Tropical disease is rampant. And Japanese resistance was as fierce as on the islands. It took the Fourteenth Army a month to establish firm beachheads across the Irrawaddy. Troops depended completely on airborne supplies, and 7500 tons had to be airlifted weekly from Assam. A total of

315,000 soldiers were flown to the front lines, and 110,000 casualties were airlifted back out during the campaign.

In March, fighting in northern Burma had all but ended. Lashio, the old Burma Road terminal, fell on the 7th. By the end of February, most of the Burmese coastline along the Bay of Bengal had been cleared. In the center the British stormed beyond the Irrawaddy bridgeheads towards Meiktila and Mandalay; the former fell on March 4, the latter after heavy fighting on the 19th. Six weeks later Allied armies fought in the outskirts of Rangoon, the capital, after a spectacular drive to the south. On May 3, when the guns were beginning to fall silent in Europe, the British re-entered the city they had left in flames and ruins three years before.

Fighting continued in Burma for several months; it was no longer a full-fledged campaign, but more of a mopping-up operation on the Philippine model.

In June, 1945, then, the Japanese position was utterly hopeless. A final offensive on the Chinese mainland had stalled. American ships blockaded the home islands so that no supplies could reach them, and it even prevented fishing boats from gathering the harvest of the sea. Hunger and deprivation spread. Overhead, American B-29s flew daily fire raids that reduced vast areas of Japan to rubble, burning whole cities to the ground.

Most Japanese knew many months earlier that the war was lost. Even Premier Koiso had acknowledged there was little hope in January, 1945. But he wanted to win the best terms from the Allies he could—despite "unconditional surrender"—and bent every effort to build up Japan's home defenses. He raised a large army of volunteers and improved the home islands' air defenses. But when Iwo Jima fell, Koiso's government fell with it—in disgrace. His successor, Admiral Baron Kantaro Suzuki, was a man of more moderate outlook who gradually pushed the warlords into the background. Still, he dared not sue for peace on the basis of unconditional surrender. The Japanese thought their emperor was a Godlike figure; they needed assurances that he would stay on the throne. In fact, the Supreme War Council decided on June 18 to try through a neutral power to get terms that would keep Hirohito as emperor.

But it was already too late. Work had been completed on a terrifying new weapon, the atomic bomb. The vast energy stored inside the smallest known unit of matter had been harnessed and was about to be released.

Scientists had long known about the power hidden inside the atom. Indeed, the atom was first "split" in a laboratory in 1932. And in 1938, German scientists had carried out the first chain reaction. British research proved subsequently that manufacture of a nuclear bomb was a definite possibility. All through 1939 refugee scientists from Italy and Germany and their British, French and American colleagues thought about the feasibility of the bomb —not because they relished the idea of unleashing so destructive a force on mankind, but because they were afraid the Nazis would if the West didn't.

Early in 1939 Enrico Fermi, a refugee from Mussolini's Italy, had repeated the trail-blazing German chain-reaction experiment in the United States. He and his colleagues—Leo Szilard and Edward Teller of Hungary and Victor Weisskopf of Austria among them—decided to get U.S. government help in pushing nuclear research. But how to get FDR's ear? There was only one scientist with the stature to do it: Albert Einstein, one of the towering geniuses of this or any other century. Einstein too had realized the awful possibility of nuclear fission in the hands of the dictators. In August, 1939, he wrote FDR a letter: "This new phenomenon would also lead to the construction of bombs. A single bomb . . . exploded in a port, might . . . destroy the whole port." FDR's interest was definitely aroused.

Gradually the evidence mounted in U.S. and British laboratories, and slowly the commitment to build a bomb took shape. Soon all work was moved to the United States, where Fermi headed up the Manhattan Project.

A distinguished team of international scientists and administrators was soon hard at work on a scheme that would cost $2 billion before it was finished. Among the most prominent were Fermi himself, Teller, Robert Oppenheimer, the Danish scientist Niels Bohr, Sir Henry Tizard, Otto Frisch, Arthur Compton, James Conant and General Leslie Groves. Work was under way at Columbia University in New York, at the University of Chicago, later at Oak Ridge, Tennessee, and then, in the final stages, at Los Alamos, New Mexico.

It was there that the new weapon would undergo its first test. And, as Japan sought feverishly to find a way to squirm out of unconditional surrender, preparations for the first nuclear explosion in history ground inexorably on. The date was set for July 16, 1945. The bomb had been placed on a tall steel tower in the middle of the desert. It was one of only three bombs the United States had built. The first one, made of uranium, had already been flown across the Pacific. The United States did not dare test it: all the Uranium-235 in Allied hands had been used up. It had to work—on the enemy. The bomb at Los Alamos used plutonium, another fissionable material. And S-1, its official designation, already had an offspring: a second plutonium bomb known as "Fat Man." S-1 was selected for the test.

A tense group of scientists huddled in a timbered shelter jammed with instruments and protected by a massive earthen bunker some 10,000 yards from the tower. At 5:10 A.M. Sam Allison, one of the Los Alamos scientists, announced into a telephone mouthpiece: "It is now zero minus twenty minutes." In the shelter and in other posts scattered across the desert, tension quickened. Scientists fastened on welders' goggles to guard against the expected glare. Slowly the minutes ticked by. Zero minus ten, zero minus five, zero minus two. Now the counting was down to seconds—fifty-five, fifty, forty-five. The men inside the control shed felt their nerves twang like bow strings. Oppenheimer, crunching his battered old hat in his hands, wondered if he would faint. At zero minus five seconds automatic cameras switched on.

It blew at 5:29:45, a ball of fire such as man had never seen before on earth. It was four times hotter in the middle of that fireball than in the center of the sun. As Robert Oppenheimer listened to the thunder and watched the light, he thought of a Hindu verse:

If the radiance of a thousand suns
Were to burst at once into the sky,
That would be like the splendor of the
          Mighty One. . . .
I am become Death,
The shatterer of worlds.

It was at once descriptive fact and prophecy, as the citizens of two Japanese towns named Hiroshima and Nagasaki would learn only weeks later.

Harry Truman spent the dawn of the atomic age in Potsdam, outside Berlin, where he had gone to attend a big-four conference to settle the future of the post-war world. He had already determined to use the bomb on Japan—if it worked. The president, like his generals, was convinced it would take 18 months and cost half a million American lives to invade Japan. The signals the Tokyo government sent up in June and July indicating Japan's readiness to quit were either not understood or not believed. Finally, there was another reason for using the bomb in war: to impress the Russians, to use the power of the atom as a diplomatic hammer.

But Truman could not bring himself to spell out just what the atomic bomb was, what it could do. He told Stalin at Potsdam that the U.S. had set off a big bomb. The Russian leader looked at him through hooded eyes and in effect told Truman that was nice, and what else was new?

The Potsdam Declaration, issued by the United States, Britain and China, was equally misunderstood in Tokyo. It was moderate enough, softening unconditional surrender to mean only of the armed forces and promising not to enslave the Japanese people, while warning of dire consequences if resistance continued. But before a neutral intermediary could deliver it to the Tokyo government, the declaration was broadcast on the radio. The Japanese took it for another declaration of war aims and announced they would do nothing about it.

There the matter rested, and on August 2, having heard nothing further from the Japanese, Truman ordered the dropping of the two atomic bombs, already stored in the Central Pacific, on Japan. Weather held up the operation. Not until 2:45 P.M. local time, August 6, did a B-29 bearing the picturesque name of *Enola Gay* taxi down a specially lengthened runway at Tinian and, with a gigantic effort of her huge engines, lift off the ground. In her bowels the plane carried "Little Boy," the untested uranium bomb.

Colonel Paul Tibbets steered his plane towards Hiroshima, the primary target. In the morning a weather plane reported perfect visibility over the city. At 8:09 A.M. on August 6, Hiroshima came into view. Tibbets and his crewmen clanked down the welder goggles. Two minutes later, at 8:11, Tibbets began his bombing run. At 8:15 the plane roared over the city at 285 miles an hour; 17 seconds later the bomb bays swung open and "Little Boy" began its six-mile descent. *Enola Gay* veered round at a sharp 150-degree angle and fled the scene. It was 15 miles away 51 seconds later when Little Boy exploded 1850 feet above Hiroshima and only 200 feet from target. For a blinding moment after the explosion, the ball of fire that shot skyward behind the fleeing Americans registered a temperature of one million degrees Fahrenheit. In a matter of seconds the billows of smoke had shot up 40,000 feet and formed an awesome mushroom cloud—the billboard poster of the atomic age.

The bomb devastated an area of four square miles. It destroyed 10,000 houses, and the fires that it spawned burned 50,000 more. At least 78,000 persons were killed by the blast, 37,000 hurt, 13,000 missing. Thousands more died later from the effects of radiation. Even stones bled, emerging from the ordeal by fire covered with blisters. The bomb left an atomic desert behind. The fires of hell had indeed descended on earth.

Still, it was not enough. The Americans didn't really give Tokyo time to collect its thoughts, to plead surrender. On August 9 another B-29, *Bock's Car*, dropped "Fat Man," the offspring of the Los Alamos bomb, on the city of Nagasaki. Actually, Nagasaki was not the prime target, but when *Bock's Car* arrived over the city of Kokura, where the bomb was to have been dropped, it found the weather impossible for a bomb run and headed for Nagasaki. "Fat Man" was a more sophisticated bomb than "Little Boy"—in fact, it made "Little Boy" obsolete the minute it was dropped. Thus, even though "Fat Man" fell further from target and was detonated in a valley where its blast could not do as much damage, the power of the explosion was greater: 35,000 died in "Fat Man's" firestorm, 60,000 were hurt. Destruction was more uneven here, largely as a result of the geography, and oddly, train service was not disrupted.

On the morning of August 9, 1945, Russia went to war against Japan. The night before, Foreign Minister Molotov had handed the declaration to the Japanese ambassador in Moscow, after having refused to see him for more than a week despite the envoy's desperate pleas. Tokyo had pinned all its hope on Moscow's mediation. Stalin, of course, wanted no part of it. Now, when not even the Americans wished the Soviet in the war, he was eager for the spoils. And Russian arms did carve large chunks out of Manchuria, plunge deeply into Korea and slice off part of the northern Japanese islands in a brilliant 24-day campaign fought against stubborn enemy resistance.

In Tokyo the War Council met in emergency session that crucial morning of August 9, and talks continued all through the day. The council was divided three to three on whether to accept the Potsdam surrender formula. Premier Suzuki refused to break the tie. Finally, at 3 A.M. on August 10, they asked Emperor Hirohito to decide. The Emperor urged capitulation. Messages flowed through Sweden and Switzerland to Washington, the Japanese still pleading to keep their Emperor. The Americans equivocated, holding out hope but making no promises. On August 14 the Japanese agreed to U.S. terms. On the 15th the Emperor broadcast the details of defeat to his people. It was the first time they had ever heard the demi-god's voice.

Two weeks later ships of Halsey's Third fleet and of the British Pacific Fleet sailed into Tokyo Bay and dropped anchor. And on September 2, 1945, the 45,000-ton U.S.S. *Missouri* was berthed peacefully in the shadow of Fujiyama. Her great 16-inch guns pointed skyward to make room for the mass of men crowded on deck. Douglas MacArthur stood behind a table on the galley deck, flanked by Jonathan Wainright of Corregidor and Arthur Percival, the British general who had lost Singapore. Both men had been freed from Japanese prisons only days earlier.

A nine-man Japanese delegation was piped aboard. Six of them were in uniform, and three wore the formal clothes of traditional diplomacy replete with cane and top hat. Foreign Minister Mamoru Shigemitsu limped forward on his wooden leg until he stood before the table on which the surrender documents lay spread out.

This time MacArthur eschewed dramatics. He made a simple, almost poignant speech: "It is my earnest hope and indeed the hope of all mankind that from this solemn occasion a better world shall emerge out of the blood and carnage of the past—a world so dedicated to the dignity of man and the fulfillment of his most cherished wish—for freedom, tolerance and justice."

The documents of surrender were then signed. In Washington President Truman proclaimed September 2, 1945, as V-J Day. The war was over.

WARSAW COMMUNITY PUBLIC LIBRARY
WARSAW, INDIANA

Epilogue

So the war was over—and much more than the war: a whole history of human existence. For the mushroom clouds over Los Alamos and Nagasaki had profoundly changed the condition of man. Henceforth he would live in the atomic age, under constant threat of destruction —indeed, under the threat of his planet's annihilation. Cosmic fear had entered human consciousness. The scars of the bomb live on in the genes of those who were exposed to its blast. And the debate on the justice of dropping it over Japan will never end. There were American scientists who went out into the desert and retched when they realized what they had helped perfect.

But the new age was only dimly perceived by the world at large. There was a gigantic job of clean-up and reconstruction, of starting life anew, of hopes for a better world. First, there was the matter of reckoning with those who had plunged mankind into so cataclysmic a disaster. An Allied war tribunal was set up in Nuremberg and Hitler's henchmen put on trial in proceedings that lasted for a year. Eleven were sentenced to death, three to life imprisonment and four others got varying jail terms. On October 16, 1946, Hermann Goering swallowed poison, an hour before he was supposed to lead his colleagues to the gallows. But the others did not cheat the hangman: Ribbentropp, Seyss-Inquart, Jew-baiting Julius Streicher, ideologue Alfred Rosenberg and two of Hitler's generals, Keitel and Jodl. Similar trials were held in Japan, where Tojo was hanged.

Nor did the Grand Alliance survive the war. The Potsdam conference of July, 1945, signaled its disintegration. Truman had taken Roosevelt's place at the conference table, and before the meeting was out Clement Attlee was in Winston Churchill's chair. On July 25 the ballot boxes were opened in Britain to reveal that the "man of the century" had, as he would later write, been "dismissed by the British electorate from all further conduct of their affairs." The Labour Party had scored a landslide victory.

The tensions inherent in so unnatural an arrangement as an alliance between Communist dictatorship and Western democracy bubbled at once to the surface. Within months they led to the Cold War. And two years later what Churchill—a far-seeing statesman in and out of office—would call an "iron curtain" had divided Europe.

Years of trouble and upheaval followed: confrontation and near-war in Europe, turmoil in Africa and Asia and local wars in Korea and Vietnam. Yet the war-torn world was rebuilt and reached a level of prosperity man had never dreamed he could attain. With the secret of the atom unlocked, science went on a rampage of discovery and progress unmatched in all history. The bomb, the computer and the satellite have changed the earth beyond recognition. And for all man's power to destroy himself and his universe, he has not yet done it—and, with the light of reason as his guide, he may even manage his own survival.

Suggested Further Reading

Bradley, Omar, *A Soldier's Story*, Holt & Co., New York, 1951.
Bryant, Sir Arthur, *The Turn of the Tide*, Collins, London, 1957.
————, *Triumph in the West*, Collins, London, 1959.
Bullock, Allan, *Hitler, A Study in Tyranny*, Harper & Row, New York, 1964 (rev. ed.).
Churchill, Winston S., *Memoirs, The Second World War*, Houghton-Mifflin, Boston, 1948–1953 (6 vols.).
Collier, Barnard, *The Second World War, A Military History*, William Morrow & Co., New York, 1967.
Davis, Kenneth S., *Experience of War*, Doubleday, Garden City, N.Y., 1965.
Eisenhower, Dwight, *Crusade in Europe*, Doubleday, Garden City, N.Y., 1948.
Fuller, J. F. C., *The Second World War*, Duel, Sloan & Pierce, New York, 1948 (reprinted 1962).
Halsey, William F. and Bryan, J., III, *Admiral Halsey's Story*, Whittlesey House, New York, 1947.
Hershey, John, *A Bell for Adano*, Knopf, New York, 1955.
Jungk, Robert, *Brighter Than a Thousand Suns*, Harcourt, Brace & World, New York, 1958.
Lamont, Lansing, *Day of Trinity*, Athaneum, New York, 1965.
Mailer, Norman, *The Naked and the Dead*, Rinehardt & Co., New York, 1948.
Murphy, Robert, *Diplomat Among Warriors*, Doubleday, Garden City, N.Y., 1964.
Plievier, Theodore, *Stalingrad*, Athaneum, London, 1948.
————, *Berlin*, Hammond, London, 1956.
Pyle, Ernie, *Here Is Your War*, Holt, New York, 1943.
————, *Brave Men*, Holt, New York, 1944.
Roper, H. Trevor, *Blitzkrieg to Defeat, Hitler's War Directives 1939–1945*, Holt, Rinehart and Winston, New York, 1964.
Ryan, Cornelius, *The Longest Day*, Simon & Schuster, New York, 1959.
————, *The Last Battle*, Simon & Schuster, New York, 1966.
Shirer, William L., *Rise and Fall of the Third Reich*, Simon & Schuster, New York, 1959.
Snyder, Louis L., *The War, A Concise History*, Simon & Schuster, New York, 1960.
Thomas, Hugh, *The Spanish Civil War*, Harper & Row, New York, 1961.
Truman, Harry S., *Year of Decision*, Vol. I of the Truman Memoirs, Doubleday, Garden City, N.Y., 1955.
Toland, John, Battle, *The Story of the Bulge*, Random House, New York, 1959.
Werth, Alexander, *Russia at War*, Dutton, New York, 1964.

Index

Caen, 138, 139, 141, 145
Cairo, 105, 106, 154
Calais, 51, 52
Cape Esperance, 184, 185
Caribbean, 99
Caroline Islands, 188, 194, 195
Carpathian Mountains, 28, 157
Casablanca, 108, 112, 113, 114
Caspian Sea, 83, 86
Cassino, 120-122
Caucasus, 74, 76, 81, 82, 83, 88
Chamberlain, Neville, 19, 20, 21-23, 24, 26, 27, 34, 44
Catholics, 15, 20
Chennault, Claire, 177
Chequers, 98
Cherbourg, 138, 139, 142
Chiang Kai-shek, 173, 176, 207
China, 156, 173, 176, 177, 208
Choiseul, 191
Cholitz, General von, 146-147
Churchill, Winston S., 15-16, 17, 34, 35, 36, 38-39, 44-45, 49, 50, 52, 53, 54, 57, 58, 60, 62, 64-65, 66, 67, 69, 71, 74, 98, 99, 100, 102, 103, 105-106, 108, 112, 113, 114, 116, 122, 125, 133, 134, 137-138, 141, 153, 154-156, 162, 163, 166, 215, 216
Copenhagen, 41
Coral Sea, 179, 183
Courageous, 35
Cossack, 39
Chuikov, General, 84, 85, 86, 87, 89, 164
Clark, General Mark, 110, 111, 119, 120, 122
Collins, General, 159
Cologne, 159
Columbia University, 210
Communists, 12, 13, 24, 131
Compiegne, 54, 56
Compton, Arthur, 210
Conant, James, 210
Constantine, 114
Corregidor, 178, 179, 203, 204, 214
Cracow, 29, 31, 157
Crete, 67, 71-72, 122
Crimea, 76, 80, 81, 128, 129, 153, 155, 162
Cumberland, 37
Cunningham, Admiral, 186
Cyprus, 72
Cyrenaica, 65, 66, 102, 105
Czechoslovakia, 20-23, 24, 96, 164

Dachau, 92

Dakar, 55, 68
Daladier, Édouard, 20, 24
Danube River, 9, 131, 161, 162
Danzig, 23, 156, 157, 161
Darlan, Admiral Jean, 111, 112, 118
Denmark, 39, 41, 164, 166
Deutschland, 35, 36, 40
Dietl, General, 40, 42, 43
Dijon, 55, 147
Dnieper River, 75, 76, 124, 127, 128, 129
Dniester River, 128, 129, 131
Doenitz, Admiral, 136, 137, 165, 166
Dollfuss, Engelbert, 15
Don River, 82, 83, 84, 87, 88, 124
Donets Basin, 75, 76, 81, 82, 89, 125, 128
Doolittle, Colonel Jimmy, 179
Doric Star, 36
Dresden, 152
Duesseldorf, 158, 159
Dumbarton Oaks, 153
Dunkirk, 50, 51, 52-54, 71, 99, 106, 120, 176
Dutch East Indies, 173, 174, 177

East Prussia, 24, 28, 134, 142, 143, 152, 156, 157
Egypt, 63-66, 67, 71, 72, 81, 100, 101, 103, 104, 105, 183
Eichmann, Adolf, 95, 97
Einstein, Albert, 210
Eisenhower, General Dwight D., 108, 110, 111, 112, 117, 119, 138, 146, 148, 151, 155, 158, 162, 163, 164, 166,
El Alamein, 81, 103, 105, 108, 125, 160, 187
Emmanuel III, King Victor, 16, 117
English Channel, 49, 58, 60, 112
Eniwetok, 195
Enola Gay, 212-213
Enterprise, 180, 184, 186
Estonia, 32, 128, 134
Ethiopia, 16, 17, 66
Exeter, 36-37

Falange Party, 17-18
Falkenhorst, Nicholas von, 39, 42
Farben, I. G., 93
Fermi, Enrico, 210
Finland, 32-34, 38-43, 69, 73, 129
Flying Tigers, 177
Foch, Marshal, 56
Formosa, 200

France, 8, 11, 15, 18, 19, 20, 22, 23,
27, 31, 34, 44, 46-47, 48, 50, 51, 52,
54-57, 60, 68, 69, 72, 88, 108, 109,
111, 112, 113, 135, 138-142, 145-148,
156, 173
Franco, Francisco, 17-18
Frank, Hans, 31
Frankfurt, 148, 158, 160
Franklyn, General, 51
Free French, 55, 68, 104, 112, 113,
146-147
French Indochina, 173, 174
Freyberg, General Bernard, 71, 72,
121-122
Friessner, General, 158, 161
Frisch, Otto, 210
Fujiyama, 214

Gamelin, General, 50
Gaulle, Charles de, 55, 68, 112, 113,
146-147
Gavin, General James, 149
Geneva, 16
George VI, King, 44, 166
Germany and Poland, 7, 23-31; and
World War I, 8, 9; between the
Wars, 8-14; and Austria, 14-15, 19-
20; and the Rhineland, 17; and the
Spanish Civil War, 17-18; and
Czechoslovakia, 20-23; and Norway,
38-44; and Denmark, 41-44; and
Belgium and Holland, 46-53; and
France, 54-57; and England, 58-62;
and Africa, 66-68, 100-115; and
Russia, 68-69, 73-90, 124-134; and
the Balkans, 69-72; and Jews, 91-
96; and Italy, 118-123; defeat of,
145-167. *See also*, Weimar Republic
Gibraltar, 57, 111
Gilbert Islands, 182, 188, 194, 196
Giraud, General Henri, 111, 112, 113
Gneisenau, 35, 36, 44, 136
Goebbels, Joseph, 11, 12, 23, 34, 77,
125, 141, 144, 154, 162, 163, 165
Goering Hermann, 11, 12, 23, 27, 47,
48, 52, 53, 56, 58-62, 72, 88, 89, 152,
164, 165, 167, 215
Govorov, General, 129, 134
Graziani, Marshal, 64
Great Britain, 8, 15, 18, 19, 20, 22, 23,
25, 33, 41-45, 46, 48, 56, 57-62, 63-
68, 70, 71-73, 92, 99, 100-108, 112,
113, 156
Greece, 64, 65, 66, 67, 69, 70, 71, 132,
152, 154, 155
Groves, General Leslie, 210

Guadalcanal, 115, 183, 184-187, 188,
190
Guam, 175, 196, 197, 198, 204
Guderian, General Heinz, 28, 30, 49,
50, 51, 52, 74, 75, 77, 79, 148
Gulf of Finland, 33, 129
Gulf of Riga, 130, 134

Hague, the, 47
Halsey, Admiral William, 188, 190,
193, 199, 200-202, 214
Harriman, Averell, 98
Harwood, Commodore, 36-37
Hawaii, 171, 174, 175, 179, 193
Hebrides Islands, 34
Helsinki, 33
Henderson, 184
Henderson Field, 184, 185
Hess, Rudolf, 56
Heydrich, Reinhardt, 96
Himalayas, 177
Himer, General Kurt, 41
Himmler, Heinrich, 14, 92, 94, 95, 164,
165, 167
Hindenburg, Paul von, 12, 14
Hipper, 35, 40
Hirohito, 209, 214
Hiroshima, 206, 212
Hitler, Adolf, 7, 8-28, 30, 31, 32, 35,
38, 39, 41, 44, 47, 50, 51, 55, 56,
57-58, 60, 61, 63, 64, 66, 67-68, 69-
71, 73, 75-77, 79-83, 84, 85, 88, 89,
91, 96, 97, 101, 103, 105, 106, 118,
119, 120, 126, 129, 131, 133, 142-144,
150, 152, 159, 161, 163, 164-167
Hodges, General, 159, 161
Hoeppner, General, 79
Holland, 44, 47-48, 148, 161, 166, 173
Homma, General, 178
Hong Kong, 174, 175
Honolulu, 171
Hood, 136
Hopkins, Harry, 99
Hornet, 180, 186
Hoth, General, 74, 82, 83, 84
Hull, Cordell, 172
Hungary, 69, 70, 81, 131, 132, 161

Iceland, 36
India, 67, 68, 100, 101, 103, 107, 176,
182, 208
Indian Ocean, 175, 182
Indochina, *see* French Indochina
Iraq, 67, 68, 100
Iran, 100

RAF, 58-62, 67, 72, 103, 106
Rangoon, 176
Rastenburg, 143, 144, 145
Rawalpindi, 36
Reichenau, General von, 28, 29, 49
Reinhardt, General, 49, 74
Rendova, 190
Renown, 40
Repulse, 175
Reynaud, Paul, 49, 50, 54, 55
Rhine River, 17, 48, 148, 149, 158, 159, 160, 161
Rhineland, 17
Ribbentrop, Joachim von, 25, 56, 164, 167, 172, 215
Roehm, Ernst, 9, 14
Rokossovsky, Marshal, 87, 88, 89, 90, 130, 132-133, 157, 161
Rome, 54, 119, 121, 122, 123
Rommel, Erwin, 49, 50, 51, 52, 54, 66-68, 81, 100-108, 114-115, 118, 125, 141, 144, 148, 176
Roosevelt, Eleanor, 163
Roosevelt, Franklin D., 98, 99, 100, 106, 112, 113, 114, 133, 137-138, 141, 153, 155-156, 162, 163, 172, 173, 177, 210, 215
Rosenberg, Alfred, 215
Rosenthal, Joe, 205
Rostov, 76, 81, 82, 83, 124
Rotterdam, 47, 48, 152
Royal Oak, 35
Ruhr, 10, 14, 148, 159, 160, 161
Rumania, 69, 70, 73, 74, 81, 82, 84, 87, 89, 128, 129, 131, 132, 162, 207
Rundstedt, Karl Gerd von, 28, 29, 46, 47, 49, 51, 54, 58, 74, 75, 76, 79, 141, 145, 150
Russell Islands, 190
Russia, 8, 11, 18, 24-25, 31, 32-34, 43, 57, 63, 68-69, 70, 72, 73-90, 91, 92, 97, 99, 100, 113, 124-134, 152, 153-156, 190

Sahara, 55
Saigon, 173, 175
Saipan, 196, 197, 198, 204
Saito, General, 197
Salerno, 120, 121
San Francisco, 156, 180
San Francisco, 186
San Bernardino Straits, 200, 201
Santa Cruz, 186
Saratoga, 184, 195
Sardinia, 112, 119

Savo Island, 184
Scapa Flow, 35
Scharnhorst, 35, 36, 44, 136
Schleicher, Kurt von, 12
Schlieffen, Alfred Graf von, 46
Schoerner, General, 130
Schoup, Colonel David, 194
Schuschnigg, Kurt von, 19, 20, 69
Scotland, 34, 107
Sea of Azov, 80, 83, 128
Sebastapol, 80, 81, 82, 129
Sedan, 46, 49
Seine River, 54, 145, 146, 147
Selassie, Haile, 16, 66
Seraph, 110,
Seyss-Inquart, Arthur, 20, 167, 215
Shigemitsu, Mamoru, 214
Shima, Admiral, 200-201
Short, General Walter, 171
Sicily, 102, 112, 113, 116-119, 120, 190, 193
Siegfried Line, 17, 28, 34, 47, 149
Silesia, 28, 157
Singapore, 174, 175, 176, 214
Sittang River, 176
Skorzeny, Colonel Otto, 119-120
Slovakia, 28, 29, 69
Smolensk, 74, 76, 80, 125, 126, 134, 142
Socialists, 12, 13, 15, 20
Solomon Islands, 177, 179, 182, 183, 184, 186, 188, 190, 193
Somaliland, 16
Somme River, 46, 50
South Africa, 65,
South America, 36, 95
South Atlantic, 35, 36, 38
South China Sea, 175
Spain, 7, 17-18, 19, 57, 139
Spanish Morocco, 18
Sprague, Admiral, 201-202
Spruance, Admiral Raymond, 196, 197
S. S., 10, 14, 92, 93, 94-95, 96, 142, 143, 144, 149, 150-151, 164
Stalin, Josef, 24, 31, 32, 34, 73, 76, 97, 125, 126, 134, 137, 138, 153, 154-156, 162, 212, 213
Stalingrad, 81, 82, 83, 84, 85, 86, 87, 88, 89, 94, 124, 146, 183, 187
Stauffenberg, Count von, 142-144
Stillwell, General Joe, 177, 208
Stockholm, 34
Straits of Dover, 38
Strausbourg, 57
Streicher, Julius, 215

WARSAW COMMUNITY PUBLIC LIBRARY
WARSAW, INDIANA

BOOKSALE